"The quality of a book about millennium prophecies is determined in large measure by the quality of the prophets to which it refers. For me as a physicist it is interesting that Tom Kay not only enumerates and interprets high quality prognostications, but also cites books like the *Grail Message* explaining the *laws* governing the coming events. His book is therefore not another doomsday book, but *the* book that can lead the reader to understand the spiritual reasons and necessity of the throes of a new age and...the right inner preparation."

—Dr. Friedbert Karger, Plasmaphysicist, Max Planck Institute, Munich

"Tom Kay has done humanity a great service...not just by bringing to life ancient visions and prophecies that can be of help to people, but by casting light on the instrument of a 'new science.' For without the intuition, which Tom Kay's book urgently requires, one cannot grasp prophecies, the 'new science,' or most importantly, the purpose of life; that each individual *must* reach full conscious maturity of the spirit."

—Dr. Micah Rubenstein, Associate Professor, Kenyon College, Ohio

Books by Tom Kay

Dear Amy: Making Sense of the Voyage of the Soul

WHEN THE
COMET
prophecies for the
new millennium *runs*

TOM KAY

HAMPTON ROADS
PUBLISHING COMPANY, INC.

Cover design by Marjoram Productions
Cover painting by Francine Barbet

For information write:

Hampton Roads Publishing Company, Inc.
134 Burgess Lane
Charlottesville, VA 22902

Or call: (804) 296-2772
FAX: (804) 296-5096

If you are unable to order this book from your local
bookseller, you may order directly from the publisher.
Quantity discounts for organizations are available.
Call 1-800-766-8009, toll-free.

ISBN 1-57174-059-7

10 9 8 7 6 5 4 3 2 1

Printed in Canada

CONTENTS

ACKNOWLEDGEMENTS

I want to thank all of the people who have helped at various stages during the preparation of this book. If I've forgotten anyone, you know who you are, and please accept my apology.

I want especially to thank Wayne Emley, A.R.E. Reference Librarian, who was always there when I needed him. And thanks to Jeannette Rowden and the other members of the library staff, and Susan Aaron, David Osborne and the staff of the bookstore.

I am beholden to Dr. Phillip Ianna of the Astronomy Department of the University of Virginia who unselfishly, and without ridicule, gave of his time on numerous occasions and patiently offered his expertise from a scientific perspective. I also want to thank Dr. Bryan Marsden of the Smithsonian Astrophysical Observatory at Harvard University for answering my questions when I inquired.

The assistance and advice of Gordon-Michael Scallion, Cynthia Keyes and Harold Barnes has been invaluable. And the same is true of Doris and Aron Abrahamsen.

My thanks to Lynn Hill for gratuitously sending me his newsletter every month, and to David Solomon for sending me information whenever I asked.

Words cannot express my gratitude to Dr. Micah Rubenstein and his wife, Carol, of the Grail Foundation Press. Whenever I was despondent and downhearted, they came to the rescue with words of encouragement and got me back on track.

As always, my long-time friend and mentor Jess Stearn was willing to offer his counsel when queried. And I'm grateful to my publishers, Bob Friedman and Frank DeMarco who had to spend a great deal of time working with my manuscript.

My thanks to Lora Gardner, Walene and Paul James, Day and Joe Schwartz, David Alexander, Paul Perry, Jack Scovil, Nat Sobel, Duncan Roads, Mary Burke, Hildy Becker, Donna Paxson, Ed Birchmore, my brother Bob and his wife Ginger, and all of the others along the way for their interest.

I want to thank my family, Judie, Timmy and Amy, for their patience and understanding throughout the two years I struggled with the manuscript.

Finally, my thanks to Francine Barbet and Jonathan and Matthew Friedman for the artwork and cover design of the book.

AUTHOR'S PROLOGUE

$\mathbf{A}$ significant number of individuals in many countries and of all religions are familiar with at least some of the disturbing prophecies for the current period in the history of the planet we share. For many, the warning signs of the "End Times" seem to be manifesting before their very eyes.

There are the prophecies of the Old Testament and of Jesus and His Apostles in the New Testament; prophecies of saints, monks and nuns, in the mathematical interpretations of the Great Pyramid, of Nostradamus, and of Mother Shipton. There are warning communiques from Mary, the Holy Mother, as She reportedly makes Her presence known in diverse settings. Finally, there are the numerous predictions of more contemporary seers such as Edgar Cayce, Gordon-Michael Scallion, Paul Solomon, Aron Abrahamsen, Dannion Brinkley, the Hopi Indians, Mary Summer Rain, Sun Bear, the prophet of Ramala, Mieshu Sama, the prophet of the *Grail Message*, and so forth.

Recently, a new source of apprehension has been added: All of the meaningful prophecies for the millennium refer to celestial disturbances in the heavens, with the leading role played by a large, bright comet that at times is referred to as a "star." Recently, the comet Hyakutake paid a visit, and now a large, bright comet known as "Hale-Bopp" approaches our solar system. Scientific evidence suggests that this particular comet may be the one that fulfills the visions of numerous prophets and seers dating back hundreds, even thousands, of years.

The multitude of prophesied events that are supposed to occur in the next five to ten years raises questions in the minds of both believers and non-believers alike concerning the "doomsday" predictions that are a pervasive ingredient in the information we digest from radio, television, and articles and books on the subject:

(1) Is there any truth to all this doom and gloom?

(2) Isn't this just another case of "millennium fever," a repeat episode of the frantic reaction of many persons and groups as the year 1000 drew near?

(3) Should I pay any attention to those making these predictions? Have they been checked out? Have their claimed "gifted abilities" been documented somewhere that I can look to? Have any of their predictions come true?

(4) Many passages in the Bible are subject to numerous interpretations. Which ones are right? And why should I have faith in Biblical prophecies?

(5) How can I tell for certain the dates in which these predicted events may occur?

(6) The year 2000 is just another calendar year with a bunch of zeros preceded by "2" instead of "1"! Why does it have special significance?

(7) Is this the time of the "Tribulation" spoken of in that confusing and frightful book, *The Revelation of John?*

(8) Is the Second Coming of Jesus at hand?

(9) Are we fast approaching the time of the Last Judgment?

(10) If we are, does the Last Judgment mean an *either/or* (heaven or hell) for each human soul meeting its Maker?

(11) Is there any place to hide?

(12) If I can't hide. . .why me? Why us? Why the world? What is the justification for this portended chastisement?

(13) Am I guilty of something? Did I play a part in bringing about the distress humanity is supposed to experience?

(14) If the predicted events are inevitable, what can I do about it? I'm only one person.

(15) Is it possible for humanity to cancel the "Tribulation" subscription? Mark it *Return To Sender?*

(16) If we have signed on for the duration, can we rewrite the script?

(17) This entire matter is too overwhelming and upsetting! Would it not be advisable to put it out of my mind and get on with my life?

(18) Is there hope for humanity and our Mother — planet Earth?

The answers to these questions are interspersed throughout the prophecies themselves. For there is a definite pattern to the prophecies, regardless of whether they were given thousands of years ago, hundreds of years ago, or last week. There are clues. There are codes. There are cryptic passages and allegories. There are similarities from different ages and sources.

The apostle Paul wrote in First Corinthians:

> *Put love first, but there are*
> *other gifts of the Spirit at*
> *which you should aim also, and*
> *above all, prophecy. . .when a*
> *man prophesies, he is talking*
> *to men, and his words have*
> *power to build, they stimulate*
> *and encourage. (14:1)*

With respect to the catastrophic prophecies, it is difficult to understand how they could "encourage"—for they are not comforting. They will, however, "stimulate!"

The Bible designates these times as "The birth pangs of the New Age." (Matt. 24:8) The carefully selected words in this passage have much to say. Any mother will attest that giving birth is attended by a certain amount of pain. But the short period of suffering is soon forgotten as she becomes caught up in raising her child.

The prophets tell us that the human spirit will have many an incentive to change course. They claim that, in a few years, every human soul will find it must adjust to a new cycle, an upward evolution in the rhythm of the universe; that people will need to change because the spiritual environment of the New Age will no longer provide a life-support system for negative consciousness. They claim that humanity will not be the same once the predicted events come to pass and that future generations will look back and understand that the "birth pangs" were a necessary part of the soul's evolution. They say that the New Age inhabitants of the planet will once again have found their connection with God and that each person will be given the opportunity to participate in the transformation of personal consciousness.

The prophecies for the millennium include abundant signs and omens, for we are told that no important future event occurs without humanity first being warned many times and shown the signs. In addition, the prophecies offer the counsel of the prophets themselves with respect to the necessary action they suggest will be required of each individual in order to survive the events they have predicted. When the entire puzzle is assembled, a map of the terrain ahead emerges, a blueprint with directional signs marked along the way.

And as most will conclude, the stumbling blocks we are unable to avoid as we traverse our individual paths into the New Millennium are the birth pangs of the New Age. As the New Age draws its first breath of fresh air, it will signal a marvelous era for all of humanity. It will be the *end of an age—not the end of the world*. At first glance, it may appear that writing a book on prophecy is a simple, linear undertaking—just organize them and write them down! Unfortunately, this is not the case. Dozens of major events have been predicted, along with many more events of lesser importance. For the most part, the sequence of specific events is impossible to determine. There may seem to be a causative force connecting certain prophesied events, but actually trying to tie specific events together in a sensible, systematic order, is strictly a guessing game. At any time certain prophesied events can become historical events if a particular prophecy is accurate.

Another problem: One short sentence in a given prophecy will often portend several significant events that are different in scope. Therefore, a certain amount of repetition will always be present, depending on the circumstance of the moment.

Once in a while, the credibility of a given prophecy can be enhanced by presenting scientific evidence. However, other predicted events are not only immensely catastrophic, but based on our knowledge at this time, next to impossible. In fact, most scientists would scoff at them as being more than just a little ridiculous. At the same time, belief systems, dogma, denial systems and opinions are always part of the picture. In short, the entire proposition is a mixed bag!

There are no experts in the field of prophecy. There are no college courses, no Ph.D.'s, nothing! The prophetic utterances offered by various individuals were meant to warn humanity so that those who choose to do so could prepare. At the very least, those who read this book will become knowledgeable about this body of enigmatic information.

This book is a collection of prophetic information gleaned from hundreds of sources. Most authors who write about the millennium prophecies paraphrase the information in their own words, adding a few quotes here and there. However, so that prejudice or partiality doesn't creep into the subject matter, whenever possible, the millennium prophets themselves have been quoted verbatim so that they stand on their own. This way, the interpretation is left to the reader, and intuitive connections may perhaps arise within the reader that otherwise would not.

The dramatic events known as the millennium prophecies are predicted to take place from "anytime now" into the first decade of the 21st century. They are expected to increase in intensity as the end of this century approaches. If they *do not* take place during this period, one thing is certain: Millions of books will be discarded, or they will be relegated to the fiction shelves in book stores and libraries—perhaps under a new heading such as "Bizarre" or "Credulous!" In addition, many large and small organizations alike will have to fold their tents and fade into the abyss, numerous magazines and newsletters will cease publication, and selected passages in the Holy Bible and other sacred books will be subjected to further re-examination, re-interpretation and controversy.

Many prophets have predicted that we are living in one of the most important periods in recorded history. As you read on, you will see why. One researcher of the millennium prophecies recently wrote me: "The tempo has long been increasing, moving swiftly now towards the 21st century's entrance into the New Golden Age of Spiritual Renaissance, an inner awakening that man has never experienced while in the physical body on this planet."

And just think, we're down to "crunch time." It won't be long until we will all know for sure.

Tom Kay

THE PROPHETS FOR THE MILLENNIUM

Anyone can forecast the future—people from all walks of life do it every day. Some people even make forecasting their profession—weather people, investment gurus, government officials, and so forth. Their predictions are based on their education, their knowledge of the subject matter, current events, the conclusions of their contemporaries and past trends.

Professional forecasters are not prophets or seers; they are simply making an educated guess. True prophets or prophetesses do not rely on the information of others, nor do they do formulate their forecasts based on the limitations of the conscious mind. They receive their information from another source—a source that is directly connected with an unseen consciousness. The Apostle Peter boldly declares: "For it was not through any human whim that men prophesied of old; men they were, but, impelled by the Holy Spirit, they spoke the words of God." (2 Pet. 1:2)

Prophets have been around since the beginning of time. Without *time* there would be no prophecy. Minutes, hours, days and years are simply a measurement determined by the movement of the earth in relation to the sun, and anything measured has limits: a beginning and an end. Because life is eternal (limitless) the impression of time is much different in the *beyond*. The Bible declares: "With the Lord, one day is like a thousand years and a thousand years like one day." (2 Pet. 3:8) Albert Einstein said, "For us believing physicists, time has the value of mere illusion, however tenacious."

It has been theorized that the human brain functions to slow down our everyday consciousness of time, so that, as developing souls in a physical body, we can experience and function in the physical world of time and space. But once the ghost-like "ethereal" soul body is released by death, its awareness is altered as it enters an immense sphere with a myriad of spiritual dimensions. It is in this ethereal beyond that the records of the actions of all souls are housed—and information concerning the earth's past, present and future is accessible.

Many souls on the other side can *read* and *interpret* the information about the future to a greater or lesser degree. The same is true of certain gifted persons while their soul dwells in a physical body. Some are able to access the information directly; others do so by communicating with a departed soul or with a spiritual entity such as an angel. However, the accuracy of their predictions is subject to many variables. The reliability of the *source* from which the person receives information is one of the variables. The most trustworthy source is that known as the Universal Records—the all-knowing Mind of God. But the information of the Universal Records is the most difficult to access.

History is full of examples of people who claim the ability to predict the future. It is no different today. In fact, the Bible warns that this will be a time of many false prophets. As a guide for everyday life, we are told in the first letter of John: "But do not trust any and every spirit, my friends; test the spirits, to see whether they are from God, for there are many prophets falsely inspired." (4:1-2)

Information on the millennium prophecies has been published in hundreds of books. A few of these, by authors who are recognized as the finest researchers in this field, will be referenced throughout this one.

Most people are familiar with the prophets from the Old and New Testament; the millennium prophecies of the Bible are very meaningful as we approach the year 2001. But other prophets have appeared whose prophecies for the millennium are meaningful. Many prophets have been "put to the test," as the apostle John says, and have proven themselves because their predictions have come to pass. This tells us that it would be to our advantage to seriously consider their predictions that have not yet occurred. A number of prophets have predicted events for our times which, in their day and age, would have been scoffed at as impossible. Finally, many individuals have had unique and captivating visions of an event that coincides with the millennium prophecies.

Bible scholars distinguish between the "major" and "minor" prophets of the Old Testament. Researchers in the millennium prophecies rely not only on the Biblical prophets, but on the predictions of certain "major" prophets who have become distinguished because of their exceptional insights. Once the prophecies of the Bible and of the other major prophets are integrated into a single work, a clear, synergistic picture emerges.

The prophets of the Bible will be credited when appropriate. Following are short biographical sketches of the other major prophetic sources who will appear with various prophecies:

Hildegard of Bingen (1098-1179), also known as Saint Hildegard (though she was never canonized) was born in Bockelheim, Germany and educated at the Benedictine Convent of Disenberg, where she became the Mother Superior in 1136. She later founded the convent of Rupertsberg, near Bingen. She is renowned for her mystical experiences, which were recorded between 1141 and 1150. They were first published in 1513. Her prophecies for the United States are remarkable because she describes a nation that did not exist when she prophesied. Also, as we approach the millennium, her classical music compositions have become very popular.

Michel De Notredame (1503-1566) is known by the Latinized form of his name, Nostradamus. Born in Saint Remi, France and educated as a physician, he first achieved distinction for his treatment of those stricken with the plague during its outbreak in France and later became the court physician to Charles IX. His book *Prophecies* was first published in 1555 in the form of verses known as "quatrains," and his fame quickly spread throughout France. In her book, *The Man Who Saw Tomorrow*, Erika Cheetham says, "Nostradamus is probably the only author who could claim that his work has never been out of print for over four hundred years, apart from the Bible. On the average, about thirty books, either editions of the *Prophecies*, or critical appreciations of them, have been published each century since his death."

Mother Shipton (1488-1561) was reputedly born Ursula Sonthiel in Norfolk, England. At 24, she married Toby Shipton, and soon thereafter, she became known as Mother Shipton. It is said she exhibited prophetic abilities from an early age. Her simple verses have been quoted for hundreds of years, and have appeared in books, pamphlets, and articles on prophecy. Recently, a large number of unknown Mother Shipton millennium prophecies were discovered. Her time-honored status as a seeress and the message of her prophecies are impossible to ignore as the millennium approaches.

Oscar Ernst Bernhardt (1875-1941) was born in Bischofswerda (Saxony), Germany. He was living in London in 1915 when, with the outbreak of World War I, he was interned on the British Isle of Man and there had a deep inner awakening. In 1924 he began to write the first essays that eventually became the three volumes titled *In the Light of Truth*—more popularly known as the *Grail Message*. Arrested in 1938 by the Nazis, he and his family were placed under house arrest and kept under the constant supervision of the Gestapo. Prevented from further fulfillment of his task, he died on the 6th of December 1941.

In the Light of Truth has been translated into thirteen languages and is distributed in over fifty countries. Many other books and booklets have been published based on the essays in the *Grail Message*. In his writings, under the pen name Abd-ru-shin, he was sometimes stern, inflexible, and foreboding. Of course, when one considers the times and the environment in which he lived, it is understandable that many of his pronouncements and warnings would be harsh. Many have found his theories of Creation and Divine Laws to be very perceptive. His supporters claim that "His living knowledge is no earthly learnedness; he draws it from purest and highest Sources."

Edgar Cayce (1877-1945), born in Hopkinsville, Kentucky, was a humble and religious man of limited means whose formal education never went beyond the eighth grade. Yet, when he entered a coma-like trance, he told how to heal incurable diseases and predicted the future. According to one researcher and author, Edgar Cayce [pronounced Kay-see] "was the world's greatest prophet of record. He has made by far the highest number and percentage of accurate predictions ever recorded."

More than one hundred books have been published about the life and work of Edgar Cayce since the first biography, *There is a River*, was first published in 1943. In addition, thousands of booklets, magazine and newspaper articles have been written about him. He has been acknowledged around the world as the "Sleeping Prophet" as a result of the 1967 publication of the best-selling book of the same title by well-known author Jess Stearn. Moreover, the *Journal of the American Medical Association*, in March, 1979, stated, "the roots of present-day holism (holistic medicine), probably go back 100 years to the birth of Edgar Cayce," and numerous Christian scholars as well as many of the Jewish faith have referred to him as a "Christian Mystic." Other than the Bible, the prophecies of Edgar Cayce are the ones against which all others are usually measured and put to the test. His well-known ability as a gifted healer adds credibility to the entire collection of his work.

Transcripts of Cayce's 14,000-plus discourses on a variety of subjects recently became available on CD-ROM. This enormous collection of more than 24 million words includes reports, letters and background data. With the Cayce information (known as "readings") now available on computer, people familiar with the work of Edgar Cayce are finding unique information and new discoveries with respect to his prophecies for the millennium.

Mokichi Okada (1882-1955) was born in Tokyo, Japan. For a good part of his life he was an avowed atheist, and his life was riddled by chronic health problems and other hindrances. However, after the death of his wife and third child, he became associated with the Shinto religion. He did not find all of the answers he had hoped to in his newly adopted religion, but his intense seeking eventually bore fruit. At the age of 45, he began to receive numerous spiritual revelations and became known by the spiritual name, Meishu Sama. The Johrei Fellowship and "Nature Farming" are the outgrowth of his teachings.

Sun Bear (1929-1992) was the Medicine Chief and founder of the Bear Tribe Medicine Society and one of the best known visionaries in America. He was critically important in keeping the door open between the Native and non-Native cultures and informing the non-Native people about Native American philosophies and prophecies. He was also the author or co-author of nine books. His prophecies for the millennium are the subject of the book, *Black Dawn/Bright Day*.

Paul Solomon (1939-1994) was born in Rogers, Arkansas. He received prophetic information while in a self-induced trance using the same basic technique as Edgar Cayce. Trained as a Baptist preacher, Solomon came from a family of Baptist ministers including his grandfather, father and uncle. He changed his baptismal name of William Dove when he left the conventional ministry of his upbringing. His physical appearance was that of an Old Testament prophet: silver-white hair, a full gray beard and gentle eyes. His presence was captivating, and he was an excellent speaker and was especially popular in England, Australia, and Japan.

In 1972 Solomon founded the Fellowship of the Inner Light in Virginia Beach, an inter-faith church which explores the common threads of truth inherent in all religions. He authored *The Meta-Human*, a definitive work on the development of man's capacity, for which he received an honorary doctorate from Rabbi Joseph Gelberman, spiritual director of the interfaith New Seminary in New York City. Recently, *The Prophetic Revelations of Paul Solomon*, by W. Alexander Wheeler, Ph.D. was published. Dr. Wheeler writes:

Paul Solomon was a prophet unto many nations. . . .Although he was received by kings and queens, prime ministers, and statesmen from all corners of the globe, Paul Solomon offered his life in the service of all humanity—especially the poor, the oppressed, the enslaved. He was inflexibly faithful to the principles of eternal justice which are the unchanging laws of God. Only one week before he passed on, he was seriously injured attempting to free an 11-year-old girl from slavery in Thailand. For his efforts on behalf of the enslaved children of Thailand, Paul Solomon was nominated for the Nobel Peace Prize in 1993.

Gordon-Michael Scallion, a present-day prophet, is known and respected internationally as a futurist and spiritual visionary, and considered by many to be one of the most accurate intuitives of our time. He was busy with his avocation in the field of electronics when he experienced a serious health crisis in 1979 that gave birth to a spiritual awakening which left him with the gift of prophecy. At times he receives his information in a Cayce-like trance, and at other times he formulates and interprets his predictions from visions. Scallion's abilities have been favorably compared to those of Edgar Cayce.

Some of his more notable published prophecies are: the April 22, 1992 Los Angeles earthquake, the June 28, 1992 Landers and Big Bear, California quakes, and the January 17, 1994 Northridge quake. He also accurately predicted four of the most significant natural disasters of our times—Hurricane Andrew, the Blizzard of '93, the Mississippi floods of '93, and the January 17, 1995 quake of Kobe, Japan. He has appeared on the Fox Television programs "Sightings," and "Encounters," and was featured on NBC television's two prime-time specials, "Ancient Prophecies." He has often appeared as a guest on well-known radio talk-shows.

Gordon-Michael is the author of the acclaimed "Future Map of the United States 1998 - 2001," which portrays vastly different boundaries than those of the present. A few years ago he started publishing his prophecies in a monthly newsletter, *The Earth Changes Report*. His accuracy is well established by the tens of thousands of people who scrutinize his predictions. He updates his prophecies every month in his newsletter which enjoys a wide circulation in numerous countries. It has been estimated that one or more of his prophetic messages reach more than two million people each month.

Aron Abrahamsen, another present-day prophet, was born in Norway. At 19, as the clouds of World War II gathered over Europe, his parents shipped him to America, where he has lived ever since. After the war he received a degree in electrical engineering from California Polytechnic State University. He participated in the feasibility study of sending a manned expedition to the moon which paved the way for the Apollo Program. As an engineer he authored several technical papers. Early in his engineering career, he had a very meaningful spiritual experience which changed his outlook, goals and purpose. After many years of studying the Scriptures, and through prayer and meditation, he started to give readings which eventually opened up new and meaningful avenues of service to mankind. Edgar Cayce's son, the late Hugh Lynn Cayce, favorably compared Abrahamsen's readings to those of his father.

Abrahamsen's work has been written about in such books as Dr. Jeffrey Goodman's *We Are the Earthquake Generation* and *Psychic Archeaology*; John White's *Pole Shift*; Dr. Laile Bartlett's *Psi Trek*; Dr. William Kautz and Melanie Branon's *Channeling, The Intuitive Connection*, and other publications in Japan and Europe. His life story is the subject of the autobiography, *On Wings of Spirit*. He is the author of the monthly newsletter *The Abrahamsen Report*.

Mary Summer Rain, a present-day visionary, is the author of numerous books based on the teachings of her American Indian teacher, She-Who-Sees, a Shoshoni who was born blind but was gifted with highly developed extrasensory abilities. (She-Who-Sees, who lived alone in a humble cabin in the mountains of Colorado, preferred to be addressed by the name "No-Eyes.") As her student, Mary Summer Rain recorded the millennium prophecies of No-Eyes and eventually developed intuitive abilities of her own.

Mary Summer Rain and No-Eyes were also featured on the NBC television special, "Ancient Prophecies," which portrayed their prophecies for the millennium as set forth in several of Mary Summer Rain's books—*Phoenix Rising* and *Spirit Song* being the most notable.

The *Ramala* Prophecies: In the 1970s a young man from Great Britain, David Jevons, began to give readings on a variety of subjects. The hundreds of readings he has dispensed during the last two decades have become known as the "Ramala readings." In the *Metaphysical Bible Dictionary*, similar terms such as "Ram"—"Ramah" —"Ramiah" and so forth are defined as signifying an "exalted spiritual understanding in consciousness." Three popular books comprising the Ramala readings have been published and are distributed in a number of countries. Prophecies for the millennium are interspersed throughout. The information in the Ramala readings is considered by many to be "exalted" and elucidating in its message to humanity.

The Hopi, who occupy the rocky mesas in northern Arizona, believe they were the very first people to inhabit America. There is little doubt that their community of Oraibi has been established longer than any other in the United States. The translation of the word "Hopi" is "peace." Their religion has embraced prophecy for hundreds of years. It has been well documented by researchers that many of the Hopi prophecies for the twentieth century have come true as they predicted. Their other prophecies for the millennium still await confirmation.

As we approach the year 2000, certain people will claim that we are in for a lot of "millennium hype." Most likely they will point to the events that took place in Europe as the year A.D. 999 drew to a close. In *Doomsday 1999 A.D.*, published in 1981, author, researcher and investigator Charles Berlitz, who is fluent in twenty-seven languages, wrote about the mass hysteria that occurred in Europe as the year A.D. 999 came to a close. It is a narrative that the scoffers can look to when they are convincing others that history is about to repeat itself.

In his chapter "Doomsday—December 31st, 999 A.D." he tells in dramatic style how the population tried desperately to prepare for Judgement Day. For the most part, forgiveness and unheard of generosity were practiced by most. However, anarchy also played a part among certain segments of the population. The fear that gripped the people continued to grow as the appointed time drew near. The churches, monasteries, and convents were continually inundated by people seeking forgiveness for their sins and absolution. Then the moment of truth was upon them—December 31st, 999 arrived. For those who could gain entrance, it was imperative that they depart the mortal world in the most advantageous way possible: by attending midnight Mass, the Sacrament of the Eucharist, in the Cathedral of St. Peter in Rome. The following is the description of the Mass as told by author and historian Frederick H. Martens in *The Story of Human Life*:

. . .Pope Sylvester II stood before the high altar. The church was overcrowded, all in it lay on their knees. The silence was so great that the rustling of the Pope's white sleeves as he moved about the altar could be heard. And there was still another sound. It was a sound that seemed to measure out the last minutes of the earth's thousand years of existence since the coming of Christ. It echoed in the ears of those present as the pulse-beat does in the ears of a man with a fever, and its beat was loud and regular and never stopped. For the door of the church sacristy stood open, and what the audience heard was the regular, uninterrupted tick, tock of the great clock which hung within, one tick for every passing second.

The Pope was a man of iron will-power, calm and collected. He had probably left the sacristy door open purposely, in order to secure the greatest amount of effect at this great moment. Though his face was pale as death with excitement, he did not move nor did his hands tremble.

The midnight mass had been said, and a deathly silence fell. The audience waited. . .Pope Sylvester said not a word. He seemed lost in prayer, his hands raised to the sky. The clock kept on ticking. A long sigh came from the people, but nothing happened. Like children afraid of the dark, all those in the church lay with their faces to the ground, and did not venture to look up. The sweat of terror ran from many an icy brow, and knees and feet which had fallen asleep lost all feeling. Then, suddenly—the clock stopped ticking!

Among the congregation the beginning of a scream of terror began to form in many a throat. And, stricken dead by fear, several bodies dropped heavily on the stone floor.

Then the clock began to strike. It struck one, two, three, four. . .It struck twelve. . .The twelfth stroke echoed out, and a deathly silence still reigned!

Then it was that Pope Sylvester turned around, and with the proud smile of a victor stretched out his hands in blessing over the heads of those who filled the church. And at the same moment, all the bells in the tower began to peal out a glad and jubilant chime, and from the organ-loft sounded a chorus of joyous voices, young and older, a little uncertain at first, perhaps, but growing clearer and firmer moment by moment. They sang the *Te Deum Laudamus*—'Thee God, we praise!'

The whole congregation united their voices with those of the choir. Yet it was some time before cramped backs could be straightened out, and before people recovered from the dreadful sight offered by those who had died of fright. When the *Te Deum* had been sung, men and women fell in each other's arms, laughing and crying and exchanging the kiss of peace. Thus ended the thousandth year after the birth of Christ!

The other documentation presented by Berlitz in his book dispels any doubt that the circumstances in 999 A.D. were much different than they are in today's world. For today there is a great deal of scientific evidence that seems to support an abundant number of prophecies for the millennium.

THE FIERY MESSENGER

In the late 1970s, a group of students and supporters in Great Britain asked intuitive David Jevons to request information from his Ramala Master in the spiritual beyond concerning the Earth Changes that had been predicted by so many seers to take place near the end of this century. A pronouncement with respect to the "Fiery Messenger" was volunteered in the reading, although it does not appear that this particular celestial event was included in previous readings or group discussions. The following is from *The Wisdom of Ramala* chapter titled, "The End of The World?":

I must begin by emphasizing that there is a question mark after the title of this talk. I have not deliberately chosen this title in order to be provocative but merely to reflect the viewpoint of many people in your World today. Even amongst spiritually-minded people there are those who question the reason for the events now taking place on this planet, who ask whether the earth can survive, whether it should survive, who ask whether the Earth Changes to come are something to be avoided or welcomed. All I want to do in this talk is to present a point of view from another plane of life and to ask you to hold it in your minds in the years to come.

I will begin by making the simple statement that the earth, like you, is imbued with spirit. It will, therefore, never die. Whilst its physical form might change as it experiences periods of transformation and transmutation, the spirit that is responsible for its creation will never die. In the same way that you in your physical bodies die and are born again onto a higher plane of life so the earth, on another level, undergoes a similar experience. It is a cosmic fact that all forms of life, no matter what the level of evolution, are born, die and are born again in the endless cycle of evolution. The earth has done this many times. . .

Those of you on the plane of earth who fear death, who do not understand the real nature of this act of transformation, will also fear the ending of the World because the result is apparently the same: the ending of physical life as you know it. But those of you who are aware of life beyond death, who recognize that death on the plane of earth is but the opening of a door to a higher level of consciousness, a return to the place of your true being, must also see that the same is true for the earth as a whole. . .

The changes of which we talk now are the Earth Changes that are associated with the introduction of the Aquarian Age. It is essential that those of you who live at this time of transition should understand the nature of and the *purpose* for these Earth Changes. . .

Remember that the symbol of the Aquarian Age is the phoenix. The phoenix is the mythical bird which consciously sacrifices itself on the cosmic fire, releasing its old form in order to come forth purified in the new. Does not the phoenix symbolize the desire within your own spiritual being for the purification of the earth to take place so that the old human form can be cast off and the new Aquarian form may come forth?

As you look around the World today you cannot help but notice the increasing tempo of human conflict all over the globe as both nations and individuals oppose each other for political, ideological, and religious reasons. But humanity is not only suffering from an outer level through famine, earthquake, disease, and war but also on an inner level through its lack of spirituality, its self-centredness, its greed, its concern only for self at the expense of its fellow human beings and the other Kingdoms of the earth [animal-vegetable- mineral]. All these events bear witness to the approach of Armageddon and the ending of the Age. Humanity needs to be purified. Humanity needs to experience the cosmic fire of purification in order to come forth reborn in the Aquarian Age.

I know there are people, some spiritually motivated, who believe that this event will not come about and that it will be prevented either by the intervention of some great Master or by Humanity reversing the path upon which it is now set. I would ask you to remember the impact of the last great impulse of the Christ energy, of the Master Jesus who came on the earth two thousand years ago. Consider how long it took for that energy to become an effective force on the plane of earth even after that Master's great sacrifice. Even if the Christ energy was to return at this time it could not move Humanity from the course on which it is set. That is why the prophets and seers of old could make their prophecies with such certainty. To ground cosmic knowledge on the earth, to manifest it through the cycle of human evolution, takes time, human time. The spiritual consciousness needed to save this World cannot be grounded in the time that is now left before the Earth Changes. . .

As to the timing of this event there are many opinions but, in truth, there is only one being who posses that knowledge and that is your God, the Creator of us all. Furthermore that knowledge will not be released to anyone until the actual moment in time draws near.

I believe that the major Earth Changes will be initiated by what I will call the "Fiery Messenger." There is even now a *star* of great power proceeding towards our Solar Body. The star, at this moment, is invisible to the human, or even telescopic eye, but it is set on a path which will bring it into conjunction with our Planetary System. As it passes by it will affect the motions of all the planets of our System, therefore, will bring about changes on the surface of the planets themselves. The effect of the passage will be to set in motion the Earth Changes that are prophesied. Various lands will sink, others will rise. . .

Humanity has the power to influence this transformation through its behavior now, through its use of nuclear technology, through its use, or abuse, of the three Kingdoms of Matter on this earth. It can either add to, or moderate, the path and the influence of this great star. How you as individuals behave now, how you lead your lives and manifest your consciousness will affect the great transformation of the earth. So I say to you now, as I said to you five years ago, that these Earth Changes are coming. They cannot be avoided. They are part of the destiny of the earth.

Is it not strange how Humanity finds it difficult to plan beyond the year 2000. It is almost as if the end of the century is the ending of a cycle. Now I'm not saying that this is the year when these changes will come to pass, but certainly the final ending of the Piscean cycle will indeed take place around that time.

This therefore gives you two decades in which to prepare yourselves, to prepare your lifeboats, to establish your true values, to shine your light and to prepare for the ending of your world. I hasten to say *your* world, not *the* World, for it is your world that must change, not the World. . .The divinity of planet earth will not be extinguished by any human action. . .

Although Humanity has the power to destroy itself, it will destroy itself not by nuclear explosions, not by destroying the planet which it abuses out of ignorance and greed, but by *destroying its own soul.*

Question: The star that was spoken of, has it passed through this Solar System before?

Answer: Yes.

Question: Is it Halley's comet?

Answer: No. It is far bigger than that.

It is amazing how many Bible prophecies describe turmoil in the sun, planets, and stars. Several of the Old Testament figures recognized as prophets had visions of a future age they believed signaled the end of an era. They beheld the turbulent events that would accompany the New Age, characterized at times as "The Last Judgement" or "The Day of the Lord" or "Armageddon."

The following excerpt is from one of the prophet Joel's visions. Some researchers speculate that the "pillars of smoke" is the column-like smoke that appears to support the mushroom cloud from a nuclear explosion.

The earth shall quake before them; the heavens shall tremble; the sun and the moon shall be dark, and the stars shall withdraw their shining. (Joel 2:10)

And I will shew wonders in the heavens and the earth, blood, and fire, and pillars of smoke. The sun shall be turned into darkness, and the moon into blood, before the great and terrible day of the Lord come. (Joel 2:30-31)

The following excerpt from the prophet Amos is said to be relevant to our times:

And it shall come to pass in that day, saith the Lord God, that I will cause the sun to go down at noon, and I will darken the earth in the clear day. (Amos 8:9)

The prophet Isaiah is one of the most respected of the Old Testament. He began his prophecy mission about 740 B.C. Among the *Dead Sea Scrolls* discovered in 1947, there was found a scroll of the Book of Isaiah. It was essentially as we know it now. The following excerpt is also from the thirteenth chapter:

Behold, the day of the Lord cometh, cruel both with wrath and fierce anger, to lay the land desolate. . .For the stars of heaven and the constellations thereof shall not give their light; the sun shall be darkened in his going forth, and the moon shall not cause her light to shine. . . .Therefore I will shake the heavens, and the earth shall remove out of her place. . .(Isaiah 13:9-13)

". . .and the earth shall remove out of her place. . ." This could be Isaiah's description of the shifting of the earth on its axis.

Most New Testament prophecies are those of Jesus. When His disciples asked Him in private for the signs and omens that would signal the "end of the age," He was very specific. His answer is recorded in the Gospels of Matthew, Mark, and Luke:

The time is coming when you will hear the noise of battle near at hand and the news of battles far away; see that you are not alarmed. Such things are bound to happen; but the end is still to come. For nation will make war upon nation, kingdom upon kingdom; there will be famines and earthquakes in many places. With all these things the birth pangs of the New Age begin. (Matthew 24:6-8)

For there will be great distress, unequaled from the beginning of the world until now—and never to be equaled again. . .Immediately after the distress of those days, the sun will be darkened, and the moon will not give its light; the stars will fall from the sky, and the heavenly bodies will be shaken. . .(Matthew 24:29)

But in those days, after that distress, the sun will be darkened, the moon will not give her light; the stars will come falling from the sky, the celestial powers will be shaken. (Mark 13:24-25)

When you hear of wars and revolutions, do not be frightened. These things must happen first, but the end will not come right away. . .Nation will rise against nation, and kingdom against kingdom. There will be great earthquakes, famines and pestilences in various places, and fearful events and great signs from heaven. There will be signs in the sun, moon, and stars. On the earth, nations will be in anguish and perplexity at the roaring and tossing of the sea. Men will faint from terror, apprehensive of what is coming on the world, for the heavenly bodies will be shaken. (Luke 21:9-11)

The Revelation of John, also known as the *Apocalypse*, has been the subject of many diverse interpretations. It is said to have been recorded by the Apostle John long after the death of Jesus, when the Romans had banished John to the island of Patmos in the Mediterranean. John apparently entered an altered state of consciousness and then recorded his visions using enigmatic symbols of dragons, beasts and demons. He also describes celestial catastrophes which are much the same as those recorded in the Old and New Testaments.

For instance, in verses 8:10 and 16:21 he describes meteor showers striking the earth that could be caused by a wayward asteroid or comet:

> And there fell a great star from heaven, burning as it were a lamp, and it fell on a third part of the [earth's] rivers."
> And there was a great earthquake, such as was not since men were upon the earth, so mighty an earthquake and so great. . .And every island fled away, and the mountains were not found. And there fell upon men a great hail out of heaven, every stone about the weight [25+ lbs.] of a talent." (Nostradamus writes that hail falling from the sky will be larger than an egg).

Meteor storms are referred to in numerous millennium prophecies. The ancient Hindu prophecies refer to our times as the Kali Yuga, the "Age of Destruction." It is recorded in the *Mahabharata*, an ancient Hindu composition:

> And the course of the winds will be confused and agitated, and innumerable meteors will flash through the sky foreboding evil. And then the Sun will appear with six others of the same kind. And all around will be din and uproar, and everywhere

there will be conflagrations. . .and fires will blaze on all sides. . .when the Yuga comes. . .

Some speculate that John and the Hindu prophet of a much earlier time may have visioned the Leonid meteor storm expected to occur again in 1999. The Leonid meteors, from the comet Temple-Tuttle, are believed to be extremely dense. The storm has been awesome and frightening in the past. In addition, the year 1999 will be very unusual because, between February and August, there will be two Solar eclipses and a Lunar eclipse.

Many prophecy students reason that certain elements of the Bible prophecies are materializing in this period. We see famine, battles and revolution; weather patterns are changing; earthquakes are intensifying and their number increasing; previously unknown disease—pestilence—is making an appearance. The cataclysmic prophecies, however, are still a matter of speculation. Will they soon be on the horizon? Is there any way to know?

Many prophets have predicted that our solar system will be stirred up by a mysterious star or a large comet. A number of astronomers theorize that we may be visited by another planet rather than a comet or a star—a planet that enters our solar system at regular intervals and causes havoc. They call it "Planet X."

A January, 1981, headline in The Detroit News read: "10th planet? Pluto's orbit says 'yes.'" The report stated that an astronomer from the U.S. Naval Observatory "told a meeting of the American Astronomical Society. . .that irregularities in the orbit of Pluto. . .indicates that the solar system contains a 10th planet, and noted that this "announcement comes as no surprise to Zecharia Sitchin, whose book, The 12th Planet, came out three years ago." Sitchin claims that Planet X visits our solar system every 3600 years.

Zecharia Sitchin is not an astronomer, yet his expertise as a researcher is well recognized in the scientific community. Born in Russia and raised in Palestine, Sitchin acquired a profound knowledge of modern and ancient Hebrew, other Semitic and European languages, the Old Testament, and the history and archaeology of the Near East. A graduate of the University of London, he was a leading journalist and editor in Israel for many years. One of the few scholars able to read and understand Sumerian, his books deal with the earth's and man's histories and pre-histories, and the information and lore etched on clay tablets. His book, Genesis Revisited, is the main reference for the following information. In 1982 the U.S. Naval Laboratory announced that it was "seriously pursuing" the search for Planet X. In 1983 The New York *Times* reported: "Clues Get Warm in the Search for Planet X," and quoted an astronomer from the Ames Research Center as saying, "Astronomers are so sure of the 10th Planet that they think there's nothing left but to name it." Of course, Sitchin already knew the name. To the Sumerians it was known as Nibiru, and to the Babylonians as Marduk.

Other reports appeared in several daily newspapers. "Giant Object Mystifies Astronomers"; "Mystery Body Found in Space"; "At Solar System's Edge Giant Object is a Mystery." And so a debate arose, and a new dimension! An article by the science service of The Washington *Post*, based on "Infrared Astronomical Satellite" (IRAS) data from the Pioneer spacecraft, said, "Astronomers do not know if it is a planet or a giant comet," and added "When IRAS scientists first saw the mystery body and calculated that it could be as close as 50 billion miles, there was some speculation that it might be moving toward earth."

In 1985 numerous astronomers were intrigued with the "Nemesis Theory" first proposed by Walter Alvarez of the University of California and his father, the Nobel-prize-winning physicist Luis Alvarez. Noticing regularity in the extinctions of various species (including the dinosaurs), they proposed that a "death star" or planet with a highly inclined and immense elliptical, comet-like orbit periodically stirs up a shower of comets that then bring death and havoc to the inner Solar System, including earth. (In *The Twelfth Planet*, Sitchin says "The Planet's periodic appearance and disappearance from earth's view confirms the assumption of its permanence. In this it acts like many comets.")

An illustration in The Washington *Post* in 1987, based on information from the U.S. Naval Observatory and *Discover* magazine, portrayed the orbit of Planet X far out in space between the "outer" planets. However, Sitchin's illustrations locate it between Mars and Jupiter, in the area of the Asteroid Belt, an assemblage of tens of thousands of "planetoids" of various dimensions (Ceres being the largest with a diameter of 481 miles). What's more, Sitchin depicts Planet X's orbit as *retrograde*. If Planet X, (or any other celestial body) enters the Asteroid Belt in a retrograde orbit, our solar system might be more than just a little stirred up! Perhaps the prophecies of meteor showers or stars falling from the sky, were not as far fetched as some surmise.

Sitchin claims that Planet X is about the size of Neptune. So again, it was no surprise to Sitchin when, in August of 1988, a report by Dr. Robert S. Harrington of the U.S. Naval Laboratory calculated that "its mass. . .is probably four times that of earth."

Many quatrains from the prophecies of Nostradamus refer to comets and similar heavenly or celestial bodies. *The Man Who Saw Tomorrow* cites two examples from Erika Cheetham's translation of the quatrains:

> After great misery for mankind an even greater approaches when the great cycle of the centuries is renewed. It will rain blood, milk, famine, war and disease: In the sky will be seen a fire, dragging a trail of sparks. [II-46]
>
> Mabus will then soon die and there will come a dreadful destruction of people and animals. Suddenly vengeance will be revealed, a hundred hands, thirst and hunger, when the COMET will pass. [II-62]

Cheetham states that Nostradamus wrote in an obscure style and that "in order to avoid being prosecuted as a magician, Nostradamus writes that he deliberately confused the time sequence of the *Prophecies* so that their secrets would not be revealed to the non-initiate." (The word "Mabus" in quatrain II, verse 62 is a mystery. Many speculate that it is the proper name of a future powerful world tyrant.)

The following prophecy about the "Fiery Messenger" is from a *Grail Message* presented shortly before the devastation and suffering of World War II swept the globe:

THE GREAT COMET

For years now, *knowing ones* have been speaking of the coming of this especially significant STAR. The number of those who await it is continually increasing, and the indications become more and more definite, so much so in fact it is to be expected soon. But what it really signifies, what it brings, has not yet been rightly explained. It is thought that it brings upheavals of an incisive nature. But this STAR portends more.

It can be called the Star of Bethlehem, because it is of exactly the same nature as that was. Its power sucks the *waters up high,* brings *weather catastrophes* and still more. When encircled by its rays the *earth quakes*.

Since the event in Bethlehem there has been nothing like it. Like the Star of Bethlehem, the STAR has also detached itself from the Eternal Realm of Primordial Spirit at such a time as to take effect on this earth exactly when the years of spiritual enlightenment are to come to all mankind.

The STAR takes its course in a *straight* line from the Eternal Realm of this part of the Universe. Its core is filled with high spiritual power; it envelopes itself in material substance, and will thereby also become visible to men on earth. Unerringly and unswervingly the COMET pursues its course, and will appear on the scene at the right hour, as already ordained thousands of years ago.

The first direct effects have already begun in recent years. For anyone who wishes neither to see nor to hear this, and who does not perceive how ridiculous it is still to maintain that all the *extraordinary* things which have already happened are of everyday occurrence, there is naturally no help. He either wishes to act like an ostrich out of fear, or he is burdened with an extremely limited understanding. Both types must be allowed to go serenely on their way; one can only smile at their easily refutable assertions.

But the knowing ones could also be told where the first *powerful* rays are striking. However, since the rays are gradually also encompassing the whole earth, there is no use being more explicit. It will take years to come to this point, and years before the COMET again releases the earth from its influence.

And then the earth is *purified* and *refreshed* in *every* respect for the blessing and joy of its inhabitants. It will be more beautiful than it has ever been. Therefore every believer shall look forward to the future with tranquil confidence, and not be alarmed at anything that may happen in the coming years. If he can look up with confidence to God, no harm will come to him.

The essay contains statements that may be of the utmost importance to the human race at this time. "Its core is filled with high spiritual power" and its "rays are gradually also encompassing the whole earth." The following is from a book published in 1980, *Rolling Thunder, The Coming Earth Changes:*

A TWELFTH CENTURY PROPHECY ABOUT AMERICA

Perhaps the earliest vision ever made concerning the future of the United States was made by Saint Hildegard, three centuries before the New World was discovered. She predicted that one day there would come forth "a great nation across the ocean that will be inhabited by peoples of different tribes and descent"—a good description of the American "melting pot" of immigrants from many foreign countries. For this future nation, however, the Saint sounded several warnings, all of which would come about approximately at the time of the appearance of a "great comet." Some translators believe what she had in mind as Halley's comet, scheduled to light up our heavens in 1986-87.

"Just before the comet comes," Saint Hildegard forecast, "many nations" including America, "will be scourged by want of famine." When the comet does finally pass over. . ."the great nation will be devastated by earthquakes, storms, and great waves of water, causing much want and plagues. The ocean will also flood many other countries, so that all coastal cities will live in fear, with many destroyed. . ."

Fortunately, however, Saint Hildegard looked beyond, and also forecast that after the great comet, and after the earth upheavals and wars are finished, the globe will eventually enter a peaceful age.

It will be a time when citizens of the "great nation" will carry no weapons, and the only use men will have for iron will be to make plowshares for cultivating a land brought back to abundance and tranquility.

A translation of the original prophecy by Saint Hildegard, published in 1941 in *The Prophets and Our Times* by Rev. R. Gerald Culleton also stated: "The Comet by its *tremendous pressure*, will force much out of the ocean and flood many countries. . ."

About 30 years ago, the Brazilian spiritualist, Ramatis, predicted the approach of a gigantic celestial body from deep in outer space. Although this body was not destined to intersect any of our planets' orbits, Ramatis proclaimed that it will cause serious disturbances in our planetary system during the 1980s, and by the 1990s its powerful gravitational energy would draw the earth's axis to a vertical position. Many of the prophecies seem to be predict that the comet/star is going to be the one, single momentous event of the millennium because of its gravitational effect on the earth. Further, if it returns to our solar system at periodic times, this fact may explain the reason numerous prophets and seers going all the way back to those of the Old Testament could make their pronouncements with such intensity and confidence.

Hundreds of prophecies are attributed to church clergy, saints and seers. Many mention *cosmic* disturbances and turmoil of numerous descriptions. The following revelation was foretold by the eminent thirteenth-century Austrian monk, Johannes Friede (1204-1257) of the order of St. John:

> When the great time will come, in which mankind will face its last, hard trial, it will be foreshadowed by striking changes in nature. The alteration between cold and heat will become more intensive, storms will have more catastrophic effects, earthquakes will destroy greater regions and the seas will overflow many lowlands. Not all of it will be the result of natural causes, but mankind will penetrate into the bowels of the earth and will reach into the clouds, gambling with its own existence. Before the powers of destruction will succeed in their design, *the universe will be thrown into disorder*, and the age of iron will plunge into nothingness.
>
> When nights will be filled with more intensive cold and days with heat, a new life will begin in nature. The heat means radiation from the earth, the cold the waning light of the sun. Only a few years more and you will become aware that sunlight has grown perceptibly weaker. *When even your artificial light will cease to give service, the great event in the heavens* will be near. . ."

The prediction by Friede that our "artificial light will cease to give service" is remarkable considering he lived hundreds of years before electrical power, and it is interesting that the Friede prophecy also refers to "the age of iron," the age of Kali-Yuga. We find in the *Visuddi-Magga*, a book from ancient India: ". . .there are seven ages, each of which is separated from the previous one by a world catastrophe."

Many sources discuss the "comet/star," and almost every single one claims that the phenomena is a recurring event. The only differences seem to be in the interval of time; however the majority are in the 3,000-to-4,000 years time frame, which could place its most recent appearance during the time of the Exodus as described in the Old Testament, and Noah before that. And if you accept the one-time existence of Atlantis as claimed by Edgar Cayce, Plato, and so many others, it may have influenced the destruction of Atlantis. With respect to the time of Noah, Edgar Cayce told a young girl in 1944:

> For as has been given from the beginning, the deluge was not a myth (as many would have you believe), but a period when man had so belittled himself with the cares of the world, with the deceitfulness of his own knowledge and power, as to require that there be a return to his dependence wholly—physically and mentally—upon God.
> Will the entity see such occur again in the earth? Will it be among those who may be given those directions as to how, where the elect may be preserved for the replenishing again of the earth? Remember, not by water—for it is the mother of life in the earth—but rather by the elements, fire. [3653-1]

Cayce may have been referring to 2nd Peter 3:10-13:

> But the Day of the Lord will come; it will come, unexpected as a thief. On the day the heavens will disappear with a great rushing sound, the elements will disintegrate in flames, and the earth and all that is in it will be laid bare. Since the earth will break up in this way, think what sort of people you ought to be, what devout and dedicated lives you should live! Look eagerly for the coming of the Day of God and work to hasten it on; that day will set the heavens ablaze until they fall apart, and will melt in the elements of flames. But we have His promise, and look forward to new heavens and a new earth, the home of justice.

Concerning the time of the Exodus, the following is excerpted and paraphrased from *Catholic Prophecy, The Coming Chastisement* by Yves Dupont:

> Let us recall briefly the situation which afflicted the Egyptians, the crossing dry-shod of the Red Sea and the prolonged duration of the day. In Mexico, on the other hand, a prolonged night was recorded as evidenced by archaeological discoveries. The passage of the comet at that time was recorded, not only in

the Book of Exodus, but also in other documents: the Egyptian papyrus, a Mexican manuscript, a Finnish narration, and many others. . ..

Will the comet to come be the same as that of Exodus? It is not impossible when we consider the description of the plagues as given in Exodus and those described in our Christian prophecies. When the tail of the Exodus comet crossed the path of the earth, a red dust, impalpable, like fine flour, began to fall. It was too fine to be seen. . .but it colored everything red and the water of the Egyptians was changed into blood. . . After the fine rusty pigment fell over Egypt, there followed a coarser dust—"like ash," this is recorded in Exodus, for then it was visible. . .

The narrative of the Book of Exodus confirms this and is in turn corroborated by various documents found in Mexico, Finland, Siberia, and India. It is therefore certain that a comet crossed the path of the earth more than 3000 years ago, causing widespread destruction.

This is the kind of phenomenon (if the prophecies are accurate) which is soon to strike the earth again.

A number of Prophecy researchers have speculated that the rotation of the earth may have been temporarily interrupted during the general time-frame of the Exodus. In the Book of Joshua it is written that Joshua ordered the sun to stand still, and: ". . .So the sun stood still in the midst of heaven, and hasted not to go down for a whole day (10:13)."

The Hopi Indians believe that we are living in the "Fourth Age," an age they also believe is fast drawing to an end. Their ancient legends claim that, as the earth rotates around its axes, it is held in place by two enormous celestial angels, and that the destruction of the three previous ages were caused when the two angels abandoned their posts. They predict that soon, the angels will again abandon their posts, and that this will happen when a "blue star" that is fast approaching will enter our solar system. Nostradamus may have seen an "interruption" of the earth's rotation during our times. In his Epistle to King Henry II of France, he wrote:

And it shall be in the month of October that a great movement of the globe will happen, and it will be such that one will think the gravity of the earth has lost its natural balance, and that it will be plunged into the abyss and perpetual blackness of space.

There will portents and signs in the spring, extreme changes, nations overthrown, and mighty earthquakes.

The following is from a reading offered by Paul Solomon in which he suggests the planet Mars will cause serious problems and perhaps a shifting of the earth on its axis:

> . . .the greater danger is that done to the environment, not only through the burning of fossil fuels, the creation of acids in the atmosphere, the destruction of the ozone, the depletion of oxygen and such. . .the change in the weather patterns is drastic. And it is this that changes the weight of the polar ice caps and throws off balance earth orbit. [This] allows for the approach, and we are talking after the year two thousand, of the passing of Mars at the nearest point that they [Earth and Mars] have passed in a few thousand years.
>
> Now that is verifiable. Look at the paths and see that they become close enough to have magnetic influence upon one another. And if the earth, then, is shifted even slightly out of its normal movement and rotation, orbit, you shall have the shifting of the poles. . .These come from tampering with the atmosphere in such a way as to drastically change the weather and the distribution of the weight on the earth. . . .
>
> And this area will be found in those series of changes or some three slippages of the crust of the earth. As there is the passing of that red planet, so will the crust of the earth be attracted toward it, as it would be approaching; so than that upper pole or the North Pole will point in the direction of its advance.
>
> Then as [Mars] comes close or at its point nearest the earth, so then will the pole point directly upward or in that portion, that direction that now exists or near—and in the passing away of its presence from the planet, so then would the poles shift again a third time toward the opposite direction. So that there will be three separate temperature changes in this area, making near impossible the survival of any animal species or plants, either in this area or upon most of the surface of this planet.

In one of his quatrains, Nostradamus wrote:

> The year 1999 and seventh month,
> From the sky will come a great king of terror,

To raise again the great king of Jacquerie,
Before and after, Mars will reign at will.

Jacques, translated from the Old French, means "peasant," and the term "Jacquerie" is used when referring to the bloody revolt of the French peasants against the nobility in 1358.

In *Beyond Prophecies and Predictions*, author and notable researcher, Moria Timms, also speculates about the planet Mars and this prophecy of Nostradamus:

Could this quatrain refer to the possible liberation of Mars's satellite, Phobos (meaning "terror") from its orbit? Phobos revolves centrifugally, which means it is straining to get out of orbit. It is a relatively dense body, and, were it to escape, it would gravitate toward the center of the solar system, passing close or even colliding with earth.

Riley Hansard Crabb, Director of Borderland Sciences Research Foundation, has information on this subject from sources other than Nostradamus. His source suggests this satellite of Mars may stray within earth's atmosphere and surprise our planet into a reluctant orbit out between Mars and Jupiter. . .

In the June '96 issue of the *Earth Changes Report*, Gordon-Michael Scallion describes a vision he had concerning Phobos:

. . .I am in an orbit around Mars. As I look back I can clearly see the Earth, a blue speck. Looking up, I see a moon orbiting Mars.

I look deeper into the heavens again. I observe a light near the star Arcturus that seems to be moving. I wonder if it is a comet, and somehow I know that it is.

Time speeds up, and I am watching things in fast motion, where weeks and months are occurring in minutes. Mars begins to shudder. . .It seems like an earthquake, and I wonder if this is happening everywhere. All of a sudden I find myself being moved halfway around Mars. My perspective on the comet, earth and the sun has changed. The comet is now brighter and seems to be building in strength. I wonder if the comet has something to do with the vibration.

Looking up again I see the moon of Mars. It is being pushed from its orbit. I can clearly see this movement, it is snakelike. I am watching as it appears over the horizon, from my perspective, and it has left its orbit. It begins to spiral out into space.

Now I find myself catapulted away from Mars. I am between the Earth and Mars, and I can see the moon of Mars. It seems to be moving away from Earth out into deep space. But as I watch it and the comet continue to move, I see that the path is changing. I believe that the Earth will intercept it in the future. I see a calendar that says three months.

I watch weeks pass quickly. One month, two months, two months and three weeks, and then I am watching a clock. I am seeing this moon move toward the Earth. I think it is so close that it is going to hit the Earth, but I hear this will not happen. It nears the Earth's atmosphere and turns red from heat. The angle is such that it appears that it is going to be deflected off the atmosphere. I remember thinking, "I hope this does occur," and within a second it ricochets off and continues out into space.

I am now shown the Earth, and as a result of the shockwave, the Earth shudders everywhere. There are winds. I am watching large land masses which appear to be the North American Plate and the Pacific Plate. They are moving, perhaps half of the plate structure of the Earth, shift as if in a single moment. They do not go down or up, but rather, they slip. The movement from my perspective doesn't seem far, but it might be something akin to twenty-five or thirty degrees of slippage.

I watch certain land masses that were warm become instantly cold. I see animals, grazing animals that look like herds of cattle, frozen in their paths. I watch other areas that are mile-high with snow, melting. I realize that it is the Antarctic. As I am watching, there is a time lapse which I would assume would be weeks or months. I watch Greenland, the ice is melting so fast that water levels throughout the world are rising.

The water is moving in so fast that new seaways are made. I can see inland seas in the United States, I can see a river running from the Great Lakes to Phoenix. I can see that the St. Lawrence Seaway has become a large inland sea. The Mississippi divides the United States in two. Europe has become a series of larger islands and most of northern Europe is under water.

At the same time I am seeing other land masses thrust up from the ocean bottom as a result of the shift. I see huge land masses in the Atlantic and the Pacific thrust up, even though the melting has raised the water level. Are there still twelve tectonic plates?

I move around to see how many there are. After counting I find there are twenty-four. . .

Edgar Cayce stated that the earth has experienced a "pole shift" in the past. He said many thousands of years ago: ". . .the polar regions were then turned to where they occupied more of the tropical or semi-tropical regions. . .The Nile entered into the Atlantic Ocean. What is now the Sahara was an inhabited land and very fertile. What is now the central portion of this country, or the Mississippi basin, was then all in the ocean; only the plateau was existent, or the regions that are now portions of Nevada. Utah and Arizona formed the greater part of what we know as the United States. . .The oceans were then turned about; they no longer bear their names. . ." [364-13]

Will the comet/star or other celestial visitor be the "trigger" that sets in motion the shifting of the earth on its axis? Saint Hildegard prophesied the comet will exert "tremendous pressure" on the earth. And it may not take a great deal of pressure to induce the earth's crust to start skidding on earth's slippery inner core. Albert Einstein, in the Forward he wrote for Charles H. Hapgood's *The Path of the Pole,* stated: "Such displacements may take place as the consequence of comparatively slight forces exerted on the crust, derived from the earth's momentum of rotation, which in turn will tend to alter the axis of rotation of the earth's crust."

The Hopi Indians believe their prophesied "blue star" will embody "spirit entities" such as angels they designate as "Kachinas"—angels who control its orbit, and that the Kachinas are capable of manifesting on earth in a material form:

When the Blue Star *Kachina* makes its appearance in the heavens, the Fifth World will emerge. This will be preceded by the last great war, a spiritual conflict with material matters. Material matters will be destroyed by spiritual beings who will remain to create one world and one nation, under one power, that of the Creator.

The following is excerpted from a feature article titled "The Blue Star" by Scallion in the March, 1993 issue of the *Earth Changes Report*:

Prior to the Earth Changes and major shifts in consciousness, spiritual forces send guidance to prepare us for these changes. This time period of preparation is known as Tribulation—a seven-year cycle ending in '98. On the physical/mental level these warnings are perceived as urges from within. As changes increase, outward signs occur, such as spiritual manifestations and signs in the heavens. One such heavenly sign is the Blue Star.

Now, imagine, a star—a blue star, that moves through the heavens at regular cycle, such as a comet, except this celestial object is pure spiritual energy, a star made manifest by spiritual forces—a star composed of light-beings. These angels—souls of the highest level—who by their own spiritual evolution, joined together as a singular Host to serve.

This star has moved through the heavens at various cycles, passing slowly sometimes, pausing other times, and appearing to remain still at other times. It has visited the earth many times, most recently 2,000 years ago, when it appeared briefly, moving across great expanses of time in just moments. At that time [it came] to fulfill the prophecies of old and to announce the birth of His Messenger whose task was to remind man of his divine nature. This same star also visited the earth 12,000 years ago, to warn the world of the coming flood—the sinking of Atlantis. Twenty-six thousand years ago the Blue Star manifested physical members from its Host to teach the universal laws of Oneness, or the Law of One. The Blue Star was visible for longer periods at other time frames, such as 54,000 years ago, when the turning of the poles occurred. Each time the Star came because it was called and its assistance was needed during the transitions. Once again the Blue Star returns. . .

In an essay titled "The Millennium," the *Grail Message* sums up the situation: "Men! When the hour comes in which, according to the Divine Will, the purification and winnowing must take place on earth, then *watch for the predicted and partly supernatural signs in the sky!*"

Two principle signs are said to signal the fulfillment of the millennium prophecies. The first sign has already occurred—the Jews have returned to the Holy Land. The second sign concerns the great comet/star/Planet X. Is the comet known as Hale-Bopp the celestial visitor spoken of in the prophecies? Astronomers have estimated that Hale-Bopp returns to our solar system every

3,200 to 4,200 years, which of course places it well within the norms of the predicted time-frame. Is Hale-Bopp *the* predicted comet/star—or is it a false alarm? Are the various prophecies about to be fulfilled—all of them? Edgar Cayce claimed that humanity would ". . .begin to fully understand in 1998."

Many scientists have compared Hale-Bopp to the famous great comet of 1811, the one Tolstoy described in *War and Peace:*

> . . .the radiant star, which, after traveling in its orbit with inconceivable velocity through infinite space, seemed suddenly—like an arrow piercing the earth—to remain fast in one chosen spot in the black firmament, vigorously tossing up its tail, shining and playing with its white light and the countless other scintillating stars.

But this isn't the first time the appearance of a bright comet created speculation about the End Times. *The New Madrid Earthquakes* reported that the comet of 1811 was observed in the United States from September 6, 1811 until January 16, 1812. At that time it was described as "peculiarly brilliant—beautiful." In those days too, were wars and rumors of wars, and in the United States three massive earthquakes along the New Madrid fault struck during the same period. At least one volcano erupted. Once the comet had disappeared from view and the New Madrid earthquakes had subsided, the writer of an article in the Pittsburgh *Gazette* seemed apprehensive as he pondered about the comet's message as it related to the events at that time:

> The extent of the territory which has been shaken, nearly at the same time, is astonishing—reaching on the Atlantic coast from Connecticut to Georgia and from the shores of the ocean inland to the State of Ohio. . .In North Carolina a volcano has appeared, and. . .in an eruption a few days since, a flood of lava poured out which ran to the distance of three quarters of a mile. *The period* is portentous and alarming. We have within a few years seen the most wonderful eclipses, the year past has produced a magnificent comet, the earthquakes within the past two months have been almost without number—and in addition to the whole, we consistently "hear of wars and summons of wars." May not the same enquiry be made of us that was made by the hypocrites of old— "Can ye not discern the signs of the times."

THE EARTH CHANGES—NEW
BOUNDARIES ARE DRAWN

In November, 1923, a businessman named Arthur Lammers began requesting "meaning of life" readings from Edgar Cayce that dealt with subjects of a philosophical and religious nature. Up to this point, Cayce had never been asked about such matters nor had it occurred to him that he could receive information about them. Although he was well-versed in the Bible and Christianity, he had never studied other world religions or speculated about the history of the human race on planet earth. But he would soon discover that "time travel" was not a problem when it came to the past as well as the future.

In the same month, during a personal reading for Gladys Davis, Cayce's stenographer, the first prediction surfaced about future geological upheavals: "This body (*not physically*) will be present when the earth is changed again." [288-1] More than eight years later, having transcribed several earth changes readings that predicted dire events, she requested another reading to inquire about the meaning of this statement. She asked the sleeping Cayce:

Question: What is meant by "This body, not physically, will be present when the earth is changed again?"

Answer: This means that the entity INNATELY, or thoughtly, through thought, will be—IS—in the position of knowing that the change comes, *yet not physically present. . .*at the period of the *greater portion* of the PHYSICAL change. [288-29]

Thus, according to the reading, as long as Gladys was dwelling in her physical body—not to worry! For when the "greater portion"

45

of the physical changes on the planet were to take place, Gladys would be in the beyond. Her soul chose the year 1986 to release her physical shell, and persuasive comparative evidence in the prophecies point to the year 1986 as one of crucial import for all of humanity.

In September, 1926, a real estate broker investing in commodities futures asked Cayce about future trends in the market, plus a final question about the weather in the grain-growing areas of South America. At the end of the reading he said, "That is all the questions." But for some reason, Edgar had more to say. The weather was not the only thing on his mind in 1926:

As for the weather conditions, and the effect same will produce on various portions of the earth's sphere, and this in its relation to the conditions in man's affairs: As has been oft given, Jupiter and Uranus influences in the affairs of the world appear the strongest on or about October 15th to 20th—when there may be expected in the minds, the actions—not only of individuals, but in various quarters of the globe, destructive conditions building. In the affairs of man many conditions will arise that will be very strange to the world at present—in religion, in politics, in the moral conditions, and in the attempt to curb or to change such, see? For there will be set in motion when prohibition will be lost in America, see? [Prohibition was repealed in 1933] Violent wind storms—two earthquakes, one occurring in California, another in Japan—tidal waves following, one to the southern portion of the isles near Japan. [195-32]

The year 1926 was the first crucial harbinger in the prophecy schedule for the twentieth century; 1936 would be the second, and 1986 the final, decisive year.

In 1926, certain events were taking place that would eventually develop into World War II in which seventy nations would become involved and tens of millions of people would perish.

• Hitler and his close associates began to expand the National Socialist (Nazi) party in Germany. He had recently completed his work *Mein Kampf* ("My Battle") which set forth his program for the restoration of Germany as a dominant power in Europe.
• In Italy, Mussolini was consolidating his power and that of his Fascist Party.

• In Japan, Hirohito became emperor, and soon thereafter an aggressive policy towards China was implemented.

Hundreds of years earlier, the sixteenth-century seeress, Mother Shipton, like Cayce, must have seen, "in various quarters of the globe, destructive conditions building" in 1926. In one of her recently discovered prophecies, she writes in simple, Nostradamus-like verse:

> *In nineteen hundred and twenty six*
> *Build houses light of straw and sticks*
> *For then shall mighty wars be planned*
> *And fire and sword shall sweep the land.*

As to the geological aspects, reports for 1926 show October to have been an exceptionally stormy month, with the number of days with gales considerably above normal over the greater part of the North Atlantic ocean, including a storm that wreaked havoc in Cuba and was described as one of the most severe on record. Storms in the Pacific, particularly in the Southern Hemisphere, were recorded only sketchily in those pre-satellite days, but a shock on September 18, 1926, produced a tidal wave which inundated the whole island of Kokomaruki and part of Guadacanal. On March 7, 1927, a seismic shock near the town of Minoyama, Japan, produced a sea wave that nearly destroyed it. Weak tidal waves were usually unreported. As to earthquakes—California experienced "strong shocks" on July 25 and October 22, 1926, and on January 1, 1927. A February 1932 Cayce *World Affairs* reading "forecasting the principal events for the next fifty years" predicts an *event* that would inaugurate changes on the face of the earth. There would be:

> . . .catastrophies [caused by the] outside forces to the earth in '36, which will come from the *shifting of the equilibrium of the earth itself in space* with those of the consequential effects upon the various portions of the country—or world—affected by same. [3976-10]

This is the first of several Cayce readings that foresee a "shifting" of the earth. "Outside forces" of a gravitational kind, or of some other invisible temperament, would somehow affect

47

the earth's "equilibrium" or balance that would eventually create havoc around the globe. And one of the "consequential effects" would be earthquakes.

Four years later, in January 1936, Cayce amplifies the "outside forces" statement:

Question: What is the primary cause of earthquakes?
Answer: The causes of these, of course, are the movements about the earth; that is, internally—and the cosmic activity or influence of other planetary forces and stars and their relationships produce or bring about the activities of the elementals of the earth; that is, the earth, the air, the fire, the water, and those combinations make for the replacements [in the crust of the earth] in the various activities. [270-35]

The "movements about the earth. . .internally" refers to the underground movements of rivers of lava and to the churning of the fiery liquid magma on which the earth's crust floats. If the churning of the magma increases because the earth loses equilibrium, then an increase in the magnitude and frequency of earthquakes would naturally follow. And this increase *has* been taking place.

In March, 1995, Scallion wrote: "The United States Geological Society reported that the number of earthquakes greater than magnitude 5.0 totaled 1,095 for the 1950s, 9,680 for the 1960s, 15,360 for the 1970s, and 15,929 for the 1980s. In the first three years of the 1990s (1990, 1991, 1992), 5,015. The cycle of earth change activity has reached startling proportions. The time frame may now be very short for cataclysmic changes to occur."

Returning to the year 1932, Cayce was asked:

Question: How soon will the changes in the earth's activity begin to be apparent?
Answer: When there is the first breaking up of some conditions in the South Sea (that's South Pacific, to be sure), and those as apparent in the sinking or rising of that that's almost opposite same, or in the Mediterranean, and the Etna area, then we may know it has *begun*.

Question: How long before this will begin?
Answer: The indications are that some of these have already begun, yet others would say these are only temporary. We

would say they have begun. '36 will see the greater changes apparent, to be sure.

Question: Will there be any physical changes in the earth's surface in North America? If so, what sections will be affected, and how?

Answer: All over the country we will find many physical changes of a minor or greater degree. The greater change, as we will find in America, will be the North Atlantic Seaboard. Watch New York! Connecticut, and the like.

Question: When will this be?

Answer: As to just when. . .*the period* ['36] *as is mostly given, as we find, BEGINS then and goes on rather than being the period of the greater change. . .* [311-8]

Cayce points to the South Pacific as an area to be watched. Other predictions are similar. In 1978, a young man experienced clinical death when he was crushed under his truck. After he returned from the other side, he discovered that he had developed intuitive insights. In 1993, *What Tom Sawyer Learned From Dying*, was published in which he writes: "There will be earthquakes; the floor of the ocean suddenly moving. I have predicted one earthquake that hasn't happened yet and it's overdue. Just trust me, it's overdue. I'm not worried that it isn't going to happen; I hope it doesn't. It won't be experienced as an earthquake *per se*, but it will be experienced as a tidal wave by the shorelines around the Indian and Pacific Oceans."

In a September 1994, reading, Aron Abrahamsen stated:

We shall first start with the general sequence of events which will take place in regards to the Earth Changes between the period 1994-2002. Expect the following: first there will be a severe earthquake followed by a Tsunami (tidal wave) near the East coast of India. This will cause much damage along the southern tip all the way to the northern part. The coastline will be devastated up to 45-65 miles inland. Much of that land will be under water, some parts will go as far as 75 miles inland and remain there. The tidal wave at its peak will be 235 feet high. It will be as a wall of water descending upon the land. The wall of water will be very, very wide, starting with the southern tip of India. A few days later another wave will hit the mid-section of India. Then a third wave will hit the northern area several days after the second wave. Each time the wave will increase its intensity and force. The first wave will be about 125 feet high, the second one will be 50 feet higher, and the third one will be something like 235 feet high.

Approximately 12 days after the third wave an earthquake will manifest itself at the bottom of the ocean adjacent to Japan. This will also affect the Philippine Islands in the deepest part of the ocean around these islands. This will be a very deep quake, originating many miles below the ocean floor. This will cause another tidal wave which will devastate the Philippine Islands as well as Japan. . .The people will not have much warning of this quake. There will only be this one with a magnitude of 9.5. It will devastate Japan, demolish Tokyo and Kyoto. . .

Three weeks after these events there will be a quake below the ocean floor around Hawaii. The first one will be near the island of Hawaii. There will be a rift going in the east-west direction under the islands. This quake will come with such great force that it, and the accompanying tidal wave, will cause great devastation.

Four weeks later another quake below the sea bottom will occur near California resulting in a rift which will cause lands to open up from north to south along the San Andreas fault. The San Joaquin and Sacramento valleys will sustain great damage. Following this, an opening of a rift between Seattle and Tacoma, in the state of Washington, going east-west almost into Idaho. This rift will be wide enough for water to find its way in there.

Two months later after the beginning of the rift in California, there will be an earthquake in the Palmdale and San Diego areas. It is difficult to say that these two will happen simultaneously, but it will appear to be like one in both places for the timing will be so close. But they are actually two separate quakes. The point of impact (epicenter) in Palmdale will spread out to Palm Springs and beyond. In San Diego the quake will go north and east resulting in ground breaking apart, making San Diego, for the moment, an island. The quake will creep south into the Baja California, area causing a rift from the Pacific coast going very close to the border between these two countries [Mexico and the U.S.A.]. Eventually that rift will open up and water will fill it. Along the west coast of the U.S.A. land will begin to fall apart, going from Los Angeles into San Bernadino. From Santa

Barabara to San Luis Obispo will be an island extending into the city of Modesto. This island will be called the Greater Santa Barbara Island.

Again, going back to 1932, Cayce was speaking of the prophecies that are supposed to be recorded somewhere inside the Great Pyramid in Egypt and are said by researchers to be pertinent to this period in the history of our planet:

Question: What [are the] corrections for the period of the 20th century?

Answer: Only those that there will be an *upheaval* in '36.

Question: Do you mean there will be an *upheaval* in '36 as recorded in the pyramid?

Answer: As recorded in the pyramid, though this is set for a correction, which, as has been given, is between '32 AND '38—the correction would be, for this—as seen—is '36—for it is in many [records]. These run from specific days; for, as has been seen, there are periods when even the hour, day, year, place, country, nation, town, and individuals are pointed out. That's how correct are many of those prophecies as made. [5748-5]

The Great Pyramid in Egypt is undoubtedly one of the most extraordinary as well as one of the most mysterious structures on the earth. Cayce said it took one hundred years to build, 10,490 to 10,390 B.C.

In *Doomsday 1999 A.D.*, Charles Berlitz wrote the following:

While archaeologists generally accept the Pharaoh Cheops (Khufu) of the IV Dynasty [2900 B.C.] as the builder of the Great Pyramid, this is questioned by a tradition held by the Copts, the purest descendents of the ancient Egyptian stock. The tradition declares that the Great Pyramid was there for many centuries *before* Khufu, thereby inferring that Khufu may have repaired it only and then have taken credit for its construction (a maneuver not unknown to the rulers of Egypt who often "erased" their predecessors' names from monuments and substituted their own).

. . .as has been mentioned by Egyptian Coptic writers in the intervening centuries, [the Great Pyramid] is not a tomb but a compendium of mathematical and astronomical knowledge. For example:

- Base perimeter divided by twice the height = 3.1416 (the modern value of Pi. Archimedes, the famous Greek mathematician who lived thousands of years later, never got closer than 3.1428).
- Fifty pyramidal inches = 1 ten millionth of the earth's polar axis (some among the ancient Egyptians must have had access to information indicating the true size and weight of the earth. The shape was well known to them and the concept of a round earth in space was taught to young students at the priestly schools).
- Base perimeter = 365.240 pyramidal inches (or number of days in a year).
- Height X 1,000,000,000 = approximate distance of earth to sun at autumnal equinox.
- Weight of pyramid X 1 trillion = approximate weight of earth.
- Base perimeter X 2 = 1 minute of a degree of the Equator.

A calculation by Heraclitus of Ephesus, a Greek philosopher of the Ionian school, can be interpreted as a forecast of the next world catastrophe. Ancient Greek cosmic outlook was influenced by a theory held by Plato and other philosophers that there would be periodic destructions of the earth by fire and flood. Heraclitus, who was not influenced by Plato's account of the destruction of Atlantis, since he predated him, calculated that the world would be destroyed again in 10,800 years, counting from the last time it suffered almost total destruction. If we take Heraclitus time span of recurring catastrophes and calculate it from a date in Plato's account of the sinking of Atlantis (9,000 years before *his* time) we obtain a date for the next catastrophe fairly close to the end of the second millennium.

The stone blocks of the pyramid are said to weigh up to 200 tons, or about 440,000 pounds. Yet they are fitted so tightly together a razor blade cannot be forced between the joints. How could an ancient people build such a structure and precisely heap the blocks one on top of the other to a height of 481 feet? Did they use ropes and rolling logs as so often depicted in history books and the movies? Not according to Edgar Cayce:

Question: How was this particular Great Pyramid of Gizeh built?

Answer: By the use of those forces in nature as make for iron to swim. Stone floats in the air in the same manner. This will be discovered in '58. [5748-6]

In a report written by a geologist in 1959 there is the following information relative to this Cayce prediction:

1958 A.D.—Anti-gravity? Professor W. Heisenberg announces (1958) discovery of a unidentified theory which relates to mass, energy and gravity. . .gravitation may be explicable in some other way than by Einstein's general theory of relativity. . .

Weber (1959) reports on work done in 1958 on the detection and generation of gravitational waves. . .which employ electrically induced stresses in crystals. . .Furth reports on recent experiments with magnetic pressure, which "can move mountains of metal or plasma for the engineer. . ."

Cayce said that there would be "upheavals" in 1936. In the following reading he integrates in one sentence what he meant by this term—plus the meaning of his other 1936 prophecies:

Question: What will be the type and extent of the upheaval in '36?

Answer: The wars, the upheavals in the interior of the earth, and *the shifting of same* [earth] *by the differentiation in the axis as respecting the positions from the Polaris center.* [5748-6]

In this answer the word "upheaval" has several connotations: (1) wars, (2) the churning of the earth's magma, and (3) the beginning of a shift in the alignment of the axis of the earth as sighted at the "North Star" Polaris—the one at the end of the handle of the Little Dipper.

Words—words —words! What a limitation they can impose upon our feeble attempts to properly express our thoughts when we are conscious, let alone if, heaven forbid, we were to find ourselves in a state of self-induced trance. And during the twenty year period the earth change prophecies were made, Cayce was giving thousands of readings on unrelated subjects, usually twice a day—mostly healing. In addition, Cayce read the King James version of the Bible from cover to cover once a year, and at times, depending on the subject-matter, he would use "ye"—"thee"—"thou" and so forth.

A reading in late 1933 on the predictions in the Great Pyramid included the following excerpts:

> . . .when the change was imminent in the earth; which change, we see, begins in '58 and ENDS with the changes wrought in the upheavals and the shifting of the poles, as begins then the reign in '98 (as time is counted in the present) of those influences that have been given by many in the records. . .for with the change it [the sunken Atlantis] must rise again. [378-16]

This is the first time the "pole shift" prophecy is clearly foretold. We also see that the "records" Cayce was reading at this time dealt with the 1958 to 1998 time frame.

"Must rise again!" This is also the first statement of many in which Cayce would claim the lost continent of Atlantis would rise above the waters of the Atlantic ocean. Numerous predictions from various seers say the same thing.

In *Timaeus* Plato wrote: "Now in this island of Atlantis there was a great and wonderful empire which had rule over the whole island and several others, as well as over parts of the continent, and besides these they subjected parts of Libya within the Straits as far as Egypt, and of Europe as far as Tyrrhenia."

Cayce claimed that Atlantis was occupied for tens of thousands of years by people who knew how to utilize the "forces in nature." When the destruction of the continent was imminent, many fled east and west. For the most part they resettled in Egypt and the Yucatan peninsula. They built pyramids at both locations which are still explored today.

In January of 1934 in a long, complex *World Affairs* reading, the geological Earth Changes prophecies were more specific:

> As to the changes *physical* again: The earth will be broken up in the western portion of America. The greater portion of Japan must go into the sea. The upper portion of Europe will be changed as in the twinkling of an eye. Land [Atlantis] will appear off the east coast of America. There will be the upheavals in the Arctic and in the Antarctic that will make for the eruption of volcanos in the Torrid areas, and there will be shifting then of the poles—so that where there has been those of a frigid or

the semi-tropical will become the more tropical, and moss and fern will grow. . .

The earth will be broken up in many places. The early portion will see a change in the physical aspect of the west coast of America. There will be open waters appearing in the northern portions of Greenland. There will be new lands seen off the Caribbean Sea, and DRY land will appear. . .South America shall be shaken from the uppermost portion to the end, and in the Antarctic off of Tierra Del Fuego LAND, and a strait with rushing waters. [3976-15]

A businessman who lived in San Francisco asked:

Question: Are details of the Earth's Eruptions [that begin] in 1936 so fixed that you can give me an outline of the Pacific Coast area to be affected along with precautionary measures to be exercised during and after this catastrophe?

Answer: All of these are...dependent upon individuals or groups who are in or keep an attitude respecting the needs, the desires, the necessary requirements in such a field of activity. *That some are DUE and WILL occur is WRITTEN*, as it were, but as we find—as to specific date or time in the present this may not be given. [But he saw the "outline" in a dream two years later—the Pacific ocean was lapping at the shores of Nebraska]. [270-32]

Several visionaries have published maps that depict the new boundaries of the United States as a result of the earth changes. The most popular by far is distributed by Matrix Institute, Inc., publisher of the *Earth Changes Report*. The "Future Map Of the United States 1998—2001," drawn from the visions of Gordon-Michael Scallion, is a mirror image of a combination of the earth change prophecies of Edgar Cayce.

On the night of March 3, 1936, while returning by train to Virginia Beach from Detroit where he had been jailed for giving readings, Cayce had a dream. His son, Hugh Lynn Cayce, wrote in the appendix section of his *Earth Changes Update* book:

Will the predicted Earth Changes really come to pass?

This *question* was probably a *burning one* of the psychic through whom the predictions came. It is understandable, therefore, that he [Edgar Cayce] might dream about "his" prophecies—about their meaning and about their *veracity*.

He had been born again in 2100 A.D. in Nebraska. The sea apparently covered all of the Western part of the country, as the city where he lived was on the coast. The family name was a strange one. At an early age, as a child, he declared himself to be Edgar Cayce who lived two hundred years before.

Scientists, men with long beards, little hair, and thick glasses were called to observe the child. They decided to visit the places he said he had been born, lived and worked—in Kentucky, Alabama, New York, Michigan and Virginia Beach. Taking the child with them, the group of scientists visited these places in a long, cigar-shaped, metal flying ship which moved at high speed.

Water covered part of Alabama. Norfolk, Virginia had become an immense seaport. New York had been destroyed either by war or an earthquake and was being rebuilt. Industries were scattered over the countryside. Most of the houses were of glass.

Many records of Edgar Cayce's work were discovered and collected. The group returned to Nebraska, taking the records with them for study."

On the 30th of June, 1936, a reading was given in which an interpretation of the dream-experience was requested. The answer follows:

"These experiences, as has oft been indicated, come to the body in those manners in which there may be help, strength, for periods when doubt or fear may have arisen. As in this experience [being jailed], there were about the entity those influences which appeared to make for such a record of confusion as to appear to the material, or mental-minded as a doubting or fearing of those sources that [caused] the periods through which the entity was passing in that particular period.

"And the vision was that there might be strength, that there might be an understanding, that though the moment may appear dark, though there may be periods of misinterpreting of purposes even these will be turned into that which will be the very proof itself in the experiences of the entity and those whom the entity might, whom the entity would, in its experience through the earth plane, help; and those to whom the entity might give hope and understanding.

"This then is the interpretation. As has been given, 'Fear not.' Keep the faith; for those that be with thee are greater than those that would hinder. Though the very heavens fall, though the earth shall be changed, though the heavens shall pass, the promises in Him are sure and will stand—as in that day—as the proof of thy activity in the lives and hearts of thy fellow men. For indeed in truth ye know, 'As ye do it unto thy fellow man, ye do it unto thy God, to thyself.' For, with self effaced, God may indeed glorify thee and make thee stand as one who is called for a purpose in the dealings, in the relationships with thy fellow man.

"Be not unmindful that He is nigh unto thee in every trial, in every temptation, and hath not willed that thou shouldst perish. Make thy will, then, one with His. Be not afraid.

"That is the interpretation. That the periods from the material angle [earth changes] as visioned are to come to pass matters not to the soul, but do thy duty today! Tomorrow will take care of itself.

"*These changes in the earth will come to pass, for the time and times and half times are at an end* [Daniel 7:25, 12:7 and Revelation 12:14] *and they begin these periods for the readjustments.* For how hath He given? "The righteous shall inherit the earth." Hast thou, my brethren, a heritage in the earth?" [294-185]

"These changes. . .*will* come to pass." Why? Because "the time and times and half times are at an end" and "they" having ended, herald the beginning of the "periods" of the Earth Changes. Cayce quoted the "times and half times" passages several times in readings. In explaining this Bible passage, he suggested that the earth and its people are entering a new cycle in what he termed the "fullness of time," and said:

And then these indicate as to what is to come to pass, even through these periods of the earth's journey through space; *"catching up,"* as it were, *with Time.* [Time is speeding up]. [1602-5]

Two months after Cayce's dream in 1936, he was asked:

Question: What great change or the beginning of what change, if any, is to take place in the earth in the year 2000 to 2001 A.D.?

Answer: When there is a shifting of the poles. Or a new cycle begins. [826-8]

According to Cayce, there have been several pole shifts. In 1944 he volunteered "[there were] . . .enormous animals which overran the earth, but ice, . . .*nature, God, changed the poles* and the animals were destroyed. . ." This took place he claimed, in the year 50,772 B.C. [5249-1]. Scientists are well aware that the outer skin of the earth on which we reside could possibly slide around the inner molten core. Most likely the best evidence this has previously occurred is the famous "Berezovka mammoth" that was discovered fast-frozen in Siberia in 1901. The stomach of this enormous elephant-like animal was found to contain plants that only grow in much warmer climates. And more amazing, buttercups were found in the mammoth's mouth it must have been munching on at the very moment "God changed the poles!"

In 1939 a lady asked Cayce the following:

Question: Three hundred years ago Jacob Boehme decreed Atlantis would rise again at this crisis time when we cross from this Piscean Era into the Aquarian. Is Atlantis rising now?

Answer: *In 1998* we may find *a great deal* of the activities as have been wrought [created] by the gradual changes that are coming about. These are at the periods when the cycle of the solar activity, or the years as related to the sun's passage through the various spheres of activity become paramount, or to the change between the Piscean and the Aquarian age. This is a gradual, not a cataclysmic activity in the experience of the earth in this period. [1939]

Question: Can a date be given to indicate the beginning of the Aquarian Age?

Answer: This has already been indicated as the period when it should pass, but that is when it begins to affect. It laps over from one to another. . .*As has been indicated, we will begin to understand fully in '98.* [1602-3]

A few days later, still on the subject of Atlantis, Cayce said, ". . .in the Atlantian land, that sank and *is* rising again. . ." Had it already started in 1939? Was it "gradually" making its presence known as Cayce said a few days earlier? Among the reports in the file is an article from the *New York Herald Tribune* dated June 4, 1939, headlined "Quake Records Trace Rise of a Vast New Continent Down Middle of Atlantic. . .Series of Isles Due to Ascend. . .Seismologists All Over The World Pool Findings to 'Watch' Continent's Birth."

A new continental land mass is slowly rising under the waves of the mid-Atlantic almost from pole to pole. Halfway between North America and Europe and South America and Africa there is a submarine ridge. . .Throughout the vast length of this area there is continual seismic activity, demonstrating that the ridge is in the process of building up and at some time islands will rise out of the ocean. They will continue to gain elevation until they are joined and a continental land mass is created. . .

The next year, Cayce again made a prediction that has come to pass. In commenting on one of the islands of Atlantis—Poseidia—that he claimed was in the vicinity of the Bimini islands of the Bahamas, he said, ". . .And Poseidia will be among the first portions of Atlantis to rise again. Expect it in '68 or '69; not so far away" [958-30]. In 1968, Dr. Manson Valentine discovered the celebrated "Bimini wall" along with many other underwater structures. The verification of this Cayce prediction is documented in *Atlantis: The Autobiography Of A Search.*

In August of 1941, the final detailed earth changes reading was given by Cayce voluntarily. In the suggestion for the reading, an individual requested personal spiritual guidance. There was not a single word that would imply this person wanted geological information. But, for some reason, she got it anyway:

. . .As to conditions in the geography of the world, of the country, changes here are gradually coming about. . .For many portions of the east coast will be disturbed, as well as many portions of the west coast, as well as the central portion of the U.S. . .lands will appear in the Atlantic, as well as in the Pacific. And what is the coast line now of many a land will be the bed of the ocean. Even many of the battle fields of the present will be ocean, will be the seas, the bays, the lands over which the NEW ORDER will carry on their trade as one with another.

Portions of the now east coast of New York, or New York City itself, will in the main disappear. This will be another generation, though, here; while the southern portions of Carolina, Georgia—these will disappear. This will be much sooner. The waters of the lakes will empty into the Gulf, rather than the waterway over which such discussions have been recently made. It would be well if the waterway [St. Lawrence Seaway] were prepared, but not for that purpose for which it is at present

59

being considered. Then the area where the entity is now located [Virginia Beach for reading] will be among the safety lands, as will be portions of what is now Ohio, Indiana and Illinois, and much of the southern portion of Canada and the eastern portion of Canada; while the western land—much of that is to be disturbed—in this land—as, of course, much in other lands. [1152-11]

In the above reading Cayce predicts several specific events that also have been predicted by others. Almost in passing, he recommends that the St. Lawrence Seaway should be built, but not necessarily for the purpose of inland shipping. At a lecture in May of 1995, Aron Abrahamsen refers to the St. Seaway Lawrence as well, and suggests that the Seaway may act as an "escape route" for a tremendous amount of flood waters:

The effect of the earth changes together with the disruptive forces from Lake Erie and the St. Lawrence Seaway will be very surprising, especially for the states of New York, Pennsylvania, and Ohio. Expect large inundations, not just one or two feet, but extending for ten or fifteen miles from the eastern-most part of Ohio, bordering Lake Erie, to the western-most part along the lake front. It will be severe, stretching from east to west for many miles.

This is because there is an underground fault in Lake Erie, as well as in the St. Lawrence Seaway. These faults will be activated as a result of undersea volcanic activity, causing a seismic wave which begins a tsunami right in the Seaway, pushing its way to the shoreline of Ohio, Michigan, and the Canadian shoreline. It will be devastating in all these directions, resulting in a largely widened Seaway.

Pennsylvania and New York will also be affected, those areas bordering the Lake and the Seaway. The inundation in New York and Pennsylvania will be from five to twelve miles.

There are fault lines going east-west and northwest and south-east, sort of criss-crossing Ohio. These faults have been known for some time, but not much has been said about them. There will be an activation of a fault in the mid-portions of Ohio from Columbus east-west to the borders. The magnitude will be in the region of 6. This will have some severe effects. It will be more quiet going farther south.

Edgar Cayce has predicted the "central portion of the United States" would be "disturbed" when the waters of the Great Lakes began to empty into the Gulf of Mexico by way of the Mississippi River. If this occurs, the Mississippi river would widen and "divide" the country. Scallion has stated the width would be at least 100 miles.

Saint Hildegard also states in her prophecy about the "great nation" that: "It will be *divided*, and in great part be submerged." She also predicts:

All sea coast cities will be fearful and many of them will be destroyed by tidal waves, and most living creatures will be killed and even those who escape will die from a horrible disease. For in none of those cities does a person live according to the Laws of God.

Scallion has predicted that the New Madrid fault in the central U.S. could activate at any time. The New Madrid fault, in the heart of the Mississippi valley, caused the greatest series of earthquakes in the history of the United States. From mid-December 1811 and into February, 1812, there were three great earthquakes: 8.6, 8.4, and 8.7 for 16 December, 23 January, and 7 February respectively. The tremors were felt from Quebec to New Orleans, and along the entire east coast, while a volcano erupted in North Carolina near Asheville. At that time, only a few thousand people lived within the area most severely affected. Today, more than twelve million people live in the same area, and geologists regularly record tremors in Memphis and St. Louis.

However, the most serious "disturbance" in the middle of the country is predicted to occur as a result of the pole shift. And Mary Summer Rain has also joined the chorus; she had a psychic experience in which she was shown the "complete devastation of the planet" and:

. . .the Great Lakes were flooding down through the Mississippi River as the earth tilted into its new axis position. . .and the Mississippi River will stretch its present shorelines to an incredible new width to accommodate the inrushing waters of the Great Lakes.

New scientific information about our planet, the solar system and the universe is constantly surfacing. One geologist who is familiar with the Cayce readings theorizes that "global warming" will continue to melt the ice caps at the poles, and may eventually create an imbalance that could cause the poles to shift. The precursor events would be increased quake activity and volcanic eruptions that, he points out by citing many examples, may have already started.

Many of Scallion's predictions have proven to be accurate. The accuracy of Edgar Cayce's readings, regardless of the subject-matter, are constantly being validated. On-going research and corroboration are continuing to be part of his legacy. However, the "melting of the ice sheets" may only be one of a combination of prophesied events that could cause the shifting of the earth on its axis. For Cayce also speaks of "outside forces to the earth."

In May of the year 2000, there will be a "grand conjunction" of the planets. At that time six planets will come into an almost perfect alignment with each other, with the little earth stuck near the middle of the alignment. Numerous researchers speculate that a gravitational "pull" caused by the other planets from this conjunction will bring about the prophesied earth changes, includ-ing a pole shift.

Will a comet or other celestial caller add to the "pull" in May of 2000? It does not seem unreasonable. More importantly, there are other roles that a comet or star is predicted to play as the millennium approaches, a role much greater in significance than one which solely affects our material surroundings.

A BOY'S VISION

It is indisputable that the most difficult obstacle in the field of prophecy is determining the time frame during which a given prophecy will occur. This predicament is always present along with the question of "source" and "interpretation." Prophets who set dates are really sticking their necks out. If time is an illusion, as Einstein said, then even attempting to determine a particular year is risky. There are also a large number of individuals who have experienced a spontaneous vision of a future event without having sought the information. They can only report what they have seen—they do not claim the gift of prophecy. But if they are deeply moved by the vision, they will usually conclude that a certain event is going to occur "soon." This is not much help when we realize that many of the prophecies for the millennium were offered hundreds or even thousands of years ago.

Geologists have been predicting a major earthquake in California for many years. (Current estimates are one in four by the year 2024.) Visionaries for the past 60 years have predicted that "the big one" will take place before the end of this century.

At the present time more and more everyday persons are reporting nightmarish dreams and visions that they feel are connected with this catastrophic event. However, none of their descriptions of *the* California earthquake can compare with those of seventeen-year-old Joe Brandt, who was unwillingly projected into the future.

The complete account was written by Brandt while a patient in a Fresno, California hospital room, recovering from a brain concussion. His reported visions occurred as he was passing between the conscious and unconscious state. He had no prior knowledge of geology or the prophecies about a major California earthquake. The collection of papers were discovered in 1967, and published in *California Superquake 1975-1977?* written by Paul James. James is a very adept researcher of prophecy, and although his conjecture about the time frame of the Big One was wrong, the book, published in the early seventies, contains some of the best reference material that has ever been compiled and published.

In the case of a person who has a spontaneous vision, there are certain instances when, in their attempt to describe a vision or a dream, they will include certain descriptions of the surroundings, technological advances, dress-fashions, and the activities of the people in the vision that would seem strange and incomprehensible to them at the time. This is the situation in the following material as Brandt describes his visions in 1937:

I woke up in the hospital room with a terrific headache—as if the whole world was revolving inside my brain. I remember, vaguely, the fall from my horse—Blackie. As I lay there, pictures began to form in my mind—pictures that stood still. I seemed to be in another world. Whether it was the future, or it was some ancient land, I could not say. Then slowly, like the silver screen of the "talkies," but with color and smell and sound, I seemed to find myself in Los Angeles—but I swear it was much bigger, much bigger, and buses and odd-shaped cars crowded the city streets.

I thought about Hollywood Boulevard, and I found myself there. Whether this is true, I do not know, but there were a lot of guys about my age with beards and wearing, some of them, earrings. All the girls, some of them keen-o, wore real short skirts. . .and they slouched along—moving like a dance.Yet they seemed familiar. I wondered if I could talk to them, and I said, "Hello," but they didn't see or hear me. I decided I would look as funny to them as they looked to me. I guess it is something you have to learn. I couldn't do it.

I noticed there was a quietness about the air, a kind of stillness. Something else was missing, something that should be there. At first, I couldn't figure it out, I didn't know what it was—then I did. There were no birds. I listened. I walked two blocks north of the Boulevard—all houses—no birds. I wondered what had happened to them. Had they gone away? Where? Again, I could hear the stillness. Then I knew something was going to happen.

I wondered what year it was. It certainly was not 1937. I saw a newspaper on the corner with a picture of the President. It surely wasn't Mr. Roosevelt. He was bigger, heavier, big ears. If it wasn't 1937, I wondered what year it was. . .My eyes weren't working right. Someone was coming—someone in 1937—it was that darned, fat nurse ready to take my temperature. I woke up. Crazy dream.

[The next day]. Gosh, my headache is worse. It is a wonder I didn't get killed on that horse. I've had another crazy dream, back in Hollywood. Those people. Why do they dress like that, I wonder? Funny glow about them. It is a shine around their heads—something shining. I remember it now. I found myself back on the Boulevard. I was waiting for something to happen and I was going to be there. I looked up at the clock down by that big theater. It was ten minutes to four. Something big was going to happen.

I wondered if I went into a movie (since nobody could see me) if I'd like it. Some cardboard blond was draped over the marquee with her leg six feet long. I started to go in, but it wasn't inside. I was waiting for something to happen outside. I walked down the street. In the concrete they have names of stars. I just recognized a few of them. The other names I had never heard. I was getting bored, I wanted to get back to the hospital in Fresno, and I wanted to stay there on the Boulevard, even if nobody could see me. Those crazy kids. Why are they dressed like that? Maybe it is some big Halloween doings, but it don't seem like Halloween. More like early spring. There was that sound again, that lack of sound. Stillness, stillness, stillness. Don't these people know that the birds have gone somewhere? The quiet is getting bigger and bigger. I know it is going to happen. Something is going to happen. It is happening now! It sure did. She woke me up, grinning and smiling, that fat one again.

"It's time for your milk, kiddo," she says. Gosh, old women of thirty acting like the cat's pajamas. Next time maybe she'll bring hot chocolate.

Where have I been? Where haven't I been? I've been to the ends of the earth and back. I've been to the end of the world— there isn't anything left. Not even Fresno, even though I'm lying here right this minute. If only my eyes would get a little clearer so I can write all this down. Nobody will believe me, anyway. I'm going back to that last moment on the Boulevard. Some sweet kid went past, dragging little boys (twins, I guess) by each hand. Her skirt was up—well, pretty high—and she had a tired look. I thought for a minute I could ask her about the birds, what had happened to them, and then I remembered she hadn't seen me. Her hair was all frowzy, way out all over her head. A lot of them looked like that, but she looked so tired and like she was sorry about something. I guess she was sorry before it happened —because it surely did happen. There was a funny smell. I don't know where it came from. I didn't like it. A smell like sulphur, sulfuric acid, a smell like death. For a minute I thought I was back in chem [chemistry].

When I looked around for the girl, she was gone. I wanted to find her for some reason. It was as if I knew something was going to happen and I could stay with her, help her. She was gone, and I walked half a block, then I saw the clock again. My eyes seemed glued to that clock. I couldn't move. I just waited. It was five minutes to four on a sunny afternoon. I thought I would stand there looking at that clock forever waiting for something to come. Then, when it came, it was nothing. It was just nothing. It wasn't nearly as hard as the earthquake we had two years ago. The ground shook, just an instant. People looked at each other, surprised. Then they laughed. I laughed, too. So this was what I had been waiting for. This funny little shake. It meant nothing.

I was relieved and I was disappointed. What had I been waiting for? I started back up the Boulevard, moving my legs like those kids. How do they do it? I never found out. I felt as if the ground wasn't solid under me. I knew I was dreaming, and yet I wasn't dreaming. There was that smell again, coming like from the ocean. I was getting to the 5 and 10 store and I saw the look on the kids' faces. Two of them were right in front of me, coming my way.

"Let's get out of this place. Let's go back East." He seemed scared. It wasn't as if the sidewalks were trembling—but you couldn't seem to see them. Not with your eyes you couldn't. An old lady had a dog, a little white dog, and she stopped and looked scared, and grabbed him in her arms and said: "Let's go home, Frou, Frou. Mama is going to take you home." That poor lady, hanging on to her dog.

I got scared. Real scared. I remembered the girl. She was way down the block, probably. I started to run. I ran and ran, and the ground kept trembling. I couldn't see it. I couldn't see it. But I knew it was trembling. Everybody looked scared. They looked terrible. One young lady just sat down on the sidewalk all doubled up. She kept saying, "earthquake, its the earthquake," over and over. But I couldn't see that anything was different.

Then, when it came, how it came. Like nothing in God's world. Like nothing. It was like the scream of a siren, long and low, or the scream of a woman I heard having a baby when I was a kid. It was awful. It was as if something—some monster—was pushing up the sidewalks. You felt it long before you saw it, as if the sidewalks wouldn't hold you anymore. I looked out at the cars. They were honking, but not scared. They just kept moving. They didn't seem to know yet that anything was happening. Then, that white car, that baby half-sized one came sprawling from the inside lane right against the curb. The girl who was driving just sat there. She sat there with her eyes staring, as if she couldn't move, but I could hear her. She made funny noises.

I watched her, thinking of the other girl. I said that it was a dream and I would wake up. But I didn't wake up. The shaking had started again, but this time different. It was a nice shaking, like a cradle being rocked for a minute, and then I saw the middle of the Boulevard seemed to be breaking in two. The concrete looked as if it were being pushed straight up by some giant shovel. It was breaking in two. That is why the girl's car went out of control. And then a loud sound again, like I've never heard before—then hundreds of sounds—all kinds of sounds; children, and women, and those crazy guys with earrings. They were all moving, some of them above the sidewalk. I can't describe it. They were lifted up. . .

And the waters kept oozing—oozing. The cries. God, it was awful. I woke up. I never want to have that dream again.

It came again. Like the first time which was a preview and all I could remember was that it was the end of the world. I was right back there—all that crying. Right in the middle of it. My eardrums felt as if they were going to burst. Noise everywhere. People falling down, some of them hurt badly. Pieces of buildings, chips, flying in the air. One hit me hard on the side of the face, but I didn't seem to feel it. I wanted to wake up, to get away from this place. It had been fun in the beginning, the first dream, when I kind of knew I was going to dream the end of the world or something. This was terrible. There were older people in cars. Most of the kids were on the street. But those old guys were yelling bloody murder, as if anybody could help them. Nobody could help anybody. It was then I felt myself lifted up. Maybe I had died. I don't know. But I was over the city. It was tilting toward the ocean—like tilting a picnic table.

The buildings were holding, better than you could believe. They were holding. They were holding. They were holding.

The people saw they were holding and they tried to cling to them or get inside. It was fantastic. Like a building had a will of its own. Everything else breaking around them, and they were holding, holding. I was up over them—looking down. I started to root for them. "Hold that line," I said. "Hold that line. Hold that line. Hold that line." I wanted to cheer, to shout, to scream. If the buildings held, those buildings on the Boulevard, maybe the girl—the girl with the two kids—maybe she could get inside. It looked that way for a long time, maybe three minutes, and three minutes was like forever. You knew they were going to hold, even if the waters kept coming up. Only they didn't.

I've never imagined what it would be like for a building to die. A building dies just like a person. It gives way, some of the bigger ones did just that. They began to crumble, like an old man with palsy, who couldn't take it anymore. They crumbled right down to nothing. And the little ones screamed like mad—over and above the roar of the people. They were mad about dying. But buildings die.

I couldn't look anymore at the people. I kept wanting to get higher. Then I seemed to be out of it all, but I could see. I seemed to be up on Big Bear near San Bernardino, but the funny thing was that I could see everywhere. I knew what was happening.

The earth seemed to start to tremble again. I could feel it even though I was up high. This time it lasted maybe twelve seconds, and it was gentle. You couldn't believe anything so gentle could cause so much damage. But then I saw the streets of Los Angeles—and everything between the San Bernardino mountains and Los Angeles. It was still tilting towards the ocean, houses, everything that was left. I could see the big lanes—dozens of big lanes still loaded with cars sliding the same way. Now the ocean was coming in, moving like a huge snake across the land. I wondered how long it was, and I could see the clock, even though I wasn't there on the Boulevard. It was 4:29. It had been half an hour. I was glad I couldn't hear the crying anymore. But I could see everything. I could see everything.

Then, like looking at a huge map of the world, I could see what was happening on the land and with the people. San Francisco was feeling it, but she was not in any way like Hollywood or Los Angeles. It was moving just like that earthquake movie with Jeanette McDonald and Gable. I could see all those mountains coming together. . .I knew it was going to happen to San Francisco—it was going to turn over—it would turn upside down. It went quickly, because of the twisting, I guess. It seemed much faster than Hollywood, but then I wasn't exactly there. I was a long way off. I was a long, long way off. I shut my eyes for a long time—I guess ten minutes—and when I opened them I saw [the] Grand Canyon.

When I looked at [the] Grand Canyon, that great big gap was closing in, and Boulder Dam was being pushed, from underneath. And then, Nevada, and on up to Reno. Way down south, way down. Baja, California. Mexico too. It looked like some volcano down there was erupting, along with everything else. I saw the map of South America, especially Columbia. Another volcano—eruption—shaking violently. I seemed to be seeing a movie of three months before—*before* the Hollywood earthquake. Venezuela seemed to be having some kind of volcanic activity. Away off in the distance, I could see Japan, on a fault, too. It was so far off—not easy to see because I was still on Big Bear Mountain, but it started to go into the sea. I couldn't hear screaming, but I could see the surprised look on their faces. They looked so surprised. Japanese girls are made well, supple, easy, muscles that move well. Pretty, too. But they were all like dolls. It was so far away I could hardly see it. In a minute or two it seemed over. Everybody was gone. There was nobody left.

I didn't know time now. I couldn't see a clock. I tried to see the island of Hawaii. I could see huge tidal waves beating against it. The people on the streets were getting wet, and they were scared. But I didn't see anybody go into the sea.

I seemed way around the globe. More flooding. Is the world going to be drenched? Constantinople. Black Sea rising. Suez Canal, for some reason seemed to be drying up. Sicily—she doesn't hold. I could see a map. Mt. Etna. Mt. Etna is shaking. A lot of area seemed to go, but it seemed to be earlier or later. I wasn't sure of time, now.

England—huge floods—but no tidal waves. Water, water everywhere, but no one was going into the sea. People were frightened and crying. Some places they fell to the streets on their knees and started to pray for the world. I didn't know the English were emotional. Ireland, Scotland—all kinds of churches were crowded—it seemed night and day. People were carrying candles and everybody was crying for California, Nevada, parts of Colorado—maybe all of it, even Utah. Everybody was crying—most of them didn't even know anybody in California, Nevada, Utah, but they were crying as if they were blood kin. Like one family. Like it happened to them.

New York was coming into view—she was still there, nothing had happened, yet water level was way up. Here, things were different. People were running in the streets yelling—"end of the world." Kids ran into restaurants and ate everything in sight. I saw a shoe store with all the shoes gone in about five minutes. 5th Avenue—everybody running. Some radio blasting—bigger—a loud speaker—that in a few minutes, power might be shut off. They must control themselves. Five girls were running like mad toward the Y.M.C.A., that place on Lexington or somewhere. But nothing was happening in New York. I saw an old lady with garbage cans filling them with water. Everybody seemed scared to death. Some people looked dazed. The streets seemed filled with loud speakers. It wasn't daylight. It was night.

I saw, like the next day, and everything was topsy turvey. Loud speakers again about fuel tanks broken in areas—shortage of oil. People seemed to be looting markets.

I saw a lot of places that seemed safe, and people were not so scared. Especially the rural areas. Here everything was almost as if nothing had happened. People seemed headed to these places, some on foot, some in cars that still had fuel. I heard—or somehow I knew—that somewhere in the Atlantic land had come up. A lot of land. I was getting awfully tired. I wanted to wake up. I wanted to go back to the girl—to know where she was—she and those two kids. I found myself back in Hollywood—and it was still 4:29. I wasn't up on Big Bear at all, I was perched over Hollywood. I was just there. It seemed perfectly natural in my dream.

I could hear now. I could hear, someplace, a radio station blasting out—telling people not to panic. They were dying in the streets. There were picture stations with movies—some right in Hollywood—these were carrying on with all the shaking. One fellow in the picture station was a little short guy who should have been scared to death. But he wasn't. He kept shouting and reading instructions. Something about helicopters or planes would go over—some kind of planes—but I knew they couldn't. Things were happening in the atmosphere. The waves were rushing up now. Waves. Such waves. Nightmare waves.

Then, I saw again, Boulder Dam, going down—pushing together, pushing together breaking apart—no, Grand Canyon was pushing together, and Boulder Dam was breaking apart. It was still daylight. All these radio stations went off at the same time—Boulder Dam had broken.

I wondered how everybody would know about it—people back East. That was when I saw the "ham radio operators." I saw them in the darndest places, as if I were right there with them. Like the little guy with glasses, they kept sounding the alarm. One kept saying: "This is California. We are going into the sea. This is California. We are going into the sea. Get to high places. Get to the mountains. All states west—this is California. We are going into the. . .we are going into the. . ." I thought he was going to say "sea," but I could see him. He was inland, but the waters had come in. His hand was still clinging to the table, he was trying to get up, so that once again he could say: "This is California. We are going into the sea. This is California. We are going into the sea."

I seemed to hear this, over and over, for what seemed hours—just those words—they kept it up until the last minute—all of them calling out, "Get to the mountains—this is California. We are going into the sea."

I woke up. It didn't seem as if I had been dreaming. I have never been so tired. For a minute or two, I thought it had happened. I wondered about two things. I hadn't seen what happened to Fresno and I hadn't found out what happened to that girl.

I've been thinking about it all morning. I'm going home tomorrow. It was just a dream. It was nothing more. Nobody in the future on Hollywood Boulevard is going to be wearing earrings—and those beards. Nothing like that is ever going to happen. That girl was so real to me—that girl with those kids. It won't ever happen—but if it did, how could I tell her (maybe she isn't even born yet) to move away from California when she has her twins—and she can't be on the Boulevard that day. She was so gosh-darned real.

The other thing—those ham operators—hanging on like that—over and over—saying the same thing:

"This is California. We are going into the sea. This is California. We are going into the sea. Get to the mountains. Get to the hilltops. California, Nevada, Colorado, Arizona, Utah. This is California. We are going into the sea."

I guess I'll hear that for days.

Several parts of Joe Brandt's vision deserve comment. He mentions "A smell like sulphur, sulfuric acid, a smell like death. For a minute I thought I was back in chem." This description is very similar to the California earthquake prophecy made by Nostradamus about four hundred years earlier: ". . .It will be seized and plunged into a turbulence, forced to drink water poisoned with sulphur."

Further along, Brandt recounts: ". . .and those crazy guys with earrings. They were all moving, some of them above the sidewalk. I can't describe it. *They were lifted up. . .*"

In the October 1993 issue of the *Earth Changes Report*, Scallion states the following regarding his prediction for the Northridge earthquake:

Underneath the Los Angeles Metropolis the potential for an explosive quake is locked within a network of "blind-thrust" faults. These faults do not break through to the surface and therefore cannot be seen. When they break, one side of the fault moves up over the other at a steep angle, creating mountains, hills and folds in the process. Malibu, Beverly Hills and the Hollywood Hills have been created as a result of blind-thrust faults. *The faults beneath Los Angeles are situated in such a way that if they suddenly snap and create an earthquake, people and objects directly overhead would overcome gravity and rise into the air, becoming momentarily weightless.* Or the faults may gradually slip, gently forming mountains or hills. Scientists agree on the existence of major faults under L.A., but they are uncertain as to how dangerous they are, when they last broke and how big an earthquake they could produce.

Several months later, on January 17, 1994, an earthquake that registered 6.6 struck two miles northwest of Northridge, a highly populated suburb of Los Angeles. More than 50 people were killed and more than 8000 were injured. Thousands lost their homes. On television people were describing how furniture and other items in their homes "floated to the ceiling."

In the January 31, 1994 issue of *Newsweek* magazine are the following excerpts from an article on the Northridge earthquake:

Once again, it was a fault they *couldn't* see that slammed Los Angelenos, crumpled their freeways, and toppled their buildings like Tinkertoys. Although the San Andreas fault gets all the notoriety, geophysicists are now realizing that dozens of invisible, even unsuspected, fractures in the rocks beneath the Los Angeles basin cause most of the earthquakes, large and small. And that has radically changed seismic calculus. Since these hidden faults do not have wires and meters attached to them like an intensive-care patient, scientists will not get any tip-off that a big trembler is coming—as they hope to if, say, the heavily instrumented San Andreas gives way. Worse, "if a quake jumped from fault to fault and ripped the full 100-mile fault zone," says seismologist Tom Henyey of the Southern California Earthquake Center, "there could be an earthquake that registers close to an 8 on the Richter scale—about 125 times more powerful than last week's jolt. . .

Just east of L.A., the San Andreas fault, which separates the Pacific and North American plates and usually runs north-south, turns abruptly west. Here the Pacific plate, drifting northwest, rams the North American. The battering shatters the continent's crust, creating a web of "blind thrust faults" that resembles a windshield after a car crash. . .

"There's this whole seismic hazard from buried thrust faults that we didn't even appreciate six years ago," says James Dolan of the California Institute Of Technology in Pasadena. . .If several thrust faults let go simultaneously or in close sequence, Los Angeles could suffer a quake in excess of magnitude 7.5 on the open-ended Richter scale, far more powerful than the 6.6 shock. "The lesson here," says Dolan, "is were not just concerned about The Big One"—usually defined as an 8.0 quake along the fragile San Andreas fault, which comes no closer to Los Angeles than 25 miles, "There are now several plausible sources for other Big Ones."

In describing his visions, Joe Brandt states California was ". . .tilting toward the ocean." And later: "I was over the city. It was tilting toward the ocean—like tilting a picnic table."

The following are excerpts from a vision that was experienced in 1965 by Reverend C. F. Harrell of Phoenix, Arizona:

Soon another vision came before me. I was standing at the edge of a sheer cliff, the coastline of California. Looking down a great distance, I could see those who were alive on the surface of the angry waters and on the wreckage of various kinds. All airports, harbors and coast defenses of all kinds ceased to exist. I asked the Lord, "How could this be?" In the vision the range of mountains nearest Los Angeles dissolved before my eyes and I was taken in Spirit above the United States, looking down upon it as on a map. I saw the great earthquake which will cause a break-off and the coastline changed before my eyes. All coast cities were inundated and sank out of sight forever. I saw a tidal wave that followed, which affected the Gulf of Mexico and the mouth of every river of the United States as well as the East coast, with tidal waves which caused much flooding and loss even in the inland as the rivers overflowed the land.

In a vision I also saw San Bernardino as the waters covered that city. Again I asked, "Lord, how can such a great part of the earth drop into nothing. He answered, "By three severe earthquakes preceding this disaster which will also be an earthquake."

Soon after these three warning earthquakes, we will see what has been predicted for many years—the greatest earthquake of all! The greatest earthquake of modern times. This information is not only in the hands of those to whom it has been revealed by the Lord, but scientific men have also been issuing serious warnings. However, people in general do not seem to be concerned.

This fourth earthquake, which will cause certain areas to sink under the water, will take around ten million lives. The Lord showed me the superstructure of the State of California. For some time it has been known scientifically that a good portion of the coast of California is just a shell that projects out over the water like a shelf. I saw a submarine going back and forth under this shelf to the base of the San Bernardino mountains. It is known that one can go out from the shoreline a short distance on the California coast and then one just drops off. . .there seeming to be no bottom. *The largest part of California is washed out underneath. There are only upright supports holding the coastline of California.*

Scientists inform us that the coastline of California is moving northwest at the rate of two inches a year. This places a great strain on the San Andreas Fault which extends from lower California to Palm Springs, near San Bernardino, then over to Palmdale and extending up to the San Francisco Bay area and to Point Arena. All this land west of the fault is moving every year. The stanchions or supports cannot move, as they are part of the ocean bed, making it necessary for them to incline or tip.

One day these supports will tip enough that they cannot bear the weight of the land. *This will be at the time of the Great Earthquake.* The west side of the San Andreas fault will break off and slide into the sea. . .

The earthquake will be the most severe destruction that has come upon this earth since the time of Noah's flood. This is the reason God is revealing what will take place; the people must be warned just as in the days of Noah. There will be ten million people whose lives will be lost in these disasters, and great suffering for those who remain alive. After the disaster, there will be famine and shortage of water in the areas along the coast all the way to Canada. . . There will be new diseases; new epidemics will break out which science knows nothing about. Climates will change on the west coast.

The earth is in turmoil. God is giving dreams and visions to His people of forthcoming events. Predictions are coming, some in part and some in more detail. When they begin to come from many sources and they are similar, then it is time to wake up.

Mary Summer Rain may be one of the predictor-sources that Reverend Harrell is referring to. The following excerpt is from her book, *Phoenix Rising:*

No-Eyes and I agreed that the California "big one" has been overly bellowed about by tabloid psychics and doomsday sayers for years; however, that does not negate its eventual reality. Incredible stress has been building up under the Pacific plate for many years, and is overdue to slide and release its repressed pressure. It becomes too simple to go about one's merry daily life ignoring the truth, the inevitable. People need to be made aware of the naked facts of the destructive side of nature's personality. Indeed, the stress is building. It is, at this very moment, inching its way to the greatest earthquake modern man has yet to be unfortunate enough to witness.

In *Spirit Song* Mary Summer Rain describes an experience she encountered as her American Indian mentor showed her a vision of the future that was similar to that of Joe Brandt, a vision that included a tilting of the earth on its axis:

We surveyed the entire continent of North America. The familiar geographic shape was changing its format at a rapid rate. We watched the movements as though we were viewing it through a child's ever-changing kaleidscope. Yet, this was no game. The earth was no toy. This was real. Everything had tilted down to the right. Alaska was now the tip of North America. Mexico wasn't south anymore, but rather west. New York was only partially visible.

On closer inspection, we found that all of North America's east and west coasts were gone. Florida appeared to be ripped entirely off the continent. The major fault lines had cracked. The San Andreas ripped through the land like some giant tearing a piece of paper. The torn shred drifted out into the churning ocean.

The waters of the world literally swished back in one huge movement, paused and came surging back to seek a new level of balance. The great movement washed over hundreds of islands. Hawaii was gone completely. Borneo, Sumatra, Philippines, Japan, Cuba, United Kingdom—all vanished within a blink of an eye.

We closed in on the United States. It wasn't as wide anymore due to the lessening of coastal areas. The Mitten State, Michigan, was covered with angry rushing waters. Upper Michigan had been torn away with the force of Lake Superior's emergency exit. All the Great Lake waters were forging downward, following the Mississippi River. Massive land areas on either side of the Mississippi River were flooded out of view. A great trench was being dug by the powerful force of the rushing waters. The land area below Michigan was drowned. Water was everywhere. There was no land under an imaginary line from

Houston to somewhere around Raleigh, North Carolina. Most of New York, Pennsylvania, and Ohio were under water. All of Michigan And Indiana were. The United States was now divided completely. The eastern portion was an island.

"Water go down later. [No-Eyes explains] Not always be island."

I was relieved to hear that. This was so incredible. When the time came for these changes, it would be a long time before the survivors were able to get a true and accurate picture of the extent of the damage. I looked far to my left and saw that all of the coastal land west of the Sierra Nevadas was gone.

A large portion of the Appalachian Range split and spread out. The Great Divide appeared to be fairly untouched. Volcanoes spewed in much of the western section of the land. . .

The view of the earth grew large as if we were watching it through a telescoping lens. We descended directly above Omaha, Nebraska.

I felt as if I was watching some horror movie conceived in the mind of evil. Horrible scenes were graphically played out in vivid detail. The city was in ruin. The tall buildings were left in their nakedness of iron skeletons. Concrete and glass lay scattered about in huge piles of rubble. People ran amok screaming in hysterics. Gore was everywhere. Crushed and mutilated bodies lay in agony over the dead. Fires burned like torches from the gas lines. Hot electrical wires lay sparking. It was total chaos.

We drifted out to the suburbs. The scenes here were less massive in destruction, but they were typical of the larger city. The low buildings were leveled and the ones still standing were being attacked by hordes of mindless people. They stormed in every store that had any kind of food. They trampled each other, caring little for the injuries they were inflicting upon the humans underneath their feet. I couldn't believe that civilized mankind could so quickly be reduced to such animal instincts of survival. They were down to the basest of actions. They were shooting one another. They were in throngs; some just roaming about, some storming private homes in an effort to get whatever they could find. The owners were shooting into the crowds. They were desperately trying to defend their domain. Animals ran wild. The zoo had been affected by the quake and cages were twisted, loosening wires and gates. The wild creatures were confused with their sudden freedom. Lions and cougars mauled screaming people. Elephants stampeded in a herd, trying to remain together. Reptiles roamed the streets. I felt sick.

In his vision, Reverend Harrell speaks of famine, which of course is predicted in the Bible prophecies and many others. In the *Revelation,* the rider on the black horse, the third he envisioned of the "Four Horsemen of the Apocalypse," John is told: "A whole day's wages for a quart of flour, a whole day's wages for three quarts of barley-meal!" (Rev. 6:6)

In the prophecies of the Mormon religion, we find from Brigham Young (1801-1877) the following in his *Journal of Discourses:*

You will hear of magnificent cities now idealized by people sinking into the earth entombing the inhabitants. The sea will heave beyond its bounds engulfing many countries. Famine will spread over the nation. . .The time will come that gold will hold no comparison in value to a bushel of wheat.

It's hard to believe there could be food shortages in the United States. This country is the "land of plenty," at least for most when it comes to food. Unfortunately, this may not always be the case. For not only do the prophecies warn of scarcities, scientists are more than just a little worried. The evidence is piling up. America's "cornucopia"—the horn of plenty—is threatened by disparate anomalies.

FOOD SHORTAGES—ANARCHY IN AMERICA?

During World War II many heroic individuals risked their lives—and even lost them—for the betterment of mankind. Perhaps the most unusual "ultimate sacrifice" was made by a group of Russian botanists during the Battle of Leningrad, now known by its original name the Battle of St. Petersburg.

The Germans had surrounded the city. They successfully cut off all supply routes and bombarded the population day and night, yet they couldn't force a surrender and occupy the city. In desperation, people were eating the bark from trees and anything else they could find that was edible to stay alive. In the book *Seeds of Change*, author Kenny Ausubel describes the events and circumstances that culminated in agony and death for these dedicated protectors of their seed treasure:

A brilliant botanist, Nikola Vavilov, discovered in the 1920s that there are centers of diversity around the world where wild plants originated and then evolved into their myriad forms. . .Tragically, in a conflict of scientific opinion with Stalinist Russian scientists, Vavilov was banished to a military prison camp, where he died in 1943. Meanwhile, the seed bank he had amassed came under threat during the terrible siege of Leningrad-St. Petersburg, which lasted for nine hundred brutal days during which six hundred thousand people starved to death. His loyal botanists risked bullets and bombs to venture into nearby fields to propagate potatoes for their collection. When they ran out of food to eat, they faced the awful choice of either eating their collection or starving to death. Soldiers entering the facility found their emaciated bodies amid untouched sacks of rice, potatoes, corn and wheat, a legacy they held more valuable than their own lives.

Seeds are the important element necessary for sustaining life on earth. Without seeds our planet would be as barren as the moon. Further, as the Russian botanists knew all too well, with seeds, as in most other things, *sameness is weakness*.

Mother Shipton, has been credited with prophesying the discovery in America by Sir Walter Raleigh of the tobacco "herb" and the potato "root" that were subsequently introduced in Europe:

> *Over a wild and stormy sea*
> *Shall noble sail,*
> *Who to find will not fail*
> *A new and far countree*
> *A herb and root*
> *That all men shall suit.*

However, it seems Sir Walter only introduced a single type of potato to Europe which became known as the "Lumper." In the middle 1800's the Lumper fell victim to a fungus that eventually spread and destroyed the main staple of millions of people. All of the potatoes rotted as the blight spread. It destroyed the whole potato crop in Ireland—history's Irish potato famine—and hundreds of thousands of people died of starvation while others emigrated to America.

Today, there is alarming evidence that history may repeat itself, at least with respect to the potato. The following excerpt is from a report that appeared in the July 30, 1995 issue of the New York *Times*:

Almost 150 years after the Ireland potato blight, a virulent new cousin of the same disease is threatening. . .The potent, fast-moving fungus known as "late blight" [is being called] the worst threat to America's potato crop in decades, and perhaps ever by scientists. It shows resistance to all chemical fungicides. First reported in the U.S. in the late 1980s, it has spread up the East Coast from Florida to Maine. This year, it has reached the potato-belt states of Idaho and Oregon, where heavy rains have fueled its growth. . .The new fungus has also been reported in the major potato-growing areas across the world, and some scientists predict that it could cause famine in South America. . .

In Ireland, the importance of Mother Nature's "safety net"—the abundant *genetic diversity* of her storehouse—had been ignored. The population learned the hard way that "mother knows best" or, "don't put all your eggs in one basket!" However, another old adage—"the only thing we learn from history is: we don't learn anything from history" would soon come into play.

Not long after the Irish potato famine "plant breeding" would take a foothold in Mother's soil. The "hybrid" seed began its invasion into the fields of "genetic diversity." Authors Mooney and Fowler explain in *Shattering:*

> Many seeds have long been worth more than their weight in gold. . .Perhaps the biggest single environmental catastrophe in human history is unfolding in the garden. The loss of genetic diversity in agriculture—silent, rapid, inexorable—is leading us to a rendezvous with extinction, to the doorstep of hunger on a scale we refuse to imagine.

There are untold thousands of varieties of seeds in the world. Many have been passed down from one generation to the next for hundreds of years. If one variety failed for some reason, others were still there. They could be rotated and usually several varieties were planted at the same time. Seed similarity was known to be dangerous. But just as important, seeds could be saved from healthy plants and used the next year—not so with hybrids! For the most part hybrid seeds are "sterile." If they do reproduce at all, their viability is decreased substantially. So growers and farmers are forced to go to the seed companies whenever they need seeds; unless, of course, they can locate a seed company that still sells the "standard" *open-pollinated* varieties in which case seeds can be saved from a mature plant and used the next year. And there are some sources in the United States if you know where to look.

There is an explanation for the reason standard seeds are difficult to locate. On Oct. 7, 1985, *The Virginian-Pilot* newspaper reported:

> Genetically created corn is first plant to win patent. A new corn plant genetically engineered by a suburban Minneapolis company has become the first plant to be patented. The decision by the U.S. Board of Patent Appeals and Interferences in Washington, announced by the company last week, could have a major impact in the $3 billion-a-year seed corn industry,

analysts said Friday. Seeds, plants and plant-tissue cultures produced by genetic engineering previously had not received such protection against imitations.

In one catalog source for non-hybrid seeds, Kent Whealy's *The Garden Seed Inventory*, Kent explains:

Plant patenting legislation has definitely made seed companies attractive for multinational corporations. During the first week after plant patenting legislation was passed in England, one company, RHM, bought 84 seed companies. Shell Oil of Great Britain has bought out 56 seed companies since the passing of the legislation in England. Royal Dutch Shell became the world's largest seed and agrichemical company, almost overnight. Seed company takeovers in the United States have also reached epidemic proportions: Atlantic Richfield (ARCO) took over Dessert Seed Company; Celanese bought out Joseph Harris Company; Ciba-Geigy (of Switzerland) purchased Funk's Seed; ITT now owns W. Atlee Burpee, Co. [since bought by George T. Ball, Inc. which markets its seeds to gardeners]; Amfac took over Gurney's Seed & Nursery and Henry Field Seed & Nursery Company. . .Monsanto purchased DeKalb Hybrid Wheat. And these are just a few of the more than 60 recent North American seed company takeovers. . .

In 1987 the *Reader's Digest* sounded the alarm in an article titled "SOS—SAVE OUR SEEDS." This scientifically oriented article referred to Kent Whealy's work and stated:

The global hybrid revolution has brought powerful social and economic changes, most of them positive. But there are hidden dangers we have only recently begun to address.

As our food crops change, so do diseases and pests that relentlessly develop new ways to penetrate the defenses we devise for our vast fields of grain and other crops. When one hybrid falls prey to such assaults, our bioengineers must rush to replace with hybrids carrying new, more resistant genes. But to do this we must constantly find fresh genetic raw material.

These "new genes" come from three sources: the ancient land-race plants of the Vavilov Centers, other distantly related wild varieties, and heirloom plants that went out of favor as newer hybrids came along. . .But ironically, today's hybrids are pushing many old-fashioned food plants to the brink of extinction. . .

Today, entire nations are becoming dependent on genetically identical plants. . .History teaches the dangers of such monoculture.

Moria Timms writes: "In Europe, growing or selling the seeds of plants not contained in the Common Catalog of the European Economic Community is illegal. In a deliberate attempt to clear the market as quickly as possible for the new patented varieties, sometimes hundreds of varieties a month are deleted from the catalog, and violators are prosecuted."

Long before *Seeds of Change* was published, Dr. Wolf D. Storl wrote the book *Culture and Horticulture* and voiced his concern:

The consequences of the loss of native seed germ plasm are staggering, when one thinks that within one short generation, human beings could throw away key evolutionary links in the food system—all in the name of progress. Germ plasm has been lost that took generations of careful and loving selection by farmers and gardeners to develop. They were lost because they were unsuited to machine production. . .The result of uniformization brought about by agribusiness, where hybrids have been selected for only one or two characteristics, is that our food plants are put on a very narrow genetic basis. The "miracle" wheat and rice of the Green Revolution, which is extincting locally-adapted native varieties, is completely dependent on high energy input in the form of chemical fertilizer, insecticides, irrigation and machinery. . .Rarely will hybrids reproduce true to type, so you cannot save seed from them.

Sun Bear wrote of his concern in *Black Dawn/Bright Day:*

In the United States and Europe, hybrid plants have been developed to produce high crop yields. But they have bred the immunities out of these plants in the process. Many of them can no longer fight off insects, molds or other pests. Also, the seeds have been developed to work best with the chemical fertilizers and pesticides.

Another thing to keep in mind about hybrid plants is that you can harvest the plants, but their seed is no good to plant. You have to go back to the seed companies to plant next year's crop. So the seeds, in reality, are owned by these companies which are owned by multinational corporations. Since these companies have a monopoly on hybrid seeds, farmers are finding that prices are going up every year. . .It is very frightening that we are dependent on gasoline-driven engines and petroleum-based chemicals for our farming. I look around and wonder what will happen when there is no petroleum. . .This is a very dangerous time because we are totally dependent on the oil companies for our food supply—and they are largely dependent on oil from the Middle East.

Hybrid seeds "are 'built' from existing genes and plant stock," Ausubel explains. "No breeder has yet created a new gene. . .Such breeding contributes to more varieties, *but not to diversity*. . .The world today relies on just one hundred fifty food plants, and only twenty of those produce 90 percent of our food. Nine are widely used, and account for three-quarters of the human diet. Of these, just three—rice, corn, and wheat—account for half. . ."

In 1993 the Union of Concerned Scientists asked about the growing interest in genetic engineering and agricultural biotechnology, "Does biotechnology represent a promise or a peril to humanity and our environment?" The following excerpts are their answer:

Genetic engineering is a biotechnology that allows scientists to move genes into organisms without regard to natural barriers. Technologists have already transferred genes from moths into potatoes and from flounders into tomatoes—and they are just beginning.

Biotechnology promises sheep that will serve as new sources of insulin, but also brings the possibility that the release of altered forms of life into our environment may have devastating consequences.

Biotechnology promises tomatoes with a longer shelf life, but has the potential for wiping out wild varieties of squash that harbor the genes that we might someday need to prevent a blight.

Companies are investing millions of dollars to create novel crops and animals for food and fiber products. Such organisms have a combination of traits not found in nature. Most will be intended for good purposes, but can exhibit unpredicted behavior upon release.

Traditional practices have already created environmental mistakes. From gypsy moths to kudzu, we have experienced both purposeful and accidental introduction of "exotic" species that have spread with disastrous results. Genetic engineering will permit the creation of hundreds of thousands of organisms that will be in some sense exotic everywhere on this planet. Some of these may have unexpected and harmful consequences.

Scientist have transferred growth hormones from cows to produce a faster growing fish, but they originally put their fish ponds in a flood plain, inviting an escape that could have led to the decimation of native fish.

Crops engineered to be virus-resistant could instead help to create new viruses that can damage agricultural crops. Engineered resistance to herbicides and pesticides could spread, making chemical control procedures more difficult and expensive. And engineering plants to "manufacture" potentially toxic substances like drugs and pesticides could have unplanned results, such as poisoning birds that scavenge their seeds.

It is also possible that new genes will spread to wild plants, creating new seeds whose invasive properties could seriously damage the existing remnants of the native biological diversity of North America.

It is currently impossible to predict what will happen to engineered plants, animals, or other organisms once they escape or are released. Our understanding of ecological processes simply lags behind our knowledge of genetic engineering. And since there are big profit potentials in biotech and few in ecology, the lag can be expected to widen in a business-as-usual situation.

This reality is exacerbated by the fact that the money for much of agricultural biotech today is coming from chemical companies. Monsanto, DuPont, and Ciba-Geigy want to be able to sell more herbicides and pesticides, so are developing and seeking to commercialize plants that will survive their chemicals. Big industrial companies are much more likely to be concerned with their bottom line than with the adverse effects on farm workers, consumers, and the environment.

In the June, 1996 issue of the *Earth Changes Report* Scallion reported:

At first glance, gene-splicing to produce new super-foods with longer shelf life, greater resistance to pests, or more nutrition seemed like a good idea. But now, some very troubling questions are beginning to accumulate.

In March, the *New England Journal of Medicine* reported that a gene from Brazil nuts that was engineered into soybeans made the beans allergenic. That's bad news at a time when the ability of soy-based foods to reduce the risk of heart disease and cancer ensures that their consumption will increase, probably dramatically.

And public-interest groups note that Food and Drug Administration safeguards are full of loopholes. For instance, biotech companies must alert the FDA, conduct safety tests, or label genetically engineered foods only if they plan to transfer genes from eight or ten of the most commonly allergenic foods. Besides, such reporting by companies is purely voluntary at present.

What about the lesser-known allergens to which many may be sensitive? As generations of food allergy sufferers have learned, avoidance of disruptive foods is often the best—or the only—defense.

Then there is the threat of the super-weed. It seems almost comical—legions of gardeners in combat with a weed even more resistant than usual to lawn chemicals via accidental bio-engineering.

But the implications may be enormous. Scientists in Denmark crossed a plant genetically engineered to resist a common herbicide with a weedy relative. Then they bred the hybrid with a wild form of the weed. They found the resistance to herbicide was transmitted to the next generation of the wild plants, *Scientific American* reported last month. That means the genes might spread, and would certainly be hard to find and control.

Despite the discovery genes can be spread in this way, the Department of Agriculture has proposed streamlining of the approval process for companies that want to field test genetically engineered crops. The proposal is opposed by the Union of Concerned Scientists.

Again, the *Mahabharata* from ancient India predicts that, the Kali Yuga will be close at hand when the following comes to pass: "When men begin to slay one another, and become wicked and fierce and without any respect for animal life, then will Yuga come to an end. . *And when flowers will be begot within flowers and within fruits, then will the Yuga come to an end.*"

There are many prophecies that claim severe weather will play a part in bringing about food shortages. In *Phoenix Rising*, Mary Summer Rain writes:

When the hot winds blow across the land, they will wither the earth into dust bowls. They will absorb the underground springs and evaporate artesian water and create great sink holes over the land like massive moon craters. These dry winds will leave devastating erosion in its wake. Excessively high winds will blaze across the country, caring little for the freak deaths they leave in their paths. Tornados will increase and become the rule rather than the exception in certain areas. Hurricanes will rip into the coastal regions with increased force and destruction. Summer thunderstorms will release a ten-fold energy through intensified lightening and hail. Winter will bring frigid temperatures with its ferocious blizzards causing week-long blackouts and untold fatalities.

In July, 1995, Scallion writes of a "warning" that he had been concerned about for several years:

In a vision, I witnessed a dark brown cloud over the midwestern United States. It seemed to cover many states including Texas, Missouri, Kansas, and Oklahoma. I am not sure of the others, as the cloud covered such a wide area it was impossible to be more specific. The cloud was stationary and began to glow red in color. A voice in the vision then said: "Watch temperatures to hit 125 degrees in August in places in the United States where these temperatures have not occurred before. Then know, the drought has begun. This summer, record after record shall be broken. If there can be the preparation now for what is to come, many livestock can be saved. Crops shall not. The period of crises is three years. Then the floods shall come." This ended the vision.

In the March 24, 1996 issue of *The Daily Oklahoman* was a report that at least one scientist seems to be confirming this prophecy: "The plains states are on the brink of an extreme drought that could grip the central U.S. until 1999, says Mike Smith, founder of weather data in Wichita, Kansas. . . ."

The prophet of Ramala adds another dimension:

When the Bible speaks prophetically of the plagues to come, that is indeed one of the events which will take place. . .At present Humanity controls the Insect Kingdom with its poisons and its pesticides, but that system will fail. . .The insects will begin to multiply more and more and to bring a scourge across the face of the earth, for the force which would keep them in check has been destroyed by the Human Race. The natural balance is gone. The Insect Kingdom will cover the earth and will bring about much Human destruction. There are scientists today who recognize this fact and are working desperately on new methods to control this potential and lethal invasion.

Perhaps, in one respect, the Ramala prophet was referring to Africanized "killer bees" that have spread from Texas to New Mexico and Arizona and are rapidly invading California. At the other end of the spectrum, agricultural scientists are very concerned about the threat to a "good" insect, the honey bee population, that is indispensable as the pollinators of much of our food supply.

In June of 1996, the Associated Press reported:

Crop experts in Virginia and Wisconsin are the latest to show concern about the reductions in bee population. . .Virginia bee-keepers have lost 40 to 90 percent of their hives. Farmers will have difficulty getting bee colonies for pollination. . .the Virginia State Apple Board predicted that this year's crop would be about 60 percent of normal. . .

In Wisconsin, because of cold, soggy weather and parasitic mites, the number of honey bees has dropped to its lowest level since the government started keeping records in 1945. . .The Wisconsin Bee Keepers Association, said at least 50 percent of Wisconsin's 75,000 bee colonies were wiped out by parasitic diseases and freezes. . .

One volcanic eruption created the year without summer in 1816, and volcanic activity is expected to increase. Volcanic ash spewing into the earth's atmosphere will circle the globe many times for years. Consequently, the sun's rays are blocked and the global temperature is affected.

Volcanic eruptions and earthquakes go hand in hand. They are both the result of disturbances in the earth's magma—the molten lava beneath the earth's crust.

In his vision, Joe Brandt said: "I saw a map of South America, especially Columbia. Another volcano—eruption—shaking violently. I seemed to be seeing a movie of three months before—*before* the Hollywood quake."

In the 1930s Edgar Cayce, concerning the "big one," offered a similar "three-month eruption time-frame" warning sign:

> If there are the greater activities in the Vesuvius, or Pelee, then the southern coast of California—and the areas between Salt Lake and the southern portions of Nevada—may expect, within the three months following same, an inundation [of flood waters] by the earthquakes. [270-35]

Vesuvius and Pelee are both very powerful volcanos that have a disposition to bury populated areas. Vesuvius erupted in 79 A.D. and buried the city of Pompeii. Pelee erupted in 1902, destroying the city of Saint-Pierre, and causing the death of about 30,000 people in the city and surrounding area. Saint-Pierre had only one survivor, a convicted murderer confined in a prison dungeon. Some people may be puzzled with respect to the connection between the volcano Vesuvius in Italy, the volcano Pelee on the island of Martinique in the West Indies, and earthquake activity on the west coast of the United States that, according to Cayce, would cause massive destruction and flooding.

The answer is seen in the "structural deformations" in the earth's crust. In the middle 1960s geologists accepted the theory of "plate tectonics." Picture the earth as a cracked walnut, the shell depicting the crust. Each section of the crust represents a massive raft-like plate floating atop the molten inner core; and the churning of the hot fluid core, caused by the earth's wobble as it rotates, jostles the plates. The plates move and bump against each other, causing activity along the boundaries of the different plates where most of the earthquakes and volcanoes occur. The most active boundary is that of the Pacific plate known as the "ring of fire."

The infamous San Andreas fault in California represents the adjacent sides of two massive plates (North American and Pacific) moving in different directions—or trying to move. They are presently pressed together, and moving very little. When the tension of their deadlock is released, the earth quakes. The eruption of Vesuvius could signal further activity along the boundaries on which it is located. Vesuvius and Pelee are connected by a plate boundary. The boundary then runs from Pelee westward to meet the eastern boundary of the Pacific plate on which the San Andreas fault is located. Agitated movement of underground lava along this boundary could start an earthquake.

Just to the east of the San Andreas fault there are several important food-raising areas including the San Joaquin Valley and the Sacramento Valley (the Great Central Valley). A large percentage of our country's vegetables and fruits (and seeds) are grown in the rich soil of these farming areas. However, they are from 22 to 248 feet below sea-level. Should there be a massive earthquake, tidal waves from the Pacific Ocean, or the Gulf of California, (as seen by Aron Abrahamsen) would flood the valleys.

Not only did Edgar Cayce understand the connection between Vesuvius and the San Andreas fault long before geologists, but hundreds of years earlier, Nostradamus also predicted the same sequence of events:

> *The Great Round Mountain of seven stadia,*
> *on the wake of peace, war, famine and flooding.*
> *It will roll a long way, drowning great countries,*
> *even ancient kingdoms and their great foundations.*

Vesuvius is known as the "Round Mountain." A "stadia" is an ancient Greek measure of distance of about 600 feet. Seven stadia or 4,200 feet is the approximate height of Mount Vesuvius. The eruption of Vesuvius denotes movement of underground molten lava which "rolls" like subterranean waves along the plate boundaries causing surface earthquakes and ocean tidal waves in its molten wake. The "ancient kingdom" affected would most likely be Japan. The entire country straddles the Pacific boundary of the ring of fire. And further, Edgar Cayce predicted: "The greater portion of Japan must go into the sea."

Nostradamus continues:

> *Earthshaking fire from the center of the earth,*
> *Will cause an earthquake around the New City.*
> *Two great rocks shall have long warred against*
> *each other, then Arethusa will redden a new river.*

In his visions Nostradamus referred to the metropolises of the "New World" of America as "New Cities." In this instance he is referring to Los Angeles. The fire from the center of the earth is the molten lava being forced up along the San Andreas fault—the "two great rocks" or tectonic plates. As they snap and separate from the strain they're no longer "warring against each other." Arethusa was a nymph or nature spirit from Greek and Roman mythology who was changed by the Moon Goddess Diana into an underground stream which passed beneath the sea to come out a fountain at a far distant land. Red lava flows westward like a "new river" under the Atlantic Ocean along the boundaries of the plates and eventually reaches the ring of fire.

> *Garden of the World near the New City,*
> *in the path of the hollow mountains.*
> *It will be seized and plunged into a turbulence,*
> *forced to drink water poisoned with sulphur.*

The "Garden of the World" refers to California's below sea-level food-raising valleys. The hollow mountains may be another reference to volcanic activity. The above-referenced quatrains were not written in a sequential or connecting order. The entire area is inundated by turbulent waters poisoned by the molten lava which contains sulfur, just as Joe Brandt has described in the previous chapter: "There was a funny smell. I don't know where it came from. I didn't like it. A smell like sulphur, sulfuric acid, a smell like death. For a minute I thought I was back in chem."

Mother Nature can cause disturbances for humanity in a lot of ways. She can cause things to happen, or she can cause things not to happen—like rain! Without water, all life on the earth disappears. Prolonged droughts reduce food production while at the same time the availability and quality of drinking water is placed in jeopardy. Reservoirs shrink, water tables drop, and contamination becomes a problem. Safe drinking water has always been taken for granted by most; however, many pollutants are now finding their way into the various water systems. Droughts would intensify the pollution invasion.

In June 1995, *The Australian* reported:

A recent conference on food, agriculture, and environment, called "Vision 2020," has warned that water could become the battleground of the 21st century, with severe shortages emerging in one of every five of the world's countries.

Growing hunger would spark a global refugee crisis, in which tens of millions of people would flood across international borders, the Director-General of the International Food Policy Research Institute, Dr. Per-Pinstrup-Anderson, said.

The conference held in Washington during June is considered the most important food summit in 30 years.

According to IFPRI analysis released yesterday, 800 million humans now suffer malnutrition, 1.1 billion live in absolute poverty with incomes less than U.S. $1 per day, while the number of refugees has risen tenfold in less than 20 years.

Food output has failed to keep pace with population growth in one third of all countries, and almost one quarter of the world's farmlands, pastures and forests are degraded.

Thirty-five countries are expected to face serious or severe water shortages by 2020.

Will the United States suffer food and water shortages? The predictions seem to point in that direction. In a recent reading Aron Abrahamsen warned:

One will see the severity by some very severe droughts in your land. The weather patterns will be changing. . .one will see the beginning of shortages. This time will be very severe. The shortages will be so severe that in certain localities of your country the supermarkets, the grocery stores, will be open only a few days in the week. This may seem far-fetched, particularly in the land in which you are living now where there is plenty of everything. Yet these shortages will become real. People will not believe this for they are surrounded with prosperity as far as goods and services are concerned. When these shortages come, it will be very abrupt and the shortages will last for quite a while.

On many occasions Mary Summer Rain became exasperated as she wondered if warning people would be nothing more than an exercise in futility. She expressed her concern to No-Eyes:

"No-Eyes, a lot of people don't believe things are going to change."

"What so! They gonna find out how good stuff [material possessions] be when they have no food in house, in store even! Then they can eat their great stuff. They gonna find out how great stuff be when they no can get gas! They gonna find out but good. What they gonna do with great stuff when crazy peoples running all over? What so 'bout no electricity, no natural gas, no propane? Huh, Summer Rain, what so then?"

In 1943 and 1944, Edgar Cayce warned:

Anyone who can buy a farm is fortunate, and buy it if you want to grow something and don't want to grow hungry in some days to come. [and] The hardships for this country have not begun yet, so far as the supply and demand for foods are concerned. . . [3632-1] and [257-254]

Several prophets, including Edgar Cayce, have predicted that a state of disorder and "anarchy" would ensue and take hold as we near the year 2000. This particular prophecy has been predicted to befall the societal structure of many countries including the United States. It is difficult to ascertain what may cause a breakdown in the orderly fabric of a nation. But it is not unreasonable to speculate that food shortages would play a significant role in the plot. In 1944 Cayce seemed to suggest this in a reading:

For those who are hungry do not care what may be the source of strength or power; not until there is a fulfillment of their needs. Unless there is then, a more universal oneness of purpose on the part of all, this will one day bring—here—in America—revolution! [3976-24]

The Edgar Cayce prediction that there would be anarchy in the United States is tied to another prophecy that also portends a tragic event for the nation. This specific prophecy was divided into three parts, of which the first two parts have already come to pass.

In June of 1939 a large group of A.R.E. members gathered at a hotel in Virginia Beach for the Association's annual meeting. The decade was drawing to a close, but things were looking bleak. Again they sought the advice and counsel of their sleeping benefactor. They composed a carefully worded paragraph as the "suggestion" for the "conductor"—in this instance Edgar's wife, Gertrude, to be read aloud to her husband as he went under.

Suggestion: You will have before you the *mass thought of the American nation*—its ideals, principles and purposes. You will give at this time a discourse on the major problems which confront the American people; indicating their basic causes and suggesting what attitudes we may hold, or procedures we may take individually and collectively, to help correct and balance these conditions.

A tall order to say the least! The reading is a long one, and deals with many subjects. And it was in this reading that Cayce volunteered the following prophecy:

Ye are to have turmoils—ye are to have strife between capital and labor. Ye are to have a division in thy own land *before ye have the second of the Presidents that next will not live through his office*—a mob rule! [3976-24]

In April 1945, the first president, Franklin D. Roosevelt, died in office of a massive cerebral hemorrhage while vacationing in Warm Springs, Georgia. In 1959, four years before the assassination of John F. Kennedy, Edgar's son, Hugh Lynn Cayce, added the following to the files:

Grammatical confusion and peculiar selection of words and phrases frequently obscure the meaning of passages in Mr. Cayce's psychic readings. . .In the reading which precedes this note [3976-24] we find one passage that is especially vague: "Ye are to have a division in thine own land *before there is the second of the Presidents that next will not live through his office*— a mob rule." Many of those who heard this reading assumed that this indicated that the second President would not live through office, thus dating the outbreak of violence in this country. A careful reading will show that this statement may refer to some distant date when the time of the second President who does not live through office arrives. A question would have cleared this at the end of the reading. We leave it for you to make your own interpretation. [In another reference to this prediction, Hugh Lynn stated: The "Division prophesied has for many years been interpreted by students as one that could arise out of racial inharmonies"].

This particular prophecy created confusion among Cayce authors and researchers for many years. Most notably, the words "that next" were changed to "who" in several publications. And even when the correct words were used, the interpretation was inaccurate. For in the book *Edgar Cayce on Prophecy*, edited by Hugh Lynn and published in 1968, there is the following:

We gathered around a radio and listened to the strained and conflicting reports that President Kennedy had been shot.

Then we heard the terrible news that he was dead.

We looked at one another in shocked amazement. "Edgar Cayce predicted this," we reminded ourselves. Franklin Roosevelt had been the first President to die in office since 1939, when the prophecy was given: "Ye are to have a division in thine own land before there is the second of the Presidents that next will not live through his office—a mob rule!"

John F. Kennedy was "the second of the Presidents."

The assassination of President Kennedy in November 1963, was also predicted by Washington, D.C. clairvoyant Jeane Dixon. In *The Door To The Future*, published in early 1963, author Jess Stearn quoted the following prediction that had appeared in *Parade Magazine* in 1956:

I picked up a tattered issue of the magazine, the last paragraph catching my eye. It spoke for itself. "As for the 1960 election, Mrs. Dixon thinks it will be dominated by labor and won by a Democrat. But he will be assassinated or die in office, though not necessarily in his first term."

It is well known that Jeane Dixon foresaw the assassination of John F. Kennedy and tried to warn him through an intermediary. A few weeks before Kennedy's fateful visit to Texas, Dixon "petitioned" the President's close friend, Kay Halle, to plead with the President to cancel his planned trip to the South.

Interestingly, students of Nostradamus speculate that he also predicted the assassination of Kennedy and included Dixon's efforts to warn him:

The great man will be struck down in the day by a thunderbolt.
An evil deed, foretold by the bearer of a *petition*. . .

Further, Nostradamus is said to have seen the assassination of Robert Kennedy along with Jeane Dixon's vision several years later that Robert would meet the same fate as his brother. Dixon tried on many occasions to warn Robert Kennedy. Further, she predicted the assassination would take place in California in the month of June, 1968.

Shortly after midnight, in the early morning hours of June 5th, Kennedy was gunned down at a hotel in Los Angeles.

In the same quatrain the 16th-century prophet continues:

"...*According to the prediction,* another falls at night time."

With respect to the third part of the Cayce prophecy, in 1971 Hugh Lynn added an addendum to the *Earth Changes* book:

> Reading 3976-24 indicated that this division would be apparent *before* the death in office of the second of the two presidents "that next" would not live through their office. The President at the time was Franklin D. Roosevelt, and it is this author's opinion that John F. Kennedy was only the first of two Presidents who would die in office, *next* after Roosevelt. The death of the "second of the Presidents" and the "division" in America are linked in this reading to "a mob rule."

There has not been a "mob rule" or "division" in this land. But the "anarchy" prophecy of this particular reading is similar to others Cayce gave and may yet be on the horizon.

Shortly before his death in 1945, Cayce paraphrases a passage from the 13th chapter of the New Testament Book of Romans in which the Apostle Paul writes: "There is no authority but by act of God, and the existing authorities are instituted by him." In a reading for a young man that was political in nature he states:

> Each nation, each individual head of a nation, is not in the position it occupies merely by "happen chance" but by the grace of God. [5142-1]

With respect to the leaders of any clime, there may be a destiny that is difficult to evade. And the end thereof may not be of the leader's choosing. Will another American president die in office sometime in the future? If we look to the Cayce readings for the answer, then other events must take place *before*—signs and omens will govern and forewarn us of such a tragic occurrence.

In December, 1994, Gordon-Michael predicted: "Terrorist activity hits New York, Los Angeles and other U.S. cities." A few months thereafter a federal building in Oklahoma City was the target of a terrorist bombing. In May, 1995, Scallion stated: "I cannot say there will not be another such event. I see multiple screens now showing possibilities of terrorist actions occurring in one screen and being blocked in another. I understand this to mean that as a result of the Oklahoma City bombing, many planned events will be foiled, but not all."

In *Black Dawn/Bright Day*, Sun Bear writes:

> I saw the time when the cities wouldn't exist in their present state. During the changes the most dangerous places will be near cities with nuclear and chemical plants. But all major cities will experience a breakdown in services. . . I've seen great garbage piles on the streets, the electric service out of order because of the storms and earthquakes, broken water mains and no more gasoline because of a major breakdown of the system.

> I also foresee race riots in the big cities, with street gangs engaged in uncontrolled fighting against each other, using guns to get what they want. When there is no money to pay their salaries, the police will not be there to protect the people in the city. Instead I saw the police banded together in groups calling themselves "Brothers of the Gun." They were using their guns to take whatever they wanted.

Many prophetic sources have predicted a major world-wide economic depression before the year 2000. Some believe this depression will be triggered by one major natural disaster or by a closely connected series of several. In 1992 Scallion predicted: ". . .insurance industry collapses because of high claims due to Earth Changes."

In June 1996 *The Virginian-Pilot* (Norfolk, Virginia) reported:

> . . .last month the Insurance Services Office, Inc. of New York, a research arm of the insurance industry, issued a report called "Managing Catastrophic Risk." . . .ISO's basis was a computer model and a survey of 80 insurer groups.

> The model projected a hurricane, say, of Andrew's magnitude, could cause damage exceeding $50 billion if it hit a congested city such as Miami proper. Losses of that magnitude would leave up to 36 percent of the surveyed insurers insolvent.

Even a $25 billion storm, which is to be expected every quarter century, would leave 10 percent of the insurers insolvent and leave customers with more than $3 billion worth of unpaid claims. . .

In the late 1980s the Ramala prophet said:

On your Earth at this time you do not have to be a prophet to recognise that the financial systems of your world are in the process of collapse. Whether you are a psychic, a mystic, a prophet or, indeed a banker, you know that the time is fast approaching when the present financial institutions of the world will crumble. This you can prophesy with certainty, but what can you say as to the nature of the timing of that event? You can, of course, make an inspired guess, you can give an opinion, but what will be the event that will initiate the final collapse? That event, of course, will be an act of God. An event will happen on this Earth which will then set in motion a chain of events which will lead to the destruction of the financial empires of the world. But does any being know what that trigger will be? I, from my point of consciousness, dwelling on a plane far above that of the Earth, can say—I do not know. . .

Edgar Cayce stated: ". . .there will be many changes, to be sure when the present conditions [World War II] subside, there will be more and more the upsetting of the monetary units of the land. . ." [5400-1].

In verse VIII 28 Nostradamus predicted:

The counterfeit of gold and silver inflated,
After the theft thrown away as worthless,
Discovered that all is dissipated by the debt,
Scripts and bonds are all wiped out.

In *Phoenix Rising*, Mary Summer Rain relates the insights she received from No-Eyes concerning what Cayce said would be "strife between capital and labor" in America that may result in a depression. And it is well known that major corporations are rapidly shifting to cheaper labor sources in other countries:

No-Eyes clearly saw the massive movement of strikes among the nation's blue collar workers. . .Will the vehement strikers be able to win their cause? Probably not, because many of the empty factories will remain that way—filled only with the silent specters of what once was. The owners will cease their U.S. operations and take their business overseas where they can be assured of increased monetary profits. . .The vacating companies will leave a jagged hole within the fabric of the stock market, and Wall Street will be thrown into confusion.

During this economic melee, the far-sighted investors will quickly unload their stocks, liquidate their assets, and withdraw their funds, leaving the banks embarrassingly over-balanced with liabilities. With the major banks caught off-guard, the people will be in a maddening rush to withdraw their assets. However, they will be gravely disappointed to discover that the F.D.I.C. has not been able to insure their hard-earned savings.

Such will be the contributing factors to the forthcoming deep recession that will hopelessly slip into depression.

It is impossible to ascertain the circumstances that could bring about the predicted anarchy in America. No-Eyes tells Mary Summer Rain that several events could happen "simultaneously." Edgar Cayce states that, in addition to the strife between capital and labor, there may be several other "divisions" among the inhabitants of the United States:

> Though there may come those periods when there will be great stress, as brother rises against brother, as group or sect or race rises against race—yet the leveling must come. [3976-18]

And in 1943, he seemed to indicate that even the government may be partly responsible:

> As for this, thine own land: more turmoils will come during and after peace. . .not immediately. . .but more than there are at the present. *These turmoils will come from within.* There is a lack of godliness in the hearts of some who direct the affairs of groups. [3976-28]

We find in the *Vishnu Purana* of India concerning the "Kali Yuga" the following:

> The leaders who rule over the earth will be violent and seize the goods of their subjects. . .The leaders, with the excuses of

fiscal need, will rob and despoil their subjects and take away private property. Moral values and the rule of law will lessen from day to day until the world will be completely perverted and agnosticism will gain the day among men.

Cayce also spoke of "the leaders who rule over the earth." And he predicts they will eventually meet their fate:

It is also understood, comprehended by some, that a new order of conditions is to arise; that there must be many a purging in high places as well as low; that there must be the greater consideration of each individual, each soul being his brother's keeper. . .these [conditions] shall call upon the mountains to cover many. As ye have seen those in lowly places raised to those of power in the political, in the machinery of nations' activities, so shall ye see those in high places reduced and calling on the waters of darkness to cover them. And those that have acted as teachers among men, the rottenness of those that have ministered in places, will be brought to the light, and turmoils and strifes shall enter.

And then there should be, there *will* be, those rising to power that are able to meet the needs. For none are in power but that have been given the opportunity by the will of the Father—from which all power emanates. Mahatma Ghandi summarized the transgressions of our time: Politics without principles; Wealth without work; Pleasure without conscience; Knowledge without character; Commerce without morality; Worship without sacrifice; Science and Technology without humanity. [3976-18]

ARMAGEDDON, THE ANTI-CHRIST, 666: MARK OF THE BEAST

Armageddon, in the Book of Revelation, refers to the mountain region of Megiddo in northern Israel that was the site of several great battles in the Old Testament, and is the predicted location of the final battle between the forces of good and evil prophesied to occur at the end of the world—the "End Times." The term creates a dramatic image of death and destruction brought about by a "Holy War" or World War III—a great and final war that could annihilate all of humanity.

Some Cayce researchers speculate that the opening battle cry of Armageddon was sounded in the year 1936, the second of the critical years for this century. In a *World Affairs* reading in February 1932 Cayce was asked:

Question: Please forecast the principal events for the next fifty years affecting the welfare of the human race.

Answer: This had best be forecast after the great catastrophe that's coming to the world in '36 in the form of the breaking up of many POWERS that now exist as factors in the world affairs. . .Then, with the breaking up in '36 will be the CHANGES that will make the different MAPS of the world.

Question: Will Italy adopt a more liberal form of government in the near future?

Answer: Rather that of a more monarchal government than that of the liberal. [3976-10]

In 1936 Adolph Hitler violated the Treaty of Locarno by invading the Rhineland. The Italian dictator Mussolini conquered

Ethiopia in the same year. In Spain, civil war erupted between the Fascists and the Communists. In Japan, an uprising by the military known as the "February 26th Incident" brought about a martial government. In the same year, Chiang Kai-Shek, the leader of China, declared war on Japan. In a definitive work *And I Was There* by Rear Admiral Edwin T. Layton is the following information:

> . . .a book by the popular naval author Shinsaku Hirata, published in Tokyo seven years earlier [1936]. . .Warera Moshi Tatakawaba "When We Fight". . .included a vivid portrayal of the American fleet commander at Pearl Harbor worrying about the "fearsome" possibility that Japan would send "a fast striking force of cruisers and aircraft carriers" that would be "truly matchless and invincible!". . .author Hirata's speculation had been founded on some knowledge of our naval maneuvers in which carrier-based planes had demonstrated it was possible to carry out a "successful" surprise attack on Hawaii. Within three years a Pearl Harbor concept was part of the Japanese naval war college study, "Strategy and Tactics Against the United States."

In his End Times prophecy, the Old Testament prophet Joel sounds a warning that some have interpreted as a reference to nuclear explosions: "And I will shew wonders in the heavens and the earth, blood, and fire, and pillars of smoke." Many have been concerned about this threat, first used by mankind in warfare more than fifty years ago.

At the end of World War II, there was a somber ceremony as the Japanese surrendered to the Allied Forces on the battleship *Missouri* in Tokyo Bay. A few weeks earlier, the atomic bomb had been used on the cities of Hiroshima and Nagasaki. It was the dawn of the Nuclear Age—one that threatened the very survival of the planet and its inhabitants.

Author Clayton James writes in *The Years of MacArthur* that after the representatives of the Japanese and Allied Forces signed the surrender agreement:

> . . .the Supreme Commander, General Douglas MacArthur, left the ceremony and went to a microphone. It had been arranged for him to broadcast a message to the world. The Supreme Commander spoke slowly and movingly:

"A new era is upon us. Even the lesson of victory itself brings with it profound concern, both for our future security and the survival of civilization. The destructiveness of the war potential, through progressive advances in scientific discovery, has in fact now reached a point which revises the traditional concepts of war.

Men since the beginning of time have sought peace. . . Military alliances, balances of power, leagues of nations, all in turn failed, leaving the only path to be by way of the crucible of war. We have had our last chance. If we do not devise some greater and more equitable system, *Armageddon* will be at our door. The problem is basically theological and involves a spiritual recrudescence and improvement of human character. . .It must be of the spirit if we are to save the flesh."

Less than two years before the atomic bombs were used, a young man died, found himself in the ethereal world, and was shown a scene in the future similar to the one described by the prophet Joel. Then he returned and became famous as one of the first people to admit having had what is now recognized as the "Near Death Experience" (NDE). His story is described in the book *My Life After Dying*, by George G. Ritchie, Jr., M.D. In late 1943, while stationed in Texas, a 20-year-old Army private George Ritchie succumbed to pneumonia and passed away. While his body was stretched out on the Army cot in the medical ward covered with a sheet, he found himself engaged in an amazing adventure. The following excerpts are in his own words:

Since I collapsed in front of the x-ray machine at approximately 3:10 A.M. on December 20, 1943, and remained unconscious until the morning of December 24, 1943, what is recorded here has been related to me by other people. . .

When the ward enlisted man made his rounds, he could find no vital signs. He quickly summoned the officer of the day, but this medical officer could detect no evidence of respiration, blood pressure or cardiac impulse. He pronounced me dead, and ordered the attendant to prepare my body for the morgue.

The ward boy had to finish his medication rounds before he could carry out the doctor's orders. Then he came back to the isolation room to which I had been brought.

Because I was the same age as he, and because he was having trouble accepting the pronouncement of death on someone as young, the ward boy went back to the officer of the day and told him he thought he had seen my chest move. He asked the medical officer if he wouldn't make up a hypo of adrenaline to have ready to give to me. The medical officer did this and followed the attendant back into my room.

The doctor again checked my vital signs and found none. When the medical officer was about to tell the attendant to go ahead and prep me for the morgue this young attendant asked the doctor to please give me the hypo to be sure. Though the doctor was sure of his diagnosis of death, he could see that this young man was having a hard time dealing with my death. For the ward boy's benefit, he plunged the hypo directly into my heart. To his surprise, my heart started beating. It was four more days and nights before I regained consciousness.

The doctor knew for a certainty, it had been 8 to 9 minutes between the two times I had been pronounced dead. I'm sure as an M.D. myself, the doctor must have become very worried, since no one was sure of how long my vital signs had ceased before the ward boy made his rounds. For then, as now, doctors knew the chance of brain damage after five minutes without oxygen to the brain was profound. This is why Dr. Francy made this statement in his notarized statement: "I, speaking for myself, feel sure that his [Dr. Ritchie's] virtual call from death and return to vigorous health has to be explained in terms of other than natural means."

The NDE travelog of Dr. Ritchie takes place during the same "earth time-frame" that Dr. Francy and the ward boy are dealing with his dead physical body. And although Dr. Ritchie may only have been dead for 8 or 9 minutes, time in the beyond is not the same as earth-time. Dr. Ritchie viewed his own corpse:

Now my massive denial was breaking down and I was going to have to accept the fact that I was dead. . .I have never felt so alone, discouraged and frightened. *"Oh God, where are you when I am so lost and discouraged?"* . . .

Suddenly an amazing thing began. The light at the end of the bed began to grow brighter and brighter. . .It continued to increase in intensity until it seemed to be equal to a million welder's lights. I knew if I had been seeing through my human eyes instead of those of my spiritual body I would have been blinded.

Then three things happened instantaneously. *Something deep inside of my spiritual being said: "STAND UP. YOU ARE IN THE PRESENCE OF THE SON OF GOD."*

I was suddenly propelled up and off the bed. Out of the brilliant light at the end of the bed stepped the most magnificent Being I have ever known. The hospital walls disappeared and in the place of them was a living panorama of my entire life where I saw in detail everything I had ever experienced, from my own caesarean birth through my present death. . .

After his life review, Dr. Ritchie accompanied Jesus on a tour of the beyond—of the various spheres, planes, or, as he names them—"realms." He is shown the vast dimensions of the ethereal world and the activities of souls therein. [Dr. Ritchie's description of the other side is reminiscent of a remark from an Edgar Cayce reading: "There is no difference between the unseen world and that which is visible; save that in the unseen, so much greater expanse or space may be covered."] Subsequent to their experiences in the beyond, Dr. Ritchie and Jesus return to Dr. Ritchie's sheet-covered body:

In what seemed a very short time, but an extremely long distance, we were back in front of the hospital at Camp Barkeley. He then led me directly into my hospital room and did a startling thing.

He opened a corridor through time which showed me increasing natural disasters coming upon this earth. There were more and more hurricanes and floods occurring over different areas of our planet. The earthquakes and volcanoes were increasing. We were becoming more and more selfish and self-righteous. Families were splitting, governments were breaking apart because people were thinking only of themselves.

I saw armies marching on the United States from the south and *explosions over the entire world that were of a magnitude beyond my capacity to imagine.* I realized if they continued, human life as we have known it could not continue to exist.

Suddenly this corridor was closed off and a second corridor started to open through time. At the beginning they appeared very similar but the further the second one unfolded, the more different it became. The planet grew more peaceful. Man and nature both were better. Man was not as critical of himself or others. He was not as destructive of nature and he was beginning to understand what love is. . . . The Lord sent a mental message to me: "It is left to man which direction he shall choose. *I came to this planet to show you through the life I led how to love. Without OUR FATHER you can do nothing, neither could I. I showed you this. You have 45 years.*"

He then gave me orders to return to the human plane and mentally said, "You have 45 years. . ." The next thing I remember was looking down at my left hand. . .Again I passed into unconsciousness and remained in it until [on the morning of Christmas eve, more than four days later] I opened my human eyes.

The Hopi Indians are also concerned about mass destruction. In *Beyond Prophecies and Predictions*, Timms writes:

According to the prophecies, "A Gourd of ashes" would be invented which, if dropped from the sky, would boil the oceans and burn the land, causing nothing to grow for many years. (When the atomic bomb was dropped, the Hopi knew it was the signal for certain teachings to be released to warn the world. . .) The prophecy says men will travel to the moon and stars and this will cause disruption and the time of the great purification will be near. It is bad that spacemen brought things back from the moon (In NASA experiments, three types of Earth bacteria died after exposure to an Apollo II core-tube soil sample from the moon. This resulted in quarantine procedures for astronauts). The Great Spirit says in the prophecy that man will not go any further when he builds a city in the sky. People are planning to build a space station.

Besides the potential nuclear threat, another danger has worried people for a long time: the use of biological or chemical weapons. Saint Hildegard is said to have seen an event for this period that foretells the use of chemical weapons: "A powerful wind will rise in the North carrying heavy fog and the densest dust, and it will fill their throats and eyes so they will cease their savagery and be stricken with great fear."

We have seen that the American Indians have deep and extensive insights and deserve a great deal more recognition than they have previously been granted. We have also seen that the ancient civilization of Atlantis is said by Plato and Cayce to have been "advanced" in several ways. Cayce claimed that Atlantis was the home of the "Red Race," and in one reading that included information about the settling of America, he mentioned in passing ". . .the Iroquois Indians; those of noble birth, those that were the pure descendants of the Atlanteans. . ." [1219-01].

In *America's Secret Destiny*, author and researcher, Robert Hieronimus, Ph.D., presents extensive documented evidence that the Iroquois Indians were the true model for the United States Constitution:

> . . .a group of six Indian tribes joined to promote peace and human rights—the League of the Iroquois—was a major influence on Ben Franklin and Thomas Jefferson. Franklin and Jefferson borrowed consciously and freely from the democratic methods by which these people had governed themselves for four centuries. Without the League's guidance and advice, Franklin and Jefferson would not have achieved their goal so well. . .the Iroquoian civil policy prevented the concentration of power in the hands of any single individual and inclined rather to the division of power among equals. The Iroquois prized individual independence and their government was set up so as to preserve that independence. The Iroquois confederation contained the "germ of modern parliament, congress, and legislature". . .

Here is what Cadwallader Colden, a contemporary of Benjamin Franklin, said about the Iroquois:

> [The Indians] have "outdone the Romans". . .[they have] a social and political system so old that the immigrant Europeans knew nothing of its origins—a federal union of five (and later six) Indian nations that had put into practice concepts of popular participation and natural rights that the European savants had thus far only theorized. The Iroquoian system, expressed through its constitution "The Great Law of Peace," rested on assumptions foreign to monarchies of Europe: it regarded leaders as servants of the people, rather than their masters, and made provision for their leader's impeachment for errant behavior. The Iroquois law and custom upheld freedom of expression in political and religious matters and it forbade the unauthorized

entry of homes. It provided for political participation by women and a relatively equitable distribution of wealth. . .

The Founding Fathers of the United States were religious individuals who placed their faith in God. They were also well versed in the prophecies, including the ones for the New Age—nor were they ignorant of the role they were destined to play. They designed the front and reverse sides of the "Great Seal of the United States of America" which are displayed on the reverse of our one dollar bill, complete with a Pyramid capped with the all-seeing "third" or "spiritual" eye which some interpreters claim exemplifies prophetic vision. The Latin phrase beneath the Pyramid, *Novus Ordo Seclorum*, in translation means "New Order of the Ages," and the words *Annuit Coeptus* above, "He Has Prospered Our Undertaking."

Many of the Founding Fathers belonged to secret societies that embraced prophecy as part of their overall philosophy. At least four of the nation's founders (Washington, Jefferson, Franklin and Charles Thompson) are alleged to have been Rosicrucians, and three, (Franklin, Jefferson and Adams) are thought to have been initiates in the Illuminate order. It is well documented that many, including Washington and Franklin, were Freemasons and belonged to various Masonic Lodges. It is even claimed that the founders had a mystical experience at the signing of the Declaration of Independence.

In *The Secret Destiny of America*, researcher, philosopher, and author Manly P. Hall tells of an unusual recorded incident:

Faced with the death penalty for high treason, courageous men debated long before they picked up the quill pen to sign the parchment that declared the independence of the colonies from the mother country. For many hours they had debated in the State House at Philadelphia, with the lower chamber doors locked and a guard posted—when suddenly a voice rang out from the balcony. A burst of eloquence to the keynote, "God has given America to be free!" ended with the delegates rushing forward to sign. . . The American patriots then turned to express their gratitude to the unknown speaker. The speaker was not in the balcony; he was not to be found anywhere. How he entered and left the locked and guarded room is not known. No one knows to this day who he was.

So, it isn't surprising that George Washington is supposed to have had a prophetic vision of the future of the country he was fighting to free. In his vision he was shown three distinct events of which two have come true. The original manuscript of the following account of Washington's vision is housed in the Library of Congress in Washington, D.C. Recorded by one, Masley Bradshaw, it recounts the story told to him by Washington's fellow patriot, Anthony Sherman, who fought with Washington at Valley Forge:

The last time I ever saw Anthony Sherman was on the fourth of July, 1859, in Independence Square. He was then ninety-nine years old, and becoming very feeble. But though so old, his dimming eyes rekindled as he gazed upon Independence Hall, which he came to visit once more.

"Let us go into the hall," he said, "I want to tell you of an incident of Washington's life—one which no one alive knows of except myself; and, if you live you will before long, see it verified."

"From the opening of the Revolution we experienced all phases of fortune, now good, now ill, one time victorious and another conquered. The darkest period we had, I think, was when Washington after several reverses, retreated to Valley Forge, where he resolved to pass the winter of 1777. Ah! I have often seen the tears coursing down our dear commander's care-worn cheeks, as he would be conversing with a confidential officer about the condition of his poor soldiers. You have doubtless heard the story of Washington's going to the thicket to pray in secret for aid and comfort from God, the interposition of whose Divine Providence brought us safely through the darkest days of the tribulation.

"One day, I remember it well, the chilly winds whistled through the leafless trees, though the sky was cloudless and the sun shone brightly, he remained in his quarters nearly all afternoon alone. When he came out, I noticed that his face was a shade paler than usual, and there seemed to be something on his mind of more than ordinary importance. Returning just after dusk, he dispatched an orderly to the quarters of the officer I mentioned who was presently in attendance. After a preliminary conversation of about half an hour, Washington, gazing upon his companion [the witness, Sherman] with a strange look of dignity which he alone could command, said to the latter:

"'I do not know whether it is owing to the anxiety of my mind, or what, but this afternoon, as I was sitting at this table engaged in preparing a dispatch, something seemed to disturb me. Looking up, I beheld standing opposite me a singularly beautiful female. So astonished was I, for I had given strict orders not to be disturbed, that it was some moments before I found language to inquire the cause of her presence. A second, a third, and even a fourth time did I repeat my question, but received no answer from my mysterious visitor except a slight raising of her eyes. By this time I felt strange sensations spreading through me. I would have risen, but the riveted gaze of the being before me rendered volition impossible. I assayed once more to address her, but my tongue had became useless. Even thought itself had become paralyzed. A new influence, mysterious, potent, irresistible, took possession of me. All I could do was to gaze steadily, vacantly at my unknown visitant. Gradually the surrounding atmosphere seemed as though becoming filled with sensation, and grew luminous. Everything about me seemed to rarify, the mysterious visitor herself becoming more airy and yet more distinct to my sight than before. I now began to feel as one dying, or rather to experience the sensations which I have sometimes imagined accompany dissolution. I did not think, I did not reason, I did not move; all were alike impossible. I was only conscious of gazing fixedly, vacantly at my companion.

"'Presently I heard a voice saying: 'Son of the Republic, look and learn,' while at the same time my visitor extended her arm eastwardly. I now beheld a heavy white vapor at some distance rising fold upon fold. This gradually dissipated, and I looked upon a strange scene. Before me lay Europe, Asia, Africa, and America. I saw rolling and tossing between Europe and America the billows of the Atlantic, and between Asia and America lay the Pacific. 'Son of the Republic,' said the same mysterious voice as before, 'look and learn.' At that moment I beheld a dark, shadowy being, like an angel, standing, or rather floating in mid-air, between Europe and America, dipping water out of the ocean in the hollow of each hand, he sprinkled some upon America with his right hand, while with his left hand he cast some upon Europe. Immediately a cloud raised from these countries, and joined in mid-ocean. For a while it remained stationary, and then moved slowly westward, until it enveloped America, in its murky folds. Sharp flashes of lightning gleamed through it at intervals, and I heard the smothered groans and cries of the American people. A second time the angel dipped water from the ocean, and sprinkled it out as before. The dark cloud was then drawn back to the ocean, in whose heaving billows it sank from view. A third time I heard the voice saying, 'Son of the Republic, look and learn.' I cast my eyes upon America and beheld villages and towns and cities springing up one after another until the whole land from the Atlantic to the Pacific was dotted with them. Again, I heard the mysterious voice say, 'Son of the Republic, the end of the century cometh, look and learn.'

"'At this the dark shadowy angel turned his face southward, and from Africa I saw an ill-omened spectre approach our land. It flitted slowly over every town and city of the latter. The inhabitants presently set themselves in battle array against each other. As I continued looking I saw a bright angel, on whose brow rested a crown of light, on which was traced the word 'UNION,' bearing the American flag which he placed between the divided nation, and said, 'Remember ye are brethren.' Instantly, the inhabitants, casting from them their weapons became friends once more, and united around the national Standard.

"'Again I heard the mysterious voice saying, 'Son of the Republic, look and learn.' At this the dark shadowy angel placed a trumpet to his mouth and blew three distinct blasts; taking water from the ocean, he sprinkled it upon Europe, Asia, and Africa. Then my eyes beheld a fearful scene: from each of these countries arose thick, black clouds that were soon joined into one. And throughout this mass there gleamed a dark red light by which I saw hordes of armed men, who, moving with the cloud, marched by land and sailed by sea to America, which country was enveloped in the volume of the cloud. And I dimly saw three vast armies devastate the whole country and burn the villages, towns and cities that I beheld springing up. As my ears listened to the thundering of the cannon, clashing of swords, and the shouts and cries of millions in mortal combat, I heard again the mysterious voice saying, 'Son of the Republic, look and learn.' When the voice ceased, the dark shadowy angel placed his trumpet once more to his mouth, and blew a long, fearful blast.

"'Instantly a light as of a thousand suns shown down from above me, and pierced and broke into fragments the dark cloud which enveloped America. At the same moment the angel upon whose head still shone the word 'UNION,' and who bore our national flag in one hand and a sword in the other, descended from the heavens attended by legions of white spirits. These immediately joined the inhabitants of America, who I perceived were well-nigh overcome, but who immediately taking courage again, closed up their broken ranks and renewed the battle. Again, amid the fearful noise of the conflict, I heard the mysterious voice saying, 'Son of the Republic, look and learn.' As the voice ceased, the shadowy angel for the last time dipped water from the ocean and sprinkled it upon America. Instantly the dark cloud rolled back, together with the armies it had brought, leaving the inhabitants of the land victorious.

"'Then once more I beheld the villages, towns, and cities springing up where I had seen them before, while the bright angel, planting the azure standard he had brought in the midst of them, cried with a loud voice, 'While the stars remain, and the heavens send dew upon the earth, so long shall the Union last.' And taking from his brow the crown which blazoned the word 'UNION,' he placed it upon the standard while the people, kneeling down, said 'Amen.'

"'The scene instantly began to fade and dissolve, and I at last saw nothing but the rising, curling vapor I at first beheld. This also disappearing, I found myself once more gazing upon the mysterious visitor, who, in the same voice I had heard before said, 'Son of the Republic, what you have seen is thus interpreted: Three great perils will come upon the republic. The most fearful is the third, passing which, the whole world united shall not prevail against her. Let every child of the Republic learn to live for his God, his land, and the Union.' With these words the vision vanished, and I started from my seat and felt that I had seen a vision wherein had been shown to me the birth, progress, and destiny of the United States.'

"Such my friends." concluded the venerable narrator, "were the words I heard from Washington's own lips, and America will do well to profit by them."

Washington's vision of eerie foreboding, like many others, is cloaked in puzzling symbolism. Careful scrutiny reveals, however, that the first two parts of the prophecy came true. In the first Washington is shown that America will prevail in the Revolutionary

War. In the second, he foresees the Civil War and the eventual restoration of the Union. (Anthony Sherman must have felt the Civil War was soon to break out; thus the impetus for him to tell Bradshaw in 1859: "If you live, you will before long, see it verified.")

The third component of the vision, "And throughout this mass there gleamed a dark red light by which I saw hordes of armed men, who, moving with the cloud, marched by land and sailed by sea to America, which country was enveloped in the volume of the cloud," is similar to the one of Dr. Ritchie: "I saw armies marching on the United States from the south. . ." In addition, there may be a connection between the "cloud" and the "color red" that could denote the use by the invaders of chemical or biological weapons.

In *Black Dawn/Bright Day*, Sun Bear describes a prophecy of the Hopi that includes the following excerpts:

> The Hopi were told the time would come when two powers would shake the earth twice. The symbol of one of them would be the rising sun—Japan—and the symbol of the other would be a sign of four directions—Germany. During World War I, the Germans used the Maltese Cross as their insignia; in World War II, they had the swastika, both symbols of the four directions. . .
>
> The Hopi were told. . .we would see great floods in many places, more powerful winds than we have seen before, the Earth shaking, and the great volcanoes erupting. We would be seeing earth, water, fire and air all being a part of the cleansing. This is happening right now.
>
> The other way the cleansing could come about would be by a people whose color was red. They would come over this land in one day and conquer it. If that happened, the Hopi were warned that nobody should go outside of their houses because there would be something in the air that would kill them. . .
>
> The Hopi were told to journey to a place where all the nations of the world would be gathered and try to speak to them, warn them to return to sacred ways. They went four times to the United Nations building. Three times when they asked to go in, they weren't allowed. The fourth time, my spiritual grandfather, Wallace Black Elk, went before them carrying a pipe. They were allowed through the door, but still they were able to talk

to only a few of the delegates. They wouldn't let Black Elk speak or the Hopi to address the entire General Assembly. The Hopi prophecies had told them that if this happened, the time of the cleansing was near. So the Hopi returned to their land.

The many predictions referring to an "invasion" of the United States are susceptible to a slew of disparate interpretations. For the most part, the advanced technology of the world as the millennium approached would not have made sense to the visionaries. Consequently, symbols were displayed that would hopefully be de-coded in time to warn the population that would be affected. Missiles, nuclear weapons, chemical and biological warfare, terrorism and the like, were far on the horizon when many of the visions were perceived.

Recently, however, an individual had an experience in which the visions he was shown did not include symbols. And like Dr. Ritchie, he had to leave his physical body for a short period so that he could sound the warning for humanity. Dannion Brinkley is an ex-Marine whose fascinating exploits are described in a recently published book, *Saved By The Light*. He has appeared on many talk shows, and has described his experience to audiences throughout the United States and in several other countries, including Russia.

The year was 1975. While talking on the telephone during an electrical storm, lightning struck the phone line. Brinkley was electrocuted, rushed to the hospital, and pronounced dead. He left his body, traveled to the beyond, but returned to what turned out to be a very long, painful and tedious recovery. In *Saved by the Light*, he details many of his extended adventures in the beyond before returning to his earth body. As his ethereal journey was drawing to a close, he was shown thirteen separate scenes of future events, each with multiple occurrences, that were projected on the screen of TV-like "boxes." He explains that: "At the time I didn't know these were future events. All I knew was that I was seeing things of great significance and that they were coming to me as clearly as the evening news, with one great difference: I was being pulled into the screen."

Once he returned to life, Dannion wrote down 117 future events he had been shown. Many have occurred as recorded—many are yet to be verified. (The world-famous researcher of the NDE experience, Dr. Raymond Moody, was made aware of Dannion's predictions shortly after Brinkley documented them). The following excerpts are from Dannion's final vision:

At the very end came a thirteenth vision. I don't know where it came from. I didn't see a Being of Light bring it forward. . .This vision was in many ways the most important of all because it summed up everything I had seen. . .

Through telepathy I could hear a Being say, "If you follow what you have been taught and keep living the same way you have lived in the last thirty years, all of this will surely be upon you. If you change, you can avoid the coming war."

Scenes from a horrible war accompanied this message. As the visions appeared on the screen, the Being of Light told me that the years 1994 through 1996 were critical ones in determining whether this war would break out. "If you follow this dogma, the world by the year 2004 will not be the same one you now know," said the Being. "But it can still be changed and you can help change it."

Scenes from World War III came to life before me. I was in a hundred places at once, from deserts to forests, and saw a world filled with fighting and chaos. Somehow it was clear that this final war, an Armageddon if you will, was caused by fear. . .

"The fear these people are feeling is an unnecessary one," said the Being of Light. "But it is a fear so great that humans will give up all freedoms in the name of safety."

I also saw scenes that were not of war, including many visions of natural disasters. In parts of the world that had once been fertile with wheat and corn, I saw parched desert and furrowed fields that farmers had given up on. In other parts of the world, torrential rainstorms had gouged out the earth, eating away topsoil and creating rivers of thick, dark mud.

People were starving in this vision. They were begging for food on the streets, holding out bowls and cups and even their hands in hopes that someone or something would offer them a scrap to eat. In some pictures people had given up or were too weak to beg and were curled on the ground waiting for the gift of death.

I saw civil wars breaking out in Central and South America and the rise of socialist governments in all of these countries before the year 2000. As these wars intensified, millions of refugees streamed across the U.S. border, looking for a new life in North America. Nothing we did could stop these immigrants. They were driven by fear of death and loss of confidence in God.

I saw millions of people streaming north out of El Salvador and Nicaragua, and millions more crossing the Rio Grande into Texas. There were so many of them that we had to line the border with troops and force them back across the river. The Mexican economy was broken by these refugees and collapsed under the strain. . .

The illegal immigrants that Dannion saw streaming across the border into the United States could also explain Dr. Ritchie's vision of an invasion from the south and the armed men that Washington saw in his vision. If the vision was accurate, this event would obviously add to the strain that is already present in some sections of the country. If there is a major economic depression, natural disasters, or shortages of food, then there could be a serious breakdown in law and order.

Scallion recently reported that he now believes the prophesied "Holy War" has started because of the riots that have been taking place in Ankara, Turkey among the Arab factions. Father Culleton references numerous Armageddon prophecies by church figures that are foreboding in nature. The following three are representative of many others in his book:

Pope Pius IX (1878):

"Since the whole world is against God and His Church, it is evident that He has reserved the victory over His enemies to Himself. This will be more obvious when it is considered that the root of all our present evils is to be found in the fact that those with talents and vigor crave earthly pleasures, and not only desert God but repudiate Him altogether.

"Thus it appears they cannot be brought back in any other way except through an act that cannot be ascribed to any secondary agency, and thus all will be forced to look to the supernatural and cry out: 'From the Lord is this come to pass and it is wonderful in our eyes!'

"There will come a great wonder, which will fill the world with astonishment. This wonder will be preceded by the triumph of revolution. The church will suffer exceedingly. Her servants and her chieftain will be mocked, scourged and martyred."

The Blessed Maria Taigi (1837):

"God will ordain two punishments: One, in the form of wars, revolutions and other evils, will originate on earth; the other will be sent from Heaven.

"There shall come over all the earth an intense darkness lasting three days and three nights. Nothing will be visible, and the air will be laden with pestilence, which will claim principally the enemies of religion. During this darkness artificial light will be impossible. Only blessed candles can be lighted and will afford lumination. He who out of curiosity opens his window to look out or leaves his house will fall dead on the spot. . ."

Sister Mary of Jesus Crucified of Pau (1878):

"All states will be shaken by war and civil conflict. During a darkness lasting three days the people given to evil ways will perish so that only one-fourth of mankind will survive. The clergy, too, will be greatly reduced in number, as most of them will die in defense of the faith of their country."

Bible prophecies warn of sickness, disease and epidemics—"pestilence." In the decade of the '90s, there have been numerous reports that this is happening before our very eyes. For example, in May, 1996 the Associated Press reported:

GENEVA—Over use of medicine, human settlement of un-inhabited areas, international travel and poverty have combined to produce a devastating spread of infectious diseases, a new report says.

The report of the World Health Organization [WHO] warns that the spread of untreatable forms of malaria and tuberculosis and the emergence of the killers like AIDS and Ebola threaten to undermine recent advances in health care.

"We are standing on the brink of a global crises of infectious diseases," WHO Director-General Dr. Hiroshi Nakajima said. . .

"More than 50,000 people die every day—17 million a year—from infectious diseases. And there is no respite in sight. . .the 137 page report makes gloomy reading.

"During the past 29 years, at least 30 new diseases have emerged to threaten the health of hundreds of millions of people. For many of these diseases there is no treatment, cure or vaccine," the report says.

Ebola, a contagious hemorrhagic fever that surfaced in 1977 and re-emerged to kill 245 people in Zaire a year ago, is another new disease. The hepatitis C virus, which causes liver cancer and was discovered in 1989, is another.

Diseases that have been around for centuries are popping up in incurable strains.

For instance, the two organisms that cause pneumonia—one of the biggest childhood killers—are increasingly resistant to drugs. The same is true of malaria and TB strains.

Other diseases—like cholera and yellow fever—are striking parts of the world that used to be considered safe, the report says.

The AntiChrist and Mark of the Beast

In the Book of Revelation, John writes:

And he [the beast, the anti-Christ] causeth, both small and great, rich and poor, free and bond, to receive a mark in their right hand, or in their foreheads:

And no man might buy or sell, save he that had the beast, or the number of his name. Here is wisdom. Let him that hath understanding count the number of the beast: for it is the number of a man; and his number is Six hundred threescore and six (666). (13:16-18)

The prophecy concerning the anti-Christ is a very powerful one for Christians around the world. In the spring of 1996, Christians by the thousands in Columbia began inundating the churches to have their children baptized. A fundamentalist Christian group had been warning that anyone not baptized by June 6, 1996 would be claimed by the anti-Christ. This warning was based on the interpretation that 6/6/96 was in some way relevant to the 666 beast of the Bible in the Book of Revelation. Even pregnant women were said to be trembling with fear, trying somehow to include their yet-to-be-born in the protection.

In Dannion's twelfth vision he was shown the following that could be interpreted as a reference to the anti-Christ and a clue to the meaning of the above passages from The Revelation:

The eleventh [TV-like] box was gone and I was into the twelfth box. Its vision addressed an important event in the distant future, the decade of the nineties (remember, this was 1975), when many of the great changes would take place.

In this box I watched as a biological engineer from the Middle East found a way to alter DNA and create a biological virus that would be used in the manufacture of computer chips. This discovery allowed for huge strides in science and technology. Japan, China, and other countries of the Pacific Rim experienced boom times as a result of this discovery and became powers of incredible magnitude. Computer chips produced from this process found their way into virtually every form of technology, from cars and airplanes to vacuum cleaners and blenders.

Before the turn of the century, this man was the richest in the world, so rich that he had a stranglehold on the world economy. Still, the world welcomed him, since the computer chips he had designed somehow put the world on an even keel.

Gradually he succumbed to his own power. He began to think of himself as a deity and insisted on greater control of the world. With that extra control, he began to rule the world.

His method of rule was unique. Everyone in the world was mandated by law to have his computer chips inserted underneath his or her skin. This chip contained all of an individual's personal information. If a government agency wanted to know something, all it had to do was scan your chip with a special device. By doing so, it could discover everything about you, from where you worked and lived to your medical records and even the kind of illness you might get in the future.

There was an even more sinister side to this chip. A person's lifetime could be limited by programming this chip to dissolve and kill him with the viral substance it was made from. Lifetimes were controlled like this to avoid the cost that growing old places on the government. It was also used as a means of eliminating people with chronic illnesses that put a drain on the medical system.

People who refused to have chips implanted in their bodies roamed as outcasts. They could not be employed and were denied government services.

Technological advances since 1975 seem to point to the fact that Brinkley's vision may have been more than just the result of an electrocution-hallucination or the product of an overactive imagination. In Europe, computer chips are being implanted under the skin of farm animals so that the European Common Market can keep track of them. In Canada, pets have a computer chip implanted beneath their skin for identification and medical records. The following excerpt is from an article supportive of smart cards in the July 1995 issue of *Popular Science:*

"If we had our way, we'd implant a chip behind everyone's ear in the maternity ward," says Ronald Kane, a vice president of Cubic Corp.'s automatic revenue collection group. Cubic is the leading maker of smart card systems for mass transit systems, highway tolls, parking, and other applications and one of a number companies and government agencies pushing the frontier of smart cards—the money of the future.

In June of 1996 the Chicago *Tribune* reported:

A tiny chip implanted inside the human body to send and receive radio messages, long a popular delusion among paranoids, is likely to be marketed as a consumer item early in the next century.

Several technologies already available or under development will enable electronics firms to make implantable ID locators, say futurists, and our yearning for convenience and security makes them almost irresistible to marketers. . .

Inevitably, implantable radio locators conjure up visions of Big Brother and unscrupulous scientists abusing such technology to control the masses. But the researchers laying the foundations for this technology see their work as helping humankind, not subverting privacy.

They seek to aid people using wireless phones to summon emergency help, to track soldiers who become lost on maneuvers and to enable people to get along without carrying cash by automatically crediting an account.

Animal advocates already urge pet owners to have tiny identification chips implanted in their dogs and cats so if they are lost, shelters can identify them through a national computerized database.

The notion of using implantable chips to control humans isn't entirely absent, even in these early stages of development. . .

Several systems already are in place with the potential to locate people using radio signals. The most obvious, called

GPS, for global positioning satellites, was launched by the military years ago and has become available for civilian applications. It uses satellites to map a person's position with great precision. Researchers want to combine such locators with equipment that monitors a person's health. . .

Companies already market pagers for children so parents can keep touch when youngsters are away from home. Adding the ability to pinpoint location at any time is a natural extension; keeping track of a child through a chip implanted under the skin may be another.

"People accept that increased communications makes life more convenient at the same time that it means there's no hiding place anymore," said Bernard Beck, a Northwestern University sociologist. "If I have a universal ID implanted, I can cash a check anywhere in the world. There's no worry about credit cards being stolen. These are attractive matters.". . .

But the potential loss of privacy is a large issue. Everyone likes to drop off the screen for an hour or so now and then.

". . .The legal issues of who owns this information are major," said Dan Polsby, a Northwestern University law professor. "It's one thing to have my hospital monitoring my heartbeat for fibrillation, but it's an entirely different matter to have the government monitoring my whereabouts."

Although potential problems are huge, locator ID chips may be inevitable, said Cornish of the World Future Society. . .

There are different opinions concerning the interpretation of the communication from John in the Book of Revelation. The anti-Christ is believed by many to represent, not an individual, but an overall negative consciousness that builds and builds until it takes a strangle-hold on the human race and throws the world into turmoil as the millennium approaches.

The *Grail Message* assigns the anti-Christ to that of an individualized spirit-entity, a "dark angel" of consciousness that represents the opposite of the Christ consciousness in the world, an "Antichrist" that has the power to affect the decisions and actions of people that have strayed from the will of God:

> The Revelation says that this Antichrist *will raise his head* before the Judgement, but not that he will first appear then! If it is said therein that he raises his head, this clearly indicates

that he must be here already, but not that he is yet to come. It means that *he will have reached his zenith of his dominion* just before the Judgement.

Listen to this cry of warning, you who are not yet spiritually deaf and blind. Take the trouble for once to think for *yourselves*. If you remain indolent in this respect you give yourselves up as lost.

If you lift the protecting cover from the lair of a poisonous snake that suddenly realizes it is exposed, it will naturally try to rear up and bite this ruthless hand.

It is no different here. Finding himself exposed, the Antichrist will quickly protest through his servants; on being unmasked he will make a great outcry, and try in every possible way to maintain himself on the throne which mankind so willingly offered him. But all this he can only do through those who inwardly revere him.

When Edgar Cayce was asked about the meaning of the anti-Christ he offered the following explanation:

Question: In what form does the anti-Christ come, spoken of in Revelation?

Answer: In the spirit of that opposed to the spirit of truth. The fruits of the spirit of the Christ are love, joy, obedience, long-suffering, brotherly love, kindness. Against such there is no law. The spirit of hate, the anti-Christ, is contention, strife, fault-finding, lovers of self, lovers of praise. Those are the anti-Christ, and take possession of groups, masses, and show themselves even in the lives of men. [281-16]

In January of 1991, shortly after the Gulf War (Desert Storm) broke out in the Middle East, several of Paul Solomon's supporters asked him to give a reading about the war's meaning in the context of the prophesied War of Armageddon:

Yes, there are gathered here the witnesses and the powers of creation and of life on this planet. You have called the witnesses and the witnesses have assembled.

And we would begin reading from these records by mentioning the Hermetic Law that is stated "as above, so below," which we mention for the reason that the great battle to which you refer, the battle of Armageddon, is a battle between Light and Darkness, not confined even to this planet, but to the entire system which you would refer to as your solar system in which the Sun itself is a cathedral of Light and this planet a manger. And in that perspective, know that the spiritual forces of Light battling against darkness are far greater than you can see, and more meaningful than the gathering of armies, however powerful, and however disposed against one another in the flesh.

At the same time, we point out that which manifests in the spiritual, that above, is also reflected in that which is below, or that which is material. And in that light we would answer a very certain YES, that this is the initial phase of the war of Armageddon as it manifests itself in the shadow of the real. By the shadow of the real we mean that the physical manifestation of that which occurs in the spiritual or in the heavens is the out-manifestation on your planet as a war between men. In the sense that you ask the question "Is this the literal battle of Armageddon?"—the war of Armageddon, then the answer is: what you see before you being played between the forces of nations with armies in the physical is a physical reflection of the spiritual war which is already begun, and has been for some time since the prophecy was given. And specifically since the time of the appearance of the Christ as Jesus of Nazareth as he ascended. In the moment he ascended the war began. ["Do not suppose that I have come to bring peace to the earth. I did not come to bring peace, but a sword." Matthew 10:34]

And though we do confirm that the alignment of the forces that you are seeing in that place in the Middle East, gathered around the plains of Megiddo, is in fact a physical out-manifestation of the spiritual battle. We would carefully point to you that this is only the smallest manifestation of this war. A far greater battle is raging, far more dangerous. That is the battle of man against the host planet, the Mother. A far more serious war is the war of man asserting his will over nature, to manipulate nature to his own purposes rather than harmonizing with the forces of growth, which are the manifestation of the Living One on this planet. Far more serious than the array of guns and tanks is the array of man's consciousness divided within himself, and out-manifesting in his attempt to manipulate the world around him, believing that a man himself might better control his destiny than would his Lord, his God. . .

And when in the egotistical nature of man attempts to control weather, climate, and balances of nature, denaturing the surface of the planet so you are involved in the battle of the forces of the heavens, the heavenly system, and mankind becomes rather than a guest on the planet of his Mother, becomes a parasite on the body of the Mother.

This is a far greater war than that fought by petty despots or a loose coalition of self-righteous nations. Then this war fought with missiles and guns is a small portion, and one battle, but it is in fact the sounding of the trumpet for the beginning of the orchestrated action of Armageddon as it would appear in the physical. But do be careful to remember the words of the Master as he spoke and said, "What you see in the physical is like seeing the movement of leaves on trees. But what you do not see is the wind that moves the leaves." And so when you see the tanks and armor and guns you are seeing the movement of the leaves. But the real battle is in the air in the sense of being in the subtler dimension of heaven within you and between you—about you. . .

And you would see those phenomena that are referred to as the stellar events, as if the stars have fallen, the moon turned to dripping blood, the earth renewed and wrapped in a robe of light, shining to rejoin the sun. These things may be difficult to visualize or even understand, and even frightening if you knew their implications. But it will come that as a result of the war that is being fought this day, this planet earth will be so destabilized that virtually every mountain and valley, every sea will be changed in its geographical nature quite literally. Earthquakes as have been prophesied since the beginning of time will change the face of the earth. But all this is the labor pains for a new birth of a new Eden on earth. And then you will know that mankind would never have appeared on this planet were not the planet sufficient to his every need to live and survive.

And so it shall be again, when all that is false, all that is manipulated and denatured about the face of the earth, be broken down and returned to the earth, then shall Eden bloom again, and man live in harmony and there shall be no more war. Then expand your consciousness beyond your concern for this current battle, for it is only the initial battle of the war. . .but that will only be the quiet of a moment of the heat of the day, and will resume again. . .

And yet it will be a different battle, for then the players will not be the nation of Iraq against a coalition of others, but rather it will begin to involve all nations of the region and beyond to virtually every nation in the world. And the war itself in a greater sense will be fought between this time and the year 2001. . .

The anti-Christ, who is the absolute embodiment of darkness, will appear. But he will appear as an angel of light [2 Corinthians 11:14], and many among you will be confused, for he will first appear to be a savior in the Middle East. But having gained power and favor he will become then power mad, drunk with power. . .

So watch not for those who swagger and boast, and are too obviously forces of evil. For the anti-Christ is far too clever, and will appear first as a savior. Be not swayed by everyone who comes in robes of light. . .

So the question remains unanswered! Is the anti-Christ simply a metaphor that represents the negative consciousness of the human race? Is the anti-Christ an evil spirit-entity who can influence the actions of certain people? Is the anti-Christ a real person, an individual who is presently living somewhere in the world and who is currently devising a sinister plan for all of humanity? Is the anti-Christ none of the above, some of the above, or all of the above? Only Father Time has the actual answer. But soon, supposedly, all the inhabitants of the earth will know the answer.

Once in a great while a discovery is made that is alleged to be authentic, and which is remarkable in its message as it relates to our times. An old manuscript or a group of aged writings turns up which throws new light on the future destiny of humanity. A recent illustration is the discovery of previously unknown prophecies of the notable sixteenth-century prophetess, Mother Shipton.

THE PROPHECIES OF MOTHER SHIPTON

In the world of prophecy and the paranormal, there is a great deal of prejudice as a result of hundreds of years of religious dogma. This intolerance was especially true in the sixteenth century. In all of Europe, persons who exhibited extrasensory perception in any way, shape, or form were rigorously persecuted by the church and the state. Consequently, Nostradamus confused the order of his prophecies and cloaked them in symbology in order to conceal their meaning from the civil and church authorities in France who he knew would accuse him of being a sorcerer. Mother Shipton, who was living in England during the same period, was reportedly threatened by various authority figures who warned her she would one day be burned at the stake as a witch. The burning of witches and other "heretics" as they were bound by both hands and feet to a large vertical pole or stake in the ground was one of the most popular forms of punishment administered by the "faithful."

The following historical information about "Witchcraft" is from the *Funk & Wagnall's New Encyclopedia*:

The witch-hunting mania obsessed Europe from about 1050 to the end of the 17th century; it subsided occasionally, but then attained greater fury. Children were encouraged to inform against parents, husband against wives, relatives and neighbors against each other. Witnesses were paid to testify. The most inhuman tortures were inflicted to force confessions. The inquisitors did not scruple to betray promises of pardon to those acknowledging guilt. There arose a class of professional witch finders who collected charges and then tested the accused for evidence of witchcraft. They were paid a fee for each conviction. The most common test was pricking. All witches were supposed to have somewhere on their bodies a mark, made by the Devil, that was insensitive to pain. If such a spot was found, it was regarded as proof of witchcraft. Among other proofs were additional breasts, supposedly used to suckle familiars, inability to weep, and failure in the water test. In this last-named test, if a woman sank when thrown into a body of water, she was considered innocent, if she stayed afloat, she was guilty.

By the use of such methods, charges of witchcraft were easily sustained. The number of those condemned to death for witchcraft is difficult to estimate, largely because reports of executions did not distinguish between heretics and witches. Approximately 1000 persons were executed in one year in the district of Como, Switzerland, and available records indicate that most of the victims were reputed witches. During the Inquisition in Toulouse, France, 400 witches and heretics were put to death in a single execution. The persecution of witches was particularly severe in Germany. In Nuremberg alone, between 100 and 200 persons were burned annually, chiefly on charges of witchcraft. Estimates of the total number of persons executed in Europe for witchcraft from the 11th to the 18th centuries range from 300,000 to nine million.

The witch-hunting craze spread inevitably to the New World. Throughout the 17th century, sporadic prosecutions for witchcraft took place in Massachusetts, Connecticut, and Virginia. The mania reached its peak in the notorious witch trials of 1692 in Salem, Mass. On the basis of statements extracted from children who had been stimulated to hysteria by stories by an old West Indian servant, more than 200 persons were imprisoned, 55 were tortured, 19 were hanged, and one was pressed to death.

Today, the stigma associated with extrasensory perception and prophecy is alive and well. Persons who exhibit paranormal abilities are accused of dabbling with the "occult" and are chastised from the pulpit and by the members of certain religious organizations. Edgar Cayce has been accused of being in touch with demons and the devil. Yet, the interpretations of the teachings in the Bible are subject to doubt and conjecture by some, for there are many versions of the Old and New Testament plus other historical records that for one reason or another were not accepted by the early Church or subsequently by other Christian denominations.

Edgar Cayce said: "For, much might be given respecting that ye have that ye call the Bible. This has passed through many hands. Many that would turn that which was written into the meanings that would suit their own purposes, as ye yourselves often do. But if ye will get the spirit of that written there ye may find it will lead thee to the gates of heaven. For, it tells of God, of your home, of His dealings with His peoples in many environs, in many lands. Read it to be wise. Study it to understand. LIVE it to know that the Christ walks through same with thee." [262-60]

Today, many versions of the Bible are available and there are more than half a dozen Bible programs for use on the computer. One of the best is the Logos Bible Software which is distributed by Logos Research Systems, Inc. of Oak Harbor, Washington. From the company newsletter, *LogosNews*, the following is excerpted:

Why does Logos offer four different Greek texts? The reasons may or may not be familiar to you. It all revolves around the issue of the missing autographs.

The mystery of the missing autographs may not be a mystery at all. By autograph we mean the original manuscript written by the original author, for example Paul's letter to the Romans written and hand signed by Paul himself. This document was probably passed around so many times that it finally fell apart or got lost among its own copies. The point is, we don't have any known autographs, just copies and copies of copies and the copy machines in those days had legs and could walk.

The manuscripts and their copies spread throughout the known world. Those manuscripts that went north and west became known as the "Byzantine" or "western" texts. Those that traveled south and east became known as "Alexandrian" or "eastern" texts. . .

The manuscripts that propagated in the north and west were copied extensively as Christianity spread throughout Europe. The manuscripts in the south on the other hand were copied infrequently and spent centuries in storage. As a result there are many recent (Middle ages) manuscripts in the west and few ancient (third and fourth century) manuscripts in the east. These eastern manuscripts were re-discovered in the 1800s with the result that nearly every Bible translated since that time has been based on the older eastern manuscripts to the near total abandonment of the western manuscripts of the middle ages. Many manuscripts make one text. Collections of manuscripts and manuscript fragments are necessary to put together whole testaments and whole Bibles. . .

Which text is the correct text? Let us be perfectly clear. We don't know!

With respect to Mother Shipton, her verses have been copied for hundreds of years, and have appeared in various books, pamphlets, and articles on prophecy. Yet we know very little about her. Even her existence is questioned. But if the Mother Shipton prophecies are suspect, the reference texts concerning her, replete with terms such as "may have," "supposedly," "most likely," "reputedly," and so forth are also certainly flawed because the information relied upon is from that very period when the witch hunts were flourishing in England and partiality was expected, if not demanded.

The first printed work dealing with the prophecies of Mother Shipton, published nearly 100 years after her death, was a little booklet of less than seven pages titled *The Prophesie of Mother Shipton In the Raigne of King Henry the Eighth, Fortelling the death of Cardinall Wolsey, the Lord Percy and others, as also what should happen in insuing times*. It was "Printed for Richard Lownds, at his Shop adjoyning to Ludgate, 1641."

The following excerpt is from Volume XVIII of *The Dictionary of National Biography*, published since 1917 by the Oxford University Press, London. It refers to the little booklet that was printed for Richard Lownds in 1641:

Mother Shipton, reputed prophetess, is, in all likelihood a wholly mythical personage. No reference to her of earlier date than 1641 is extant. In that year there was published an anonymous tract entitled 'The Prophecies of Mother Shipton in the Reigne of King Henry the 8th, foretelling the death of Cardinall Wolsey, the Lord Percy, and others, as also what should happen in insuing times' (London, 4to). According to this doubtful authority, Wolsey, after his nomination to the archbishopric of York, learnt that 'Mother Shipton' had prophesied he should never visit the city of York, and in consequence sent three friends, the Duke of Suffolk, Lords Percy and Darcy, to threaten her with punishment unless she recanted her prophecy. But the old woman stood firm, hospitably entertained the envoys, and at their invitation foretold in somewhat mysterious phraseology their own future and many events that were to befall the kingdom. Most of her predictions related to the city of York and its neighborhood, but some of them interpreted the approach of the civil wars and one foretold the fire of London in 1666.

For some reason, the fact that the above-referenced "doubtful authority" also verified Mother Shipton's prediction concerning the death of Cardinal Wolsey is missing. The following is from the text of the small booklet which includes the Anglican language, style, and punctuation of the period:

. . .Mother *Shipton*, said the Duke, you said the Cardinal should never see *York*; Yea, said she, I said he might see *York*, but never come at it; But said the Duke, when he comes to *York* thou shalt be burned. . .

Not long after the Cardinal came to *Cawwood*, and going to the top of the Tower, he asked where *York* was, and how far thither, and said that one had said that he should never see *York*; Nay, said one, she said you might see *York*, but never come at it. He vowed to burn her when he came to *York*. Then they shewed him *York*, and told him it was but eight miles thence; he said he will soon be there; but being sent for by the King, he died in the way to *London* at *Leisester* of a lask (A laxity, a looseness or flux [dysentery?]).

The Encyclopedia of Witches and Witchcraft designates Mother Shipton:
. . .A 15th-century English witch and seer who supposedly prophesied scientific inventions, new technology, wars and politics through several centuries, all written in crude rhymes. The books of her "prophecies" are likely the invention of later writers, among them Richard Head who published her predictions in 1667; an anonymous writer who published *The Strange and Wonderful History of Mother Shipton* in 1668, and a man named Hindley, who apparently authored Shipton predictions in 1871. . .

Her predictions included automobiles, telephone and tele-
graph, iron-clad boats, the California gold rush and the Crystal
Palace in London. Mother Shipton is also credited with predicting the Civil War in England, the Great Fire of London (1666),
the discovery of tobacco and potatoes in the New World, World
War II, and the women's liberation movement. Her memorial,
Mother Shipton's cave, is in Knaresborough.

In predicting the Great Fire of London, Mother Shipton said
that men would walk on the charred remains of the rooftops of
burned buildings that had collapsed to the ground, and the master
of a ship sailing up the Thames river would lament over the city
he remembered. In the 1641 booklet printed by Richard Lownds
is the following:

> . . .and after that a ship come sailing up the Thames till it come
> against *London,* and the Master shall weep, and the Mariners
> shall ask him why he weepeth, being he hath made so good a
> voyage, and he shall say; Ah what goodly City this was, none
> in the world comparable to it, and now there is scarce left any
> house that can let us have a drink for our money.

Shortly after the Great Fire, the famous English historian and
diarist, Samuel Pepys (1633-1703), who became Secretary of the
Admiralty under Charles II, recorded that, when Prince Rupert
was sailing up the Thames on October 20, 1666, Rupert moaned:
"Now Shipton's prophecy is out."

Mother Shipton is also credited with predicting the Great Plague
of 1665 that ravaged the population of London the year before
the Great Fire: "Triumphant Death rides London through."

It seems plausible that Irish scholar, Richard Head, decided it
was time to write about Mother Shipton's life and prophecies and
have them printed for posterity because two of her most catastrophic prophecies had come to pass. The first edition of his
work was published in 1667, but little did Head realize at the
time that his biography of her would be the focus of an embar-
rassment for another writer almost 200 years later.

The witchcraft encyclopedia reference to "a man named
Hindley" pertains to the respected British editor, Charles Hindley,
who undoubtedly is responsible for some of the controversy
regarding Mother Shipton. In 1862, Hindley reprinted in garbled

version the 1687 edition of Richard Head's biography. However, it seems Hindley changed or added a few verses of his own, the most notorious one being: "The world to an end shall come, in eighteen hundred and eighty one." Hindley's work created quite a stir, but in 1873, Hindley confessed to having embellished Richard Head's work. Nevertheless, according to Charles Berlitz, the 1881 prediction caused "near panic until the date was past."

Perhaps the most meticulous Mother Shipton reference material, *Mother Shipton's Prophecy Book*, is distributed at her memorial and historic park in Knaresborough. And with respect to Hindley's 1881 world ending concoction, it states: ". . .but Mother Shipton <u>did</u> make a Prophecy about the end of the world. It fortells; 'The world shall end when the High Bridge is <u>thrice fallen</u>.' The 'High Bridge' is in Knarsborough, right beside the entrance to Mother Shipton's cave, and has twice fallen already."

Regardless if Mother Shipton's prophecies are the "invention of later writers," there is no question that, even today, whenever her prophecies are quoted they are repetitions of previously published works dating back more than 100 years. The most recent authoritative work, Harrison's *Mother Shipton Investigated,* was published in 1881 (The world hadn't come to an end). No new prophetic stanzas attributed to her have made an appearance—that is until now!

When Mother Shipton's verses are quoted, they do not always appear in the same order, nor do they always read exactly the same. The Anglican language of her time is subject to various translations; however, the variations are usually of little significance. In addition it is unlikely that, with both Mother Shipton and Nostradamus, their visions of the future spanning hundreds of years came to them in chronological order. They could only write down their observations and wait for history to arrange the sequence.

In this day and age, the discovery of long-lost medieval and Renaissance documents happens with some frequency, and the newly-discovered prophecies of Mother Shipton seem to fit into this category. They were not discovered in England, however, but in Australia! This, of course, adds a little flavor to an already controversial subject.

Nexus Magazine, published in Australia, has a respectable circulation there as well as in New Zealand, the United Kingdom, Europe and the United States. It is an investigative type of magazine which garners information from a variety of sources in numerous countries for its articles. It delves into political, scientific, and metaphysical matters including prophecy. The following is from February/March, 1995, issue of *Nexus:*

> This rare collection of Mother Shipton's prophecies was sent to us by a *Nexus* reader who told us that, thirty years ago, she painstakingly transcribed them and managed to smuggle them out of the Mitchell Library, Sidney (now the State Library of New South Wales). The originals were kept in a locked room, along with many other volumes of prophetic writings deemed unsuitable for viewing by the general public.
>
> To our knowledge, this particular translation has never been made available to the public before appearing in *Nexus.* . .

Nexus editor, Duncan Roads stated in the strongest of terms that, on several occasions, he diligently interviewed the lady who claims to have discovered the prophecies, and that he is convinced of her integrity. He said she told him that her research led her to conclude that the prophecies, which were recorded on "scrolls" and stored in two jars, were at least 100 years old. How the verses reached Australia is a mystery.

The order of a few prophetic stanzas quoted here have been slightly rearranged for the sake of continuity, but the adjusted sequence does not alter the message. Also, a few have not been quoted because they are inconsequential for our purpose. The following four stanzas were on the outer wrapping of the scrolls or "tome" found in the museum. Currently, a tome is defined as a lengthy, scholarly work, or one of the books in a work of several volumes. However, this term from the Latin *tomus*, is also defined as a scroll or roll of paper.

The stanzas suggest that Mother Shipton was convinced of her impending execution and felt an urgency to record it for future generations. Further, she must have felt it might be destroyed if found during the inquisitions of her time, so she placed it in a container and "secreted" it away:

> *I know I go, I know I'm free*
> *I Know that this will come to be.*
> *Secreted this, for this will be*
> *Found by later dynasty.*

A dairy maid, a bonney lass
Shall kick this tome as she does pass
And five generations she shall breed
Before one male child learns to read.

This is then held year by year
Till an iron monster trembling fear
Eats parchment, words and quill and ink
And mankind is given time to think.

And only when this comes to be
Will mankind read this prophecy
But one man's sweet's another's bane
So I shall not have burned in vain.
    — Mother Shipton

In the third stanza above, Mother Shipton describes the "monster" steam-driven iron printing presses that were put into service around the middle of the nineteenth century.

The following verses are in the main part of the collection:

A Carriage without horse will go
Disaster fill the world with woe.
In London, Primrose Hill shall be
In centre hold a Bishop's See.

Most translations use "accidents" (fill the world with woe), which better suits this prediction of the automobile and its role in the mishaps that cause pain and suffering on the roads and highways around the world. London stretches for miles around Primrose Hill and Westminster Abbey (Bishop's See); however, in the sixteenth century they were some distance from central London.

There is a similar verse attributed to Mother Shipton which reads: "When London surrounds Primrose Hill, the streets of the metropolis will run with blood." This could be interpreted as referring to the constant bombardment of London by Hitler's Luftwaffe in World War II.

In the first two lines of the next stanza Mother Shipton describes the modern world's communication network:

> *Around the world men's thoughts will fly*
> *Quick as the twinkling of an eye.*
> *And water shall great wonders do*
> *How strange. And yet it shall come true.*

The translation of the third line from another source reads: "Fire and water shall wonders do." Either translation might refer to steam boilers, hydroelectric facilities, municipal water systems, and so forth.

The next stanza is an obvious reference to transportation tunnels, submarines, and military and commercial aircraft:

> *Through towering hills proud men shall ride*
> *No horse or ass move by his side.*
> *Beneath the water, men shall walk*
> *Shall ride, shall sleep, shall even talk*
> *And in the air men shall be seen*
> *In white and black and even green.*
>
> *A great man then shall come and go*
> *For prophecy declares it so.*

Because of Mother Shipton's English heritage, and because the stanza follows others of the twentieth century, the great man is most likely Winston Churchill.

Gold was discovered in California in 1848. The "gold rush" is envisioned as migrants pan gold from the stone-laden streams:

> *In water, iron then shall float*
> *As easy as a wooden boat.*
> *Gold shall be seen in stream and stone*
> *In land that is yet unknown.*

This prediction could also refer to the discovery of gold in Australia. However, European cartographers were aware of the approximate location of *Terra Australias*, as the island continent was originally known in the first half of the 16th century.

> *And England shall admit a Jew*
> *You think this strange, but it is true.*
> *The Jew that once was held in scorn*
> *Shall of a Christian then be born.*

The last verse printed in the booklet distributed at Mother Shipton's memorial reads: "Shall of a Christian be born and born."

During Mother Shipton's time there were strong prejudices toward the Jews. In 1290 the small Jewish population in England had been expelled. It was not until 1656 that they were somewhat reluctantly allowed to return. The Church's new policy of "tolerance" would "bear" the burden of the Jewish presence.

> *A house of glass shall come to pass*
> *In England. But Alas, alas*
> *A war will follow with the work*
> *Where dwells the Pagan and Turk.*

The "house of glass" refers to the famous Crystal Palace in London that was completed in 1851. Immediately thereafter, the laborers who had built the Crystal Palace were shipped to the Crimean peninsula in the Black Sea to support Great Britain's military forces in the Crimean War (1852-1856) in which Great Britain, France, and Moslem ("Pagan") Turkey defeated Russia.

The following stanza could have several interpretations and may refer to the seventeenth-century Civil War in England:

> *These states will lock in fiercest strife*
> *And seek to take each others life.*
> *When north shall thus divide the south*
> *And Eagle build in Lion's mouth*
> *Then tax and blood and cruel war*
> *Shall come to every humble door.*

The interpretation of the next stanza was previously interpreted. It envisions Germany's and Japan's aggressive plans in 1926 that eventually were carried out in the second World War:

> *In nineteen hundred and twenty six*
> *Build houses light of straw and sticks*
> *For then shall mighty wars be planned*
> *And fire and sword shall sweep the land.*

The following stanza is a good illustration of how a person in the sixteenth century would attempt to describe the modern "monster" harvesters and the advent of machinery dominated agriculture:

And roaring monsters with man atop
Does seem to eat the verdant crop
And men shall fly as birds do now
And give away the horse and plough.

The next stanza is the one which foretells the women's liberation movement. The final two lines are open to controversy, interpretation and disagreement:

For in those wondrous far-off days
The women shall adopt a craze
To dress like men, and trousers wear
And to cut off their locks of hair.
They'll ride astride with brazen brow
As witches do on broomstick now.

Bloody World Wars of the past reached new heights of death and destruction with the emergence of twentieth century technology that is described in the following:

When pictures look alive with movements free
When ships like fishes swim beneath the sea
When men like birds shall scour the sky
Then half the world, deep drenched in blood
shall die. . .

A similar stanza to the one above is engraved on an aged tombstone at Kirby Cemetery, in Essex, England. It is unlikely the tombstone marks the burial plot of Mother Shipton, for her memorial in the town of Knaresborough is far from the county of Essex. In addition, it is said she was buried somewhere on the outskirts of York, and by tradition a tombstone was raised on her grave with the following inscription:

Here lies she who never ly'd,
Whose skill often has been tried,
Her prophecies shall still survive
And even keep her name alive.

The Tombstone was later moved to a museum in York, but has since disappeared.

In the Old Testament, the angel, Gabriel, appears to the prophet, Daniel, to tell of the "time of the end." In the New Testament, Gabriel appears to Zechariah to tell him his wife, Elizabeth, will give birth to John the Baptist. Later, Gabriel appears to Mary, and tells her that she will bring Jesus into the world. Edgar Cayce said: "Gabriel is, to be sure, the announcer." [5277-1] Mother Shipton also speaks of Gabriel as she continues by painting an overall picture of her vision of the final decade of the twentieth century:

For those who live the century through
In fear and trembling this shall do.
Flee to the mountains and the dens
The bog and forest and wild fens.

For storms shall rage and oceans roar
When Gabriel stands on sea and shore
And as he blows his wondrous horn
Old worlds die and new be born.

There'll be a sign for all to see
Be sure that it will certain be.
Then love shall die and marriage cease
And nations wane as babes decrease.

And wives shall fondle cats and dogs
And men live much the same as hogs.

Actually, there are two similar signs; the sign referred to above and symbolized in the next stanza as the "fiery Dragon" is an "introductory" sign. We are told that the prophecies which follow this *initial* sign will first be announced to all of humanity by an important messenger, a "herald"—one that has passed our way before. For this will be the messenger's sixth known appearance as dated from Mother Shipton's time when she recorded the prophecy:

A fiery Dragon will cross the sky
Six times before this earth shall die
Mankind will tremble and frightened be
For the sixth heralds in this prophecy.

The "fiery Dragon" is Mother Shipton's carefully chosen symbol for a *comet*. She chose this symbol by virtue of the fact that the long-tailed Dragon spewing flames from its mouth has been used throughout antiquity by many civilizations as a descriptive metaphor for a comet. For instance, the ancient Chinese, when describing a comet, would cite a "Red Dragon." Most likely, Mother Shipton's fiery Dragon in the above verse is the comet Halley. How she knew it would return at certain intervals is a mystery. It would be more than 100 years after her death that the British astronomer Edmund Halley would predict that his namesake would have an approximate orbit of 76 years. Counting forward from the period of time after the prophecy was made, (1607, 1682, 1759, 1835, and 1910) the comet would return on its sixth orbit in the 1980's, which it did. It entered the heart of our solar system in 1985, was closest to the earth in April of 1986, and departed.

There is evidence from several sources that the period from 1986 to 1989 was a crucial one. If humanity had not changed its negative activities by that time, there would be no turning back.

The spiritual teaching that human actions can affect physical matter is at least as old as the Old Testament story of Ninevah, whose citizens repented at the urging of the prophet Jonah, averting God's threatened destruction of the city. However, in the New Testament, Jesus told his disciples: "For just as Jonah was a sign to the Ninevites, so will the Son of Man be to this generation. . .The men of Nineveh will appear at the Judgement when this generation is on trial, and ensure its condemnation, for they repented at the preaching of Jonah, and what is here is greater than Jonah." (Luke 11:30-32)

In *Beyond Prophecies and Predictions,* there is the following excerpt of the teaching "as above so below" by the Japanese prophet Meishu Sama:

> . . .human actions and speech of a violent, destructive or negative nature create clouds in the spiritual realms which gather near their source until (like rain) they are finally dissipated by natural law in the form of turbulent weather or disasters. . .the earth is going to have to face "a mighty upheaval, the greatest cataclysm in all history."

Edgar Cayce stated the same view on several occasions. For example, in 1932 he told a person:

. . .for as understood—or should be. . .there are those conditions in the activity of individuals, in line of thought and endeavor, oft keep many a city and many a land intact through their application of the spiritual Laws. . .Tendencies in the hearts and souls of men are such that these [earth changes] may be brought about. For as often indicated. . .it is not the world, the earth, the environs about it nor the planetary influences that rule man. Rather does man—by his compliance with divine Law—bring order out of chaos; or by his disregard. . .of the Laws of divine influence, bring chaos and destructive forces into his experience. [416-7]

In the November 1993 issue of "The Earth Changes Report," the following question was asked of Gordon-Michael Scallion: "Since we understand that conscious, focused attention on something has the ability to change it, to what extent can we as individuals and groups effect a mitigation of the Earth changes you see?" He answered:

In the '70s the amount of positive consciousness required to bring about a change was relatively little. But, as we entered the end of the '80s, we entered into a period of psychodynamic forces, psychic spiritual energy accelerations, which meant that whatever was in the collective consciousness was being amplified because of earth and cosmic forces. So if the consciousness was loving and benevolent and following a spiritual ideal, then the planet would flourish and many things would be altered. The time frame of '87 through '89 was the crossover point which meant that each year afterwards it was going to require a lot more people—in the millions—to bring about positive change. There is not any event that I have predicted that can not be negated if enough people are living in harmony. It would now require 30 percent of the population of the United States to negate the events I have forecast.

Scallion's time period of '87 through '89 straddles perfectly the cross-over-year Jesus gave Dr. Ritchie. The near-death experience of Dr. Ritchie took place in 1943, and in that year Jesus said humanity had 45 years to change—until 1988!

In *Black Dawn/Bright Day* Sun Bear states: "1987 was one of the most powerful years for humanity since the beginning of the

Earth changes. . .The ancient Mayan temples have a specific number of steps. The Aztecs also used a certain number of steps in their temples. The steps represent a measurement of time. The last step on the temples is 1987—it's the last date there. That is because the Mayan and Aztec prophets knew 1987 would be a time of major change in the world."

Just before Easter in 1986, the Ramala prophet told his seekers: "These are not ordinary times. This is not an ordinary Easter. This is the Easter before *the beginning* of Armageddon. This is the Easter that Jesus would have celebrated before His moment of truth."

Finally, many researchers of Nostradamus mistakenly asserted that the predicted California earthquake, the "big one," would take place on May 10, 1988. Their hypothesis was based on his following quatrains:

> *The sun in twenty degrees of Taurus,*
> *there will be a great earthquake. . .*

> *A very great shaking in the month of May,*
> *Saturn in Capricorn, Jupiter and Mercury*
> *in Taurus, Venus in Cancer, Mars in Virgo,*
> *Then stones will fall larger than an egg.*

Perhaps Nostradamus understood the year 1988 was the point of no return. The dark spiritual clouds created by human energy had become so heavy that they would have to be released at that time and eventually affect the physical structure of the earth.

Mother Shipton, along with so many other prophets, must have surmised with a great deal of confidence that the inertia of human consciousness would be difficult to reverse. The *Grail Message* is quite forthright in the following excerpt from its essay "The Millennium":

Admonitions through the prophets, then through the Son of God Himself, were not enough to change man and induce him to take the right course. He did not want to, and increasingly nourished his conceited idea of being a world-ruler, in which already lay hidden the germ for his inevitable downfall. This germ grew with his conceit, and prepared the catastrophes that must now be unleashed according to the Eternal Law in Creation, which man failed to recognize because of his conceited idea of being master prevented him from doing so.

The sole cause of the coming horrors lies in the distortion of the Divine Laws through the false volition of human Spirits in Creation. . .That is also why the end could be foreseen already thousands of years ago; because owing to the wrongly-willed attitude of men it could not possibly come about any differently since the final result of anything that happens always remains strictly bound to the Divine Laws.

Mother Shipton now continues as she deduces that the comet has only received a passing glance by "modern" humanity. However, the lack of concern is not enough to stamp a "return to sender" directive on the envelope delivered by the apocalyptic herald:

> *And when the Dragon's tail is gone*
> *Man forgets, and smiles, and carries on*
> *To apply himself—too late, too late*
> *For mankind has earned deserved fate.*
>
> *His masked smile, his fate grandeur*
> *Will serve the Gods their anger stir.*
> *And they will send the Dragon back*
> *To light the sky—his tail will crack*
> *Upon the Earth and rend the Earth*
> *And man shall flee, King, Lord, and serf.*

Based on the information in the previous chapter "The Fiery Messenger" and other comparative information, it seems most plausible that Mother Shipton had two separate visions of a comet, and assumed they were one in the same. However, whether one comet or two, nothing is changed, for the fiery Dragon has a very disruptive personality.

The destructive reputation of comets and "heavenly" invasions is well documented by scientists. In addition, legends can be found in the ancient records of many countries around the world. The following is a summation by researcher David Solomon:

The Celestial Lord Shiva, God of destruction, was known to ancient peoples as a vast, fiery body that, when it entered the solar system caused planetary catastrophes. Of this apparition Pliney, wrote, "A terrible comet was seen by the people of

Ethiopia and Egypt, to which the name Typhon, the king of the period, gave his name. It had a fiery appearance and was twisted like a coil, and it was grim to behold. And Heavenly fire is spit forth by this planet as crackling flies from a burning log."

The celestial Body was known to the Latins as Lucifer, to the ancient Greeks as Typhon, to the Mayans as Celestial Quetzalcoatl, to the ancient Sumerians as Nibiru (Planet of the Crossing), to the ancient Chinese as Gung-gung—the Great Black or Red Dragon, to the Phoenicians as the Great Phoenix, to the ancient Hebrews as Yahweh, and to the ancient Egyptians as Apep or Seth."

Over two thousand years ago, Solon [the Greek statesman and philosopher credited with being the founder of democracy] visited Egypt to exchange information concerning history and genealogies. One of the High Priests told him: "Solon, you are young in soul, every one of you. For therein you possess not a single science that is hoary with age. And this is the cause thereof—there have been and there will be many diverse destructions of mankind, of which the greatest are by fire and water, and lesser ones by countless other means. . .but *the truth of it lies in the occurrence of a shifting of the bodies in the heavens which surround the earth*, and destruction of the things on earth by fierce fire. Like a plague, the flood from heaven comes sweeping down afresh upon your people, it leaves none of you but the unlettered and the uncultured, so that you become young as ever, with no knowledge of all that happened in old times in this land or in your own. Certainly the genealogies which you related just now, Solon, concerning the people of your country, are little better than children's tales; for in the first place, you remember but one deluge [Atlantis], though many have occurred previously.

To reiterate, Halley's comet was the first "sign," the one that would herald the catastrophes that were to follow. The fulfillment of the major earth changes prophecies will be brought about by a much greater sign prophesied for the millennium. It is Sitchin's "Planet X," the "Fiery Messenger" in the Ramala prophecy, the "Great Comet" or "Star" as foretold in the *Grail Message,* the "Blue Star" of the Hopi Indians and Scallion's designation; the "Great Star" of the Book Revelation, "His Star" that, as we will see, is referred to in the Edgar Cayce Readings, and so forth.

They are one in the same, a "Fiery Dragon" of massive size with a much longer elliptical orbit than the comet Halley. It will be observed all around the globe. The gravitational effect of the Fiery Dragon on the earth was also visioned by Mother Shipton hundreds of years ago:

> *For seven days and seven nights*
> *Man will watch this awesome sight.*
> *The tides will rise beyond their ken*
> *To bite away the shores, and then*
> *The mountains will begin to roar*
> *And earthquakes split the plain and shore.*

Nostradamus describes his vision of the same heavenly event in somewhat the same fashion: "The great star will burn for seven days and the murky atmosphere will make the sun appear double."
Mother Shipton continues:

> *And flooding waters, rushing in*
> *Will flood the lands with such a din*
> *That mankind cowers in muddy fen*
> *And snarls about his fellow men.*
>
> *Man flees in terror from the floods*
> *And kills, and rapes and lies in blood*
> *And spilling blood by mankind's hands*
> *Will stain and bitter many lands.*
>
> *He bares his teeth and fights and kills*
> *And secrets food in secret hills*
> *And ugly in his fear, he lies*
> *To kill marauders, thieves and spies.*

It is well known that many people who are familiar with the prophecies have been storing weapons and non-perishable foods in remote areas for several years. But as suitable drinking water sources become scarce in the locations they have selected, they may be forced to search for water far removed from the presupposed safety of their isolated survival locations:

> *But slowly they are routed out*
> *To seek diminishing water spout*

And men will die of thirst before
The oceans rise to mount the shore.
And lands will crack and rend anew
You think it strange. It will come true.

In the above stanza Mother Shipton also describes rising ocean tides. This could occur from the melting of the ice caps or the shifting of the earth on its axis. Lands would also crack and rend anew as new boundaries created.

The next stanza is difficult to interpret. She seems to be inferring that many countries will not retain their "solid" foundations. Many other prophecies would agree. Cayce predicted "The upper portion of Europe will be changed as in the twinkling of an eye. . ."

And in some far-off distant land,
Some men—oh such a tiny band.
Will have to leave their solid mount,
And span the earth, those few to count.

Mother Shipton speaks of a "solid mount" in a "far-off distant land." The tiny band of men might refer to the leaders of a "band of Indians"—the Hopi, who live in Arizona on the top of a mountain over 3000 feet above the desert. Their prophecies tell them that they will be protected at this particular spot when the Great Purification comes. Cayce predicted: "Lands will appear in the Atlantic as well as in the Pacific. And what is the coast line now of many a land will be the bed of the ocean. Even many of the battle fields of the present [World War II] will be ocean, will be the seas, the bays, the lands over which the New Order will carry on their trade. . ." [1152-11]

According to Mother Shipton, lands appear which rise from the ocean floor, and people will settle them. [According to Duncan Roads, one word in the first verse was "unreadable" because of an ink smudge]:

Who survives this (unreadable) and then
Begin the human race again.
But not on land already there
But on ocean beds, stark, dry and bare.

Not every soul on Earth will die
As the Dragon's tail goes sweeping by.
Not every land on Earth will sink
But these will wallow in stench and stink
Of rotting bodies of beast and man
Of vegetation crisped on land.

But the land that rises from the sea
Will be dry and clean and soft and free
Of mankind's dirt and therefore be
The source of man's new dynasty.
And those that live will ever fear
The Dragon's tail for many year
But time erases memory
You think it strange. But it will be.

Few people are aware that Cayce spoke of extra-terrestrials, on two occasions. In a reading about the Atlantean period, he said: "The manners of transportation, the manners of communications through the airships of that period were such as Ezekiel described of a much later date" [1859-1]. Ezekiel has been designated as one of the four major prophets of The Old Testament who lived about 600 B.C. In the first chapter of the Book of Ezekiel, he describes the following experience:

And I looked, and, behold a whirlwind came out of the north, a great cloud, and a fire infolding itself, and a brightness was about it, and out of the midst thereof as the colour of amber, out of the midst of the fire.

Also out of the midst of the fire came the likeness of four living creatures. And this was their appearance; they had the likeness of a man. . .

As for their rings, they were so high that they were dreadful; and their rings were full of eyes round about them four.

And when the living creatures went, the wheels went with them; and when the living creatures were lifted up from the earth, the wheels were lifted up.

In 1938 while discussing the experiences of the people of the Mayan region who occupied Central America, Cayce mentioned in passing: ". . .and there were the beginnings of the unfoldments of the understanding [from] those that were visiting from other worlds or planets" [1616-1].

In *Black Dawn/Bright Day*, Sun Bear exclaims:

My people have a legend that says our teachers came down from the sky in a silver or white clamshell. When it settled onto the ground, the clamshell opened up and the teachers came out. This describes a spaceship perfectly."

The next Mother Shipton stanza of twelve lines is remarkable in many respects. First, it predicts UFO activity (excuse enough for certain governments to have "secreted" the collection). And interestingly, Mother Shipton even sees the silver serpent-like space ships that have been observed by so many in recent years. In a way, her vision resembles the dream of Edgar Cayce in 1936 in which he saw ". . .men with long beards, little hair, and thick glasses. . .[that traveled] in a long, cigar-shaped, metal flying ship that moved at high speed." Mother Shipton could also be inferring that her visioned visitors were simply returning once again to help with the "unfoldments of understanding" as Cayce said:

And before the race is built anew
A silver serpent comes to view
And spew out men of like unknown
To mingle with the earth now grown

Cold from its heat, and these men can
Enlighten the minds of future man
To intermingle and show them how
To live and love and thus endow

The children with the second sight.
A natural thing so that they might
Grow graceful, humble, and when they do
The Golden Age will start anew.

There may be another reason extra-terrestrials have decided to visit the planet earth at this time—humanity's new-found ability to use nuclear energy. And the detonation of the first nuclear bombs may have sent an apocalyptic signal-wave far out into the universe.

The first atomic bomb was exploded at the White Sands Proving Ground in New Mexico in July of 1945. The next month atomic bombs were dropped on Hiroshima and Nagasaki. It wasn't long thereafter when extraterrestrial entities were dispatched from an unknown location in the universe to investigate. They would arrive at the Proving Ground in July of 1947.

On July 1st, the military began tracking an unknown flying object above the proving ground. On July 4th, the "flying saucer" crashed in the mountains near the town of Roswell north of the Proving Ground. What took place thereafter—the "official cover-up"—is well documented in numerous books. The bodies of five strange-looking entities were recovered from the wreckage. They resembled the human form, but they obviously were not members of the human race. The descriptions of the "aliens" by those members of the military and medical profession who were witnesses are comparable. Many have recently broken their silence after more than forty years and their stories are similar. The composite written portraits picture entities that were short, weighed about sixty pounds, and had large heads with no hair. They had sunken eyes, a convex nose and small cavities for ears. Their mouths were very thin with a small cavity and without teeth.

Since the "Roswell Incident," hundreds of sightings have been reported by individuals from all walks of life. Many present-day seerers have predicted that the presence of extra-terrestrials will soon become common knowledge as we approach the millennium. Recently, in Mexico City, hundreds of thousands observed the erratic maneuvering of numerous saucer-like disks over the area. Many of the astonished citizens recorded the event on video tape. These tapes have been played on television in the United States as well as in Mexico. There is no doubt that the unidentified flying objects over Mexico City were not "weather balloons"—the Government's explanation for the Roswell visitation. Gordon-Michael recently predicted: "We will find that Roswell did exist."

According to a UFO article by author and researcher, Richard J. Boylan, Ph.D., published in the spring 1996 issue of *Nexus*, a coalition called "Stargate" made up of former astronauts, high-ranking military officers, scientists and others is gathering evidence of UFO/ET reality and plans to brief world leaders, the United Nations, scientific academies, and religious leaders after which the coalition will make a public disclosure.

Many people believe the alien visitors are attempting to increase humanity's awareness of their presence by way of the numerous "crop circles" that have been discovered around the world in the past few years. In 1994 Scallion reported: ". . .Some are false, created by some to express personal egos. Most are created by highly charged spheres of light, so compressed as to emit strong gravitational and magnetic fields of such strength as to distort time. The spheres move in stylus fashion creating the messages." In *Spirit Song,* the following exchange about extraterrestrials took place between No-Eyes and Mary Summer Rain:

"Many spirits here now. They here to bring special hope, special comfort and light to coming darkness days of all peoples. The changes, right?

"No Summer, before that even—now. It gonna be no good later. That be too late. Changes come, no more New York, no more books, no more T.V.—radio even. Peoples here to give comfort, make peoples ready now. Summer, all over, many new peoples here. Not only in mountains, that tiny part. Many new peoples all over country, other countries, other planets even. This gonna be big stuff, Summer. It gonna go on all over. Summer think Great Spirit only come here? Summer think Great Spirit only going to fight evil ones only here? He gonna get rid of evil all over. This important here. Great Spirit gonna come after many big changes on Earth Mother, after many big changes all places. We not only planet! We talk 'bout great happening all over."

There are a number of predictions that claim extra-terrestrials will intervene at some point in order to help humanity, especially concerning the nuclear waste problem, the possibility that nuclear weapons may continue to be tested or exploded on the surface of the planet, or to prevent another nuclear accident such as the one that happened at Chernobyl. And although governments and scientists claim they are concerned about nuclear accidents, the fact that the Diablo Canyon nuclear plant located on a major fault line in California is still in operation makes one wonder. In addition, chemical weapons are stored in containers around the world that may create problems in the future.

During one of her visits with No-Eyes, Mary Summer Rain was told of future nuclear accidents:

"Phoenix gonna screech loud and long. His wail gonna come same time as nuclear stuff. . .

"Summer, peoples stupid. They got live stuff buried inside Earth Mother. She no like that stuff. It hurt her bad, it burn her real bad. Earth Mother cry in pain. She gonna try to get rid of bad burning stuff peoples put there. She gonna do it too."

"Wait. We need to get the right words here. You said 'live' stuff that burns. . ."

"Yup. No-Eyes mean nuclear stuff that burn Earth Mother. What Summer's word for that?"

"Radiation. Radioactive materials and waste."

"That what No-Eyes mean. Yup. . .Earth Mother sick and tired of peoples burning waste in her breast. She gonna give it back to peoples. She gonna show peoples how bad she hurt. She give peoples back their own bad medicine even. . ."

"Is the earth going to have quakes at the dump sites?"

"Two spots only."

"How many areas will this affect altogether?"

"Ten, maybe twelve even."

"Populated areas?"

"Some gonna be."

"If two will have quakes, what will the others have? What will they seep from?"

"They just gonna ooze up."

"Just? No-Eyes, how can you be so casual about this? If toxic waste is going to leach back up to the surface, then hundreds of people will be in terrible danger."

"More even. Thousands."

These predicted catastrophic nuclear events may be the reasons extraterrestrials will land on the planet. At least this is the opinion of one researcher of the teachings and prophecies of the Unarius Educational Foundation Academy of Science in California:

The irresponsible testings of nuclear energies, which have never stopped—the dangers that, environmentally speaking, are affecting negatively all life-forms within the planetary environs in this physical universe—MUST STOP. The higher developed Intelligences will not stop the so-called buzzing of this planet with their technologically advanced space-craft. For if this planet is to survive—and it is now in a very bad way from the horrors of murderous wars and the destruction of our natural resources, then it will need the higher advanced knowledge of "how" in order to dissipate the wastes of atomic fuels, the vital need to clean and purify our oceans, rivers and creeks, and the revitalization of the soil we grow our food in.

In July, 1996 *The Virginian-Pilot* reported:

LIVERMORE, Calif.—U.S. nuclear weapons production and storage centers are vulnerable to earthquakes, tornadoes, floods, and other natural disasters, government scientists warn. In worst-case scenarios, damaged facilities could spew radioactive material and toxic chemicals into surrounding areas, according to the experts asked by the Department of Energy to evaluate the danger. . .

While the greatest danger is seismic, other threats include volcanic eruptions, and flooding in the West and Northwest, direct hits by cyclones in "Tornado Alley" plants, and lighting strikes in Texas and the Southeast. . .

Mary Summer Rain had a vision of war breaking out and asked No-Eyes to explain its meaning:

"It come from Africa."

"But the watchers will stop it, won't they?"

"Yep, soon after stuff start they gonna take control."

"I guess it wouldn't do to have the world destroyed before God lets the people do that themselves."

"Nope. . .No-Eyes tell."

"Big bombs gonna go across sky. One, maybe two more even come here. It enough to stop power. It upset Earth Mother. She gonna shake—upset gas under earth. They gonna stop that. No more bombs come then See?"

"She was telling me that missiles would be exchanged, but only a few. The missiles would target areas of major power, communication and arsenal areas. Perhaps the first missile would explode above ground and inhibit power. She referred to the Earth Watchers and that they would use their highly advanced technology to stop the exchanges. These Earth Watchers are intelligent beings who are concerned about the welfare of the earth, in respect to possible adverse chain reactions out into the universe. . .mankind was not going to be allowed to annihilate himself or his beautiful world. . .they would use a force field that was yet incomprehensible to us."

The first of the three books of the Ramala prophecies, *The Revelation of Ramala*, was published in the 1970s. The following is excerpted from information that was offered about UFO activity:

Man is not really a being of the earth. He dwells only temporarily on the surface of the earth to further his evolution. His soul first descends into the aura of the earth at the moment of conception. After the seed has been fertilized, that seed, knowing the nature of life on this earth, begins to create for itself a body within the mother's womb, a body suited to the conditions of life on the earth. Your physical bodies, therefore, are designed solely for life on this earth, and that is why man finds it so unnatural as he proceeds in his spacecraft. . .

Life on other planets, then, does exist, but in a form incomprehensible to Man. . .he cannot conceive of life beyond the physical and the true nature of his existence, so he cannot conceive of life on the other planets. But life does exist, and in a state of evolution far, far advanced beyond that which Man has attained. . .

Because of the point of evolution that they have reached, the beings who live on the other planets are able to observe life in this school of earth. Because they understand the true nature of spiritual existence. . .in no way do they interfere with Man's progression, for if Man was to conceive the idea that there are superior beings who could descend at will to help him around his difficulties, to change his path, it would remove one of the basic lessons of this earth, which is that Man has to change himself. . .

Many people have witnessed the phenomenon of unidentified flying objects. Some people have been privileged to observe a life form within them, but most of them have remained silent. Only a few have spoken of their encounters with their brothers from outer space. The reason for this is that Man on the earth is not yet ready to accept the nature and the purpose of these beings because he is largely restricted by the concepts and dogmas of organized religion and science. Just as you look down at a young child, and for example, would be reluctant to destroy its belief in Father Christmas even though you know it to be a false belief, so Man must learn to discover for himself. Therefore they wait patiently for that moment when Man will discover the falseness of much of organized religion and science, will reject it and will begin to open his mind and look elsewhere for the true concept of life within this Solar Body.

That beings from other planets come to this earth at all is not out of idle curiosity or even out of a desire to ease Man's burdens as he walks his path on the surface of this earth. They come solely for the purpose of the preservation of the earth, for Man with his intellect, his technology, but without the balancing emotion of love, is destroying this planet. . .Your brothers from outer space who come to you come in friendship. They come with understanding. . .

Dr. Boylan wrote that the Stargate coalition plans to present evidence of UFO/ET reality and to brief world leaders, the United Nations, scientific academies, *and* religious leaders after which the coalition will make a public disclosure. Further, the Ramala prophet suggests that much of the teachings of organized religion will be rejected, perhaps because of the UFO scenario. If true, the specific teachings that will be rejected are not delineated. However, it should be noted that although Edgar Cayce spoke of UFOs and extraterrestrials, until the day he died he never once in a reading or as a conscious individual wavered with respect to the Christian teaching that Jesus Christ was the Messiah and is "The Way" for all of humanity.

All of the prophecies for the millennium portend serious events for the planet. However, with respect to Mother Shipton, her assertion that the earth would be populated by "the children with the second sight" may be the most important statement among all of the prophecies because this prophecy is referring to human beings, not extraterrestrials.

The next stanza is the final one from the main collection of scrolls discovered in Australia. And although Cardinal Wolsey was unable to carry out his vow to burn Mother Shipton, it appears another state or church authority had succeeded in ordering her execution. The order would be carried out when the timekeepers in the bell towers of sixteenth-century England sounded the appointed hour over the towns and countryside:

The Dragon's tail is but a sign,
For mankind's fall and man's decline.
And before this prophecy is done,
I shall be burned at the stake, at one,

153

My body singed and my soul set free.
You think I utter blasphemy,
You're wrong. These things have come to me,
The prophecy will come to be.

The following verses were found on a scroll in a separate jar in the State Library. The lady who transcribed them concluded that they had been written at the same time because they merge well with the main collection while adding many more noteworthy predictions:

The signs will be there for all to read;
When man shall do most heinous deed.

Man will ruin kinder lives;
By taking them as to their wives.

The "kinder lives" could refer to the increasing number of stories in today's news disclosing the widespread misdeeds of fathers sexually abusing their female "kin"—their daughters.

It could also refer to sexual activities between "kind" or kinder members of the same sex. Of course, it could refer to both, or it could refer to neither. To continue:

And murder foul and brutal deed;
When man will only think of greed.

And man shall walk as if asleep;
He does not look—he many not peep.

The first two-line stanza above is self-explanatory. The following two could point to a stressful social atmosphere among certain people as they withdraw into themselves in their daily lives. The New Testament declares that, before the new millennium, "the love of many will grow cold" as mutual trust dwindles between individuals. It's also predicted that many people will not be able to distinguish right from wrong, and consequently they will show no remorse for immoral acts. Finally, there are prophecies that imply certain governments, because they are dealing with anarchy, may attempt to control their constituencies by various methods of intrusion into their private lives.

Nostradamus wrote: "Nine set aside from the rest of humanity, Removed, having divided all by their judgements and counsel, Their fates will be determined on their departure. . .dead, banished and scattered." In the 1980s No-Eyes elucidates:

"Listen Summer, this be most important stuff here. State peoples first gonna make two or three bad laws for peoples. People not gonna have say 'bout these laws. These laws be made in big building in state. . .There be seven or eight men in dark dresses."

"Could there be women in this group? Could there be as many as nine people in long black robes?"

"Yup, women too even. Summer be right. There be nine."

"No-Eyes, those people are called the Supreme Court justices. They pass laws that govern the entire country. And your saying that they'll be passing laws that aren't good for the people."

"That right."

"But two or three laws don't incite massive riots."

"No-Eyes not done speakin' here. No-Eyes *first* two or three. But they gonna make many more bad laws for peoples. They make laws to take away peoples' private life, private rights to *spirit* ways, private everything even."

"That would leave us with a police state. Are you absolutely certain about this?"

"Yup, No-eyes certain. Summer keep eye on this court, watch all laws it gonna make. It gonna look like no big thing at first, but it gonna get more and more strong over peoples' private stuff."

The next four stanzas are again self-explanatory with the exception of the first line. The word "tail" has several meanings; however, from Mother Shipton's time (tayle) to the present, one way it's used is when referring to the rear component of an army that is responsible for supplying the troops:

The iron men the tail shall do;
And iron cart and carriage too.

The kings shall false promise make;
And talk just for talking's sake.

And nations plan horrific war;
The like as never seen before.

And taxes rise and lively down;
And nations wear perpetual frown.

The next three stanzas are again eerie as Mother Shipton expresses her uncanny prophetic faculty. She speaks of towns being swallowed by earthquakes and volcanic eruptions. This, of course, is nothing unusual since both activities are on-going events on the earth and have occurred often since her death. The prominent verse is her reference to the eruption of three specific volcanos. No one can say for sure to which volcanoes Mother Shipton was referring. To her, the three eruptions in her visions were just additional signs:

Yet greater signs there be to see;
As man nears latter century.

Three sleeping mountains gather breath;
And spew out mud, and ice and death.
And earthquakes swallow town and town;
In lands as yet to me unknown.

We have seen that Edgar Cayce and Nostradamus placed special emphasis on the eruptions of the volcanoes Vesuvius and Pelee. Several present-day prophets have also seen the eruptions of Pelee and Vesuvius as precursor events to massive widespread destruction far from their location. (It should be noted that besides the Pelee in the West Indies, Pelee is the native Hawaiian name for their "god" of volcanoes of which there are several in the state of Hawaii).

The identity of Mother Shipton's third volcano, however, is not well known. It could refer to Mount Etna in eastern Sicily, the highest active volcano in Europe. It is most likely that, along with Vesuvius and Pelee, Mother Shipton is speaking of Mount Rainier in the state of Washington. Gordon-Michael Scallion and Aron Abrahamsen have repeatedly warned that Mount Rainier would erupt before Vesuvius and Pelee and start the ball rolling so to speak. Also, in the late 1960s a visionary who was a research subject at the Future Foundation of Steinauer, Nebraska predicted:

I can't see the year, but I'll tell you this, there is going to be volcanic action on Mount Rainier, it won't be long after that there will be more volcanic action in the South American and Mexican volcanoes. These things will all fall together. Watch Mount Rainier for our gauge.

In *Black Dawn/Bright Day* is the following concerning Mount Rainier—"Grandfather"—in the state of Washington:

The native people there have a prophecy that came to them a long time back. This prophecy said a time would come when the Little Sister would speak and Grandfather would answer, and the land would be swept clean to the ocean...The mountain that we call the Little Sister is Mount St. Helens in the geography books. In December, 1979, Mt. St. Helens was still considered a dormant volcano by geologists. In March of 1980, the little sister began to whisper. [Just as Mount Rainier has been doing for some time.] On May 18th of 1980, the Little Sister spoke and threw a cubic mile of mountain into the air, covering the whole Northwest, and eventually the globe, with volcanic ash.

In the June 1996 Issue of the *Earth Changes Report* is the following:

Mount Ranier erupted in the 1840s, according to Thomas Sisson of the USGS, but it has not experienced a very large eruption for at least a thousand years. He says that Mount Ranier will certainly erupt again.

The volcanoes in the Cascade Range erupt less frequently than some others, but when they do erupt they are extremely dangerous. According to the USGS, an eruption would probably start with steam release near the summit, and might result in magma flow. Debris flows and floods could be destructive over a large area.

Also in June 1996, *Life* magazine published a long, detailed feature article on increasing volcanic activity:

This very day the earth tore itself open, erupting in a fury of flame and ash. It will do so again tomorrow. And after that, worse—much worse—is COMING...

There are 1500 known active volcanoes in the world, with eight to 12 eruptions occurring at any given moment. Despite tremendous advances in early-warning systems, 29,000 people have been killed by volcanoes in the past 15 years. It's easy to say that it has ever been thus—and many volcanologists do say that, attributing high tremor statistics to more sophisticated monitoring—but Manuel Nathenson, for one, speculates that activity may be increasing. "During the Ice Age," explains Nathenson, the coordinator of the U.S. Geological Survey's Volcano Hazards program, "ice probably capped the volcanoes."

Whether volcanic activity is on the rise or not, we do know that the recent, famous blasts—Mount Saint Helens, even Pinatubo—are relatively small potatoes. Much worse is surely coming. Where? Can't be sure. When? Don't know...

They *will* be deadly. Consider: A volcano can shift ground a hundred miles off; it can create a tsunami 1,000 feet high, swamping islands an ocean away...

The editor of *Nexus Magazine* states that the next stanza "could describe the on-going conflict between Catholics and Protestants in Ireland," which makes sense:

> *And Christian one fights Christian two;*
> *And nations sigh, yet nothing do.*

Another doubtful interpretation involves the present war in the Balkans, the location where many historians claim previous conflicts resulted in World War I and World War II. The Serbs and the Croats are involved, and the Serbs belong to the Serbian Orthodox Church, but the Croats are Roman Catholics. It is improbable that this is the correct interpretation because the Moslems are also involved. The Moslem involvement in the Balkans war, however, may portend the fulfillment of an ominous future prophecy that will once again distinguish a conflict in the Balkans as a forerunner to another World War.

One of Mother Shipton's earliest recorded prophecies may be the most enigmatic of them all. She seems to be predicting that she visioned an invasion of England by armies from the "land of the moon"—one or more of the Arab nations:

Then shall come the Son of Man, having a fierce beast in his arms, whose Kingdom lies in the land of the moon, which is dreaded throughout the world. With a number shall he pass many waters, and shall come to the land of the Lion, looking for help of the beast of his country, and an Eagle shall come out of the East, spread with the Beams of the Son of Man, and shall destroy castles of the Thames. And there shall be a battle among many kingdoms. . .and therewith shall be crowned the Son of Man, and the fourth year shall be preferred. And there will be a Universal peace over the whole world, and there shall be plenty of fruits; and then he shall go to the land of the Cross.

There are a large number of prophecies attributed to Church saints, nuns, priests, and monks, that foresee a war in Europe involving many nations. Many predict the Vatican will be attacked and overrun. Perhaps the best known of the prophecies was the result of numerous visitations by the Virgin Mary in 1917 to three children in Portugal. As they knelt on their knees in the mountainous terrain, Mary would appear before them in the sky. She imparted many prophetic messages to the children, some of which have come to pass, the first being the deaths of two of the children that occurred soon thereafter. The experiences of Lucia dos Santos and her two cousins are recognized by Catholics as the "Miracle of Fatima." In the best-known appearance of Mary, over 50,000 people, many of them sceptics, accompanied the children to Fatima. As they stood in the pouring rain, the clouds suddenly parted and the sun appeared. Then, the sun erratically twirled around in the sky several times before it returned to its normal position.

About ten years later, after Lucia had joined a convent, Jesus appeared to her and told her not to disclose one of the prophetic messages until 1960. So she wrote it down and it was delivered to the Pope in Rome. In 1960, Christians around the world waited anxiously for the secret prophecy, but it was never released by the Church and hasn't been to this day. But in 1958, Jeane Dixon had an experience that may lift the veil to some degree.

While praying in church, Mary appeared to Jeane in a misty vision. The word "Fatima" appeared, and then she was shown the figure of a future bloodied Pope. But when she was shown the Pope's throne, it was empty.

Father Culleton tells of a 1914 vision by Pope Pius X:

I saw one of my successors by name fleeing over the corpses
of his brethren. He will flee to a place for a short respite where
he is unknown, but he himself will die a cruel death.

Thirty years ago it was reported in *A Gift of Prophecy* that, in
January, 1944, shortly before Roosevelt's death, he invited Jeane
Dixon to the White House for a private "consultation" in the oval
office. At that time Roosevelt asked Jeane if Russia would remain
allies with the United States. Jeane told Roosevelt that communist
Russia would eventually become allies with the United States
against "Red China." Roosevelt was startled, because at that time
China did not have a communist government. The next four stanzas
could refer to Russia, whose national symbol is the bear, and to
one or more Asian countries:

And yellow men great power gain;
From mighty bear with whom they've lain.

These mighty tyrants will fall too;
They fail to split the world in two.

But from the acts a danger bred;
An ague, leaving many dead.

And physics find no remedy;
For this is worse than leprosy.

An "ague" is a serious epidemic or p*lague*. Many nations have
developed deadly chemical and biological weapons and the technology has been exported to other countries. It is not folly to
speculate they might be used at some time, especially when one
considers the prophecies of the Hopi, Mary Summer Rain, Saint
Hildegard and others.

During Mother Shipton's time the term "physics" was used
when referring to persons of the medical profession.

In the final stanza Mother Shipton signs off:

Oh many signs for all to see;
The truth of this true prophecy.

Two decisive questions that recur: "This entire doom and gloom scenario is overwhelming—can it really happen?" And: "If it is meant to happen, how do we know when and for how long?" The "how long" is anyone's guess. As to the "when," there is a directive that was given almost two thousand years ago.

In the New Testament Book of Matthew, after Jesus narrates in very complete and distressing details of the expected events, He tells his disciples: ". . .about that day no one knows. . .not even the Son, only the Father." But in the same chapter He bestows to humanity an observation-allegory as to the approximate time frame: "Learn a lesson from the fig tree. When its tender shoots appear and are breaking into leaf, you know that summer is near. In the same way, when you see all these things, you may know that the end is near, at the very door" (24:32-33).

In April 1996, Gordon-Michael Scallion completed his *Future Map of the World* after months of intense toil. In the May issue of the *Earth Changes Report* he relates the following:

> Completing this project was difficult for me. The problem was not shortage of information; the specifics of changes were quite complete and clear to me, as was the mechanism of these changes. The difficulty lay in the emotions I experienced while doing this project. I can not count the times I said to my self, "Why does this have to occur?" I eventually had a vision that kept me moving forward.
>
> The vision was of an elderly, Oriental man, perhaps in his seventies, with a long beard and a white flowing robe. He told me that just as weather cycles occur, often causing tornadoes, cyclones, and hurricanes, geophysical cycles of changes also occur. It is part of the natural rhythm of the earth. We have only to look at the past and the most recent ice age to see that what he was saying is true.
>
> He went on to say that sometimes the cycles of change are modified either by the misuse of the forces governing nature or by the beneficial use of those same forces. In other words: cycles can be prolonged or accelerated, and the severity of these changes can be amplified or reduced; but cycles must occur eventually as a way of achieving balance.
>
> His parting words were, "Has this civilation aided or hindered God's cycles? Has Man worked with the forces of Spirit? Has Man treated the land with the same love and care he would his

children? Until these things are set right, changes greater than need be will occur, and before their time!"

About twenty years earlier, in *The Revelation of Ramala*, a similar answer was offered when someone asked:

Question: If just one hundred people were aware and would direct their energies to the healing of the planet, would this be enough to save the world?

Answer: You must understand that there are two cycles of evolution that are in operation at this time—humanity and the earth. The Earth's cycle would take place whether Humanity lived on its surface or not. It is a natural cycle which affects all the planets in our solar system. Humanity's cycle is peculiar to Humanity and is part of an ongoing evolutionary process on many levels of existence, in many Ages, which is designed to lead Humanity back to God consciousness, to merging with the Source of its creation. At this time in history the Earth's and Humanity's destinies interlock. . .The human cycle is separate from the Earth's cycle. Whilst Humanity's behavior in thought, word, and deed modifies the nature of the Earth's cycle, it cannot prevent it from taking place. You cannot stop a natural process from taking place, unless you are God, of course!"

In the same publication, under the title *The True Meaning and Significance of Cataclysm,* the Ramala prophet offers the following explanation and advice:

If I say that a cataclysm is coming, do not think that disaster looms nigh, that the purpose of your life is limited, that everything is to be destroyed in it and, therefore, that there is no point in pursuing the aims of your life. A cataclysm does bring change, but you are forever changing. In every hour of every day, as you live in your physical bodies of matter, you are changing, and you will continue to change and evolve until the moment of that cataclysm. For there will be death in it but, as you know, death is only another form of change. Therefore death in a cataclysm does not mean the extermination, the ending, of life: it is, rather, a rebirth. I would therefore invite you to regard a cataclysm not as an ending, not as a finality, but truly as a beginning. I would ask you to look at the cataclysm which is to come at the end of this century not as the ending of an Age but as the birth, the dawning of a New Age.

Cataclysms are your Creator's way of ensuring that the continuing Plan for evolution of this Earth is carried out. They are as natural as the other changes which Man can observe on the surface of this Earth—the birth and death of Man, the birth and death of Nature. . .Everything in matter is in a continuous state of change. It is up to Man's consciousness to interpret and to recognise the purpose of that change, and then evolution will take place. . .

Forces beyond your control acting both within and outside the realm of this planet set in motion the mechanism for initiating a cataclysm. . .When such influences are brought to bear upon the Earth, magnetic forces within the Earth react to these vibrations and thereby trigger off a state of fluidity in the Earth's crust which allows movement of the land masses on the surface.

When these cataclysmic changes take place, large tracts of land are moved around like pieces of a jig-saw puzzle. Large portions of the Earth's surface rise and fall, appear and disappear. This is what confuses your geologists today, for they look at the surface of this Earth as they now see it and try to deduce its whole evolution from just one small portion of its present surface.

I am asking you, therefore, to understand the need for, and the purpose of, a cataclysm, to see why Man has to change, to see why Man must change. . .for the Age of Aquarius is to be an age of great evolution. . .In this New Age Man will progress and evolve beyond your wildest dreams. The Earth will become what it should be: a vibration of Universal Love fulfilling its purpose in the Solar Body. It will be giving out its emanations not to this Solar Body but to Creation beyond.

Many men have prophesied that a cataclysm is coming. Over the last one thousand years many seers and prophets have spoken of this event. Before you dismiss these prophecies as the warnings of cranks seek to establish why they were warning you. They have long since died: the warnings were not for them. The only motivation they had in making their prophecies was to foretell what was to come. They prophesied so as to warn a race of men which would be far removed from them both in its way of life and in its evolution. You may disregard the voice of God at your peril.

Jesus highlighted the route on the prophecy map with all of the "signs" marked along the way—others have done the same. Therefore, if the signs do start filtering into our everyday lives, then once a person admits to himself or herself that the situation is getting serious, what can be done to pull through?

Edgar Cayce referred to the Ninety-first Psalm over sixty times when giving advice and encouragement for dealing with situations that troubled people:

> He that dwelleth in the secret place of the most High shall abide under the shadow of the Almighty.
> I will say of the Lord, He is my refuge and my fortress: my God; in Him will I trust. . .
> Thou shall not be afraid by night; nor for the arrow that flieth by day;
> Nor for the pestilence that walketh in darkness; nor for the destruction that wasteth at noonday.
> A thousand may fall at thy right side; and ten thousand at thy right hand; but it shall not come nigh to thee. . .
> There shall no evil befall thee, neither shall any plague come nigh thy dwelling.
> For he shall give his angels charge over thee, to keep thee in all thy ways. . .

The method for gaining access to the protection promised in the Ninety-first Psalm is explained in the first verse: "He that dwelleth in the *secret place*' of the most High shall abide under the shadow of the Almighty." Cayce, other prophets, and numerous religious teachers claim that the location of the "secret place" is within our own physical body. It is the electromagnetic Spirit used by God to form all of Creation. They often quote the fourth chapter of John from the Bible that states: "God is Spirit, and they that worship Him must worship Him in Spirit and in truth."

Cayce went even further and stated that every human being can increase or "spiritualize" the frequency of their electromagnetic-vibrational energy by practicing prayer and meditation. He told one lady who asked him to explain the reason she was having visionary experiences during and immediately following meditation that the experiences were:

...the indication of the abilities that lie within self to raise the vibration to such an extent as to bring light to the inner self. [2441-2]

Not only is the Spirit our Life Force, it is also our transmission line that connects us to God's power station. The better the connection, the more we "abide in the shadow of the Almighty." Psychic abilities are enhanced—guidance is provided—protection is granted.

First, each person will need to cleanse their soul with "positive" words, thoughts and deeds. The strength of the connection made during prayer and meditation is determined by a person's motivation, the true purpose for looking to God's Spirit for help and Guidance. In this respect Cayce often paraphrased the mandate of Jesus: "Therefore if thou bring thy gift to the altar, and there rememberest thy brother has ought against thee, leave there thy gift before the altar, and go thy way; first be reconciled to thy brother, and then come and offer thy gift." (Matthew 5:23-24)

Cayce told one individual:

For whosoever cometh to offer to self, or to make an offering to the throne of mercy and grace, and speaketh unkind of his brother, is only partially awake or aware. [281-24]

He told another:

Hurts arise from misunderstandings. Thus the injunction to forgive as ye would be forgiven. As given to each soul, if you would offer praise or honor to thy God and have aught against thy brother or thy brother against thee, first make thy peace with thy brother. Then thy offering, thy praise, may be other than sounding brass or a tinkling cymbal [1 Corinthians 13]. Otherwise, it will mean nothing to anyone except to fool thine own self. [3253-2]

He told a group of supporters in reading on meditation:

Approach not the inner man, or the inner self, with a grudge or an unkind thought held against ANY man! or do so to thine own undoing sooner or later! [281-13]

In discussing the war of Armageddon, Paul Solomon tells his supporters how they can help as individuals:

And those of you who would change the face of this war must learn that love is not simply passive. . .but those activities against war who build bonds between men in a meaningful way, one helping the other—this is love in action. And love passive and afraid, quiet as a lamb, and withdrawn, will not win a battle. But love alive, in action, healing, this will win a war. You must learn to make your love alive and active. Understand it to be as great a force as it is, for there is no force of darkness which can stand before the light. Thus you must shine your light in dark places.

Shining your light in dark places must *first* mean the dark places within you. Seeing yourself as you are that you might become what you can be, without fearing what you have contained within you, to reveal it so that you might be cleansed. . .

Sun Bear writes in *Black Dawn/Bright Day:*

Learning how to put your gifts and power to work in the most positive manner is what it's all about right now. Many people are just existing today, until one day they wake up and find out who they are. Right now, people use only about ten percent of their brain power, their ability. Once in a while we get into it a little deeper when we go into meditation or our dream world. But the Creator thinks that most people are goofy enough with what they have already. Like the governor in a car, there's a time clock on people's brains so they can't go beyond certain limits unless they are really, sincerely looking and trying.

. . .you're going to see such major changes at all levels that you won't recognize the world afterwards. Think about it. Between now and the year 2000 is the time span in which most of the major changes are going to be happening. They are happening right now, and they're going to intensify. It's not some little "maybe" thing anymore—it's for real and it's growing in strength.

The process of the Earth changes has been set in motion. One time I asked Spirit, "What about these powerful changes that we see happening? Can events be changed? If tomorrow everybody was good and got down on their hands and knees and prayed, would that change it?

"No, the changes are sealed," Spirit told me. . .

If you want to survive the coming changes, remember this: the only people who are going to survive, Spirit says, are the people who are willing to make a conscious change in the way they look at life, in the way they understand things, and in their actions towards all creation. . .

The *Grail Message* prophet promises:

Therefore every *believer* shall look forward to the future with tranquil confidence, and not be alarmed at anything that may happen in the coming years. If he can look up with confidence to God, no harm will come to him.

Once a person gets his or her words, thoughts and deeds in line with God's Will, he or she will be able to benefit from practicing prayer and the proper application and discipline of meditation. With respect to the practice of meditation, learning about the risks and rewards as well as the correct procedure for getting started is recommended as the first step in the Cayce readings. The combination of right actions, prayer and meditation will act to expand the consciousness of an individual.

THE INTENSE SPIRITUAL TRANSFORMATION

When Mother Shipton spoke of "The children with the second sight," she was referring to ESP—extrasensory perception. The prophecies suggest that every person living during the New Age will develop extraordinary psychic abilities that are far greater than any we know today. At a conference in Montreal, Canada, in May of 1995, Gordon-Michael Scallion told his audience: "In the next six-year time period, what occurs would be equivalent in history to probably tens of thousands of years. It's an unbelievable shift in consciousness that is going on. We will be able to do things that we can't even imagine with our minds and the ability to communicate with other realms, healing abilities, all this is going to become commonplace."

Then Scallion described a recent, powerful vision he had of the world after the earth changes:

> . . .there were no wars on the planet anywhere. Populations were in rural areas. Most of the cities were non-existent, but the population was still plentiful. I looked at the newborn children, and they were different. . .The race of humanity had become highly intuitive and the knowledge that everybody contained was being drawn from a central host, so that everybody had access to incredible amounts of knowledge. I found myself at a hospital. . .there was no more AIDS. . .the vibrations themselves had changed and literally eliminated the majority of the diseases that we have today. There were no cases of cancer either that I could detect anywhere.

The word psychic, from the original Greek, means "of the soul" or "an attribute of the soul." Cayce, while in a trance, said:

Many say that ye have no consciousness of having a soul—yet the very fact that ye hope, that ye have a desire for better things, the very fact that ye are able to be sorry or glad, indicates an activity of the mind that takes hold upon something that is not temporal in its nature,—something that passeth not away with the last breath that is drawn but that takes hold upon the very sources of its beginning—the SOUL—that which was made in the image of thy Maker; not thy body, no, not thy mind, but thy SOUL was in the image of thy Creator. [281-41]

The essence of the soul can be found in the word "ethereal"—juxtaposed as in "real ether." The *American Heritage Dictionary* states that the word "ethereal" is defined as "Resembling ether in lightness. . . highly refined. . .delicate. . .of the celestial spheres; heavenly. . ."

Do we have two bodies, physical and ethereal? According to many religious people, the answer is a definite "Yes!" Then what's the ethereal body made of? We find that in physics the term ether is described as "an all-pervading, infinitely elastic, massless medium formerly postulated as the medium of propagation of *electromagnetic waves*." In a recent article in *Nexus*, two-time Nobel Prize nominee Robert Becker, recognized as a pioneer in the field of electromedicine, stated: ". . .the latest scientific revolution has validated the ancient, preliterate concept of 'life energy,' not as some mystical, unknowable force but as measurable electromagnetic forces that act within the body as *organized control systems*." Our physical body and ethereal body are a single component, with the ethereal body providing the electromagnetic energy or "life force" necessary to sustain earthly life. The *Grail Message* states that they "slide together like a telescope."

This suggests that the human body has an electromagnetic force field that is completely immersed in every cell of the physical body, radiating energy. It is not part of the physical body, but the Spirit part of the soul body which gives it life. Thus the conclusion that a person has died when the doctor's instruments can no longer register electrical impulses from the brain.

The electromagnetic wavelengths that radiate from all physical matter, including the human body can be detected by the utilization of scientific instruments—and also by certain psychic individuals. The wavelengths that are seen by a psychic person as different colors—the "aura" that is familiar to many.

The first encounter that people have concerning the aura is usually of the "halo"—a luminous ring or disk of light surrounding the heads or bodies of sacred figures such as saints in religious paintings. Thoughts, actions and deeds of a person appear to influence the electromagnetic field of the person and radiate different colors for a variety of reasons. The following story, by columnist Henry Driver, appeared in a Norfolk, Virginia, newspaper, *The Ocean View Times*, in April of 1989:

> Regarding Edgar Cayce, here is a story that was passed down to me by Langley Land's mother.
>
> She was standing in her yard, when Mr. Cayce came by to be neighborly; she passed the time of day, as she usually did. While Cayce was there, a man went by with a frown on his face. Cayce, turning to Mrs. Land said, "That man has a terrible aura. In fact, he has an awful burden on his heart. He has committed some horrible crime."
>
> "Why Mr. Cayce, what do you mean?" Mrs. Land asked.
>
> "God has given me a blessing, which at times I feel is almost a curse. That is, that I can see the personality of a man or woman, which emanates from them in a glow of colors, which is called an *aura*. That man's was really frightening."
>
> Mrs. Land didn't think much of this, but two weeks later, she saw that the *Virginian-Pilot*, and the *Princess Anne Free Press* carried front-page stories with a picture of the man who had passed in front of her house that day when Edgar Cayce and she were talking. He had been arrested for murder.

Human beings vibrate within a range of cycles per second that synchronize or are compatible with the earth's vibration. Should the electromagnetic cycles of the Earth begin to resonate at a higher frequency (speed up), people would need to increase the frequency of his or her vibration in order to remain compatible with the vibration of the earth. This not only can be accomplished, but according to the prophets will be *necessary* in the New Age.

Scientists know that the magnetic poles of the earth have moved or even reversed in the past. The prophecies say that the magnetic poles will soon move to another location. The crucial question is, will the earth's physical poles also shift? The general consensus answers that they will to some extent. How long this will take is anyone's guess, but the most popular scenario speculates it will take one to three years. How a geological shift of the earth would affect physical matter is anyone's guess, and so is the new location of the poles once everything has settled down.

Aron Abrahamsen claims the North pole will relocate somewhere in China. Edgar Cayce said that once the shift is completed: ". . .where there have been those of a frigid or semi-tropical will become more tropical, and moss and fern will grow." But it doesn't appear that any previous magnetic and/or physical pole shifts changed the vibrations of the earth or of humanity in the way described by Scallion in Montreal. Nor does it appear the claimed past visitations of "Fiery Dragons" were able to change the spiritual vibrations of the human race to any great extent. Therefore, the Fiery Dragon prophesied for the New Age may have a different identity, or it may have additional spiritual energy that would be capable of increasing the spiritual vibration of everything in its path. This hypothesis is the one that is proposed by a researcher of the *Grail Message*. Dr. Richard Steinpach (1917-1992) was born in Vienna, Austria. Between 1979 and 1991, he gave hundreds of lectures throughout Germany, Austria, and Switzerland on the *Grail Massage*. He also wrote books that have been translated into several languages and are distributed by the Grail Foundation in Germany. In 1973, as the Comet Kohoutek was visiting our solar system, he was asked to give a lecture on the "Great Comet" or "Star" that had been predicted in the *Grail Message* several decades before. The following excerpts are from his lecture:

Repeatedly, the appearance of a comet in the past has caused anxiety, panic, even fear of the end of the world. The "enlightened" man of today will think himself very much above such things. Nonetheless. . .a heavy uneasiness remains. And this intuitive perception is justified. . . .But the numerous effects of its appearance can neither be predicted nor comprehended by scientific methods.

The interplay of power in the cosmic spaces is dependent upon certain definite conditions. The great law of reciprocal action inherent in creation is in effect here; only the balance between the power of attraction and centrifugal force maintains the celestial bodies in their courses. Between them, a network of the most finely shaded radiations is operative, which we can only perceive in their coarsest ramifications, perhaps as electrical or magnetic phenomena.

In this balanced reciprocity of masses is interjected a foreign body in the form of a comet, which stands outside of this system. The head and tail of a comet consists of more or less heavy masses, in which, at least, similar forces to those we know from earthly and cosmic observations are operative. Hence it would be simple-minded to contend that they remain without any influence upon the relationships in our solar system and particularly our earth. Let us imagine, in a coarser analogy, piercing a spider's web with some object. The amount of damage would depend to a large degree on the nature and size of the object. . .

The power that we designate as "energy" which in variable forms is the basis of all phenomena is of Spiritual origin. "Spiritual particles" form the innermost kernel of what we regard as the elementary particles of all matter (neutrons, protons, electrons). While they belong to the fundamental species of the spiritual, they are still of different quality than the human spirit. In particular, they are no longer, like the human spirit, capable of volition and development. They originate in high realms of Creation and fall like a fine spiritual misty rain ever downwards, since they are in themselves not strong enough to maintain themselves at their high point of origin. However, like everything spiritual, they possess a magnet-like power of attraction. So in descending, they attract to themselves the finest particles of their environment, which, pressed together, become more compact and thus heavier than the others, which are still loose and light. Through the law of spiritual gravitation this again leads to the further descent of the covered spiritual particle, whereby the process is repeated from one stage to the next. . .So it becomes ever more compact as it goes on its way, taking on one delicate covering after the other until at last it becomes recognizable to our senses as "cosmic radiation." All that we call matter comes from this radiation, as science indeed knows but still cannot explain. For every material mass contains spiritual power as the source of its operations. For this reason alone the comet means an additional thrust of such spiritual power into our solar system.

Waves of spiritual power also emanate constantly from the human spirit. . .The human spirit, through its ability to exercise its own volition, its desires and free will, is in possession of the means to create forms corresponding to its will out of the inexhaustible power-stream of creation. So every action in this earthly material world as well as every thought, every intuitive perception, results in forms corresponding to the appropriate degree of density, which remain bound to their producer. Thus, brought forth by the human spirit, an invisible delicate web originated, extending far beyond this earth. Through this web the inhabitants of earth are attached as by innumerable conducting wires to worlds of existence of a different nature and kind. Corresponding power flows through these "wires," since the strength of person's volition determines the firmness of the connection.

If now a comet, with the additional spiritual power it contains, moves through this network of circuits formed by spiritual currents, we can imagine the effects approximately as when a power line falls on a distribution system of lower voltage. The results are familiar to us all: under the influence of the higher voltage the wire no longer glows, the fuses burn out and the power line no longer completes the large circuit. Rather, through a "short circuit," the beginning and ending are connected with each other via shorter paths, causing the energy present in the circuit to be released with an explosive spark.

The coming of the "great comet" was announced in the *Grail Message* decades ago. It is said that its power "sucks the waters up high, brings weather catastrophes and. . .when encircled by its rays the earthquakes." However, it does not only bring these grave natural happenings. The increased pressure of the Light which "encompasses the earth and holds it relentlessly clasped, releases in the closing of the ring, everything that ever occurred on earth." For this comet, it is said, is "filled with high spiritual power," which would indicate a source far above the sphere of origin of the spirit particles from which all of the material creation originates.

The events so depicted become clear when they are likened to the previously given picture of a distribution system. Even though they operate in other spheres, the spiritual effects released by the comet correspond in their basic characteristics to those we can observe in an electrical short circuit. In this case, as in the other, it is in the end a question of a premature release of reaction as a result of increased energy that is spiritual power. . .

The *Grail Message* contains no prophecies in the usual sense. It states what is necessary for us to know. No more! The deep seriousness of its communications is not intended to enflame the passion for the sensational. The fulfillment of what is stated there is not meant to be awaited at set times with prickling curiosity, but rather in all happenings to be recognized and experienced continuously. So we are told scarcely more about the "great comet" than the fact of its coming and of its irrevocable necessity, for it brings the final resolution of those events which through man's own guilt must now bring about his judgement. To the attentive observer it will be no secret that we have already come very close to this period; but a short period of time still divides us from the last horrible phase of the great purification process. *First,* mankind must be perplexed and confused by the results of their own actions and their falsely established order, so that they may recognize Whose Will in Truth rules creation. . .

The comet Kohoutek is indeed the largest comet yet known and has come closest to the earth, but its mass is not sufficiently great, nor does its course come so close to the earth as to call forth the comprehensive effects attributed to the "great comet" in the *Grail Message.* . .A 12th century prophecy attributed to a monk named Johannes Friede, reads: "But first a comet will pass by the earth for a short time. This however, is only an interlude and can only be viewed as a forewarning." [Kohoutek—Halley—Hyakutake—Hale-Bopp?] In the appearance of such forerunners lies a renewed grace of the Creator. For the spiritual radiation of this comet brings a *transition.* We can envision this, perhaps as though the weaker threads of fate are set aglow and cut asunder by the increased power, thus springing back to their originator. Yet while the power is indeed increased, it is not the final high voltage that will consume everything. Thus mankind is led further into the rapidly resulting effects of their false attitudes. In the process it will be possible for many, before the final period, out of their own recognition, to let the longing for the right way to arise in themselves.

Indeed, all prophecies speak of a final judgement, bringing with it a purification of this earth. But the majority of them, by far, are of ancient origin and are often difficult to interpret. An expectation frequently mistakened, led finally to the error of depreciating the warnings. Man's growing knowledge of material things, his investigation and utilization of matter and the

resulting self-adulation make people of today vastly unrecep-
tive for the working of powers beyond their area of knowledge.
To speak of a final judgement, therefore, for many bears the
stamp of discarded superstition. The final time cannot be approaching, they say, or in their judgement, it would be heralded
by spectacular events.

To combat this human weakness, Abd-ru-shin has said: "At
the present time only what you are able to observe can serve to
expand your knowledge." But he has also clearly stated in which
direction our attention should be directed; to the unprecedented
abundance and coincidence of events in all areas, since this is
also for us a recognizable sign of the approaching final time. He
particularly emphasized the acceleration with which everything
will be accomplished: "Therefore everything develops more
rapidly, more powerfully, than has ever happened before."

Just this superabundance of everything streaming to us and
the ever-increasing tempo of developments can be observed
with all clarity by everyone who is open-minded. It is scarcely
possible for us to control this rapid rate of change any longer.
As a result of this, the assumed progress is already beginning to
rebound upon ourselves. What we produce today, learn today,
can already tomorrow be overtaken and outdated. Increasingly,
man is losing the possibility of becoming aware of change and
adjusting himself to it. Compared to the ever more rapid whirl-
ing movement of his surroundings his own movement remains
behind him and increasingly he runs the danger of losing his
support and being carried away. For ever new "waves" break
over us, closing the rings of human history.

In the *Grail Message* essay on "The Great Comet" it is stated
that, "But *what* it really signifies, what it brings, whence it comes,
has *not* yet been rightly explained. . .It can be called the Star of
Bethlehem, because it is of exactly the same nature as that
was. . .this Star has also detached itself from the Eternal Realm
of Primordial Spirit at such a time as to take effect on this earth
exactly when the years of spiritual enlightenment are to come to
all mankind. The Star takes its course in a *straight* line from the
Eternal Realm to this part of the Universe. *Its core is filled with
high spiritual power* [emphasis added]; it envelopes itself in
material substance, and will thereby also become visible to men
on earth."

In *Beyond Prophecies and Predictions*, referring to Meishu Sama, author Moria Timms states:

> Meishu Sama learned in his revelation that the earth is going to have to face a "mighty upheaval, the greatest cataclysm in all history." He declared that at the event considered as the Biblical "last judgement" a great cataclysmic action *will take place in the spiritual realm* [emphasis added] followed by a similar counter-event in the physical world. . .It was revealed to him that humanity is standing at the threshold of a great transitional period, a turning point from the old age of darkness to the New Age of light. Divine light is now being released, the tremendous spiritual vibration of which is overwhelming to the negative state that exists in the world today. He was told that only as people become attuned to this higher vibration will they change their attitudes and be better able to pass through the coming period of flux. . .

It seems reasonable that the fiery Dragon of the Millennium is a very special celestial entity. If it entered our solar system before, it must have picked up an enormous amount of spiritual energy far out in the universe before making a return trip. But regardless of the circumstances, most prophecies agree that as it approaches closer and closer, its spiritual radiations are going to cause a lot of "shorts" in the present circuitry of people and the circuitry of the earth. Scallion has said that, as the magnetic pole shift accelerates, it will bring out the best and the worst in individuals. Their true inner self will be forcibly exposed by their actions. The *Grail Message* claims that "they will be brought into the Light." In the January 1993 issue of *The Earth* Changes Report the following information is found:

> . . .the earth's magnetic field shall become erratic as it prepares for its new course. . .With the beginning of the shifting of the magnetic poles, the forces of nature react. . . Weather becomes erratic throughout the world—trade winds shift, high winds occur in many countries. The polar regions begin to melt increasing the water flow in many tributaries. . .
>
> New plagues emerge—disease of the optic system and the parasympathetic system—cause: body's electrical system unbalanced due to interaction between the body and the earth's magnetic field and electromagnetic pollution. . .

The descriptive term "electromagnetic pollution" in this statement is an interesting and foreboding one. But, once again, scientific information has surfaced that may explain the meaning of this term. On August 29, 1995 the Associated Press reported:

> The unmanned Galileo spacecraft, 39 million miles from Jupiter, is plowing through a dust storm, the heaviest it has encountered on its interplanetary voyage. Scientists aren't sure whether the electrically charged dust comes from a volcano on Jupiter's moon Io, from particle rings that circle the giant planet or from the Comet Shoemaker-Levy 9, which crashed into Jupiter's cloudy atmosphere last year. But they're getting excited at the prospects of getting answers.
>
> "Finding a source of dust like this coming out of Jupiter, with Jupiter acting like a big electromagnetic accelerator spewing dust into the solar system, is a completely unanticipated discovery," Torrence Johnson, Galileo project scientist at NASA's Jet Propulsion Laboratory in Pasadena, California, said Tuesday.

In the February 1994 issue of *Earth Changes* under the heading "Magnetic Pole Shift May Be In Process," Scallion reports:

> . . .I believe this has occurred. Witness both increased weather and seismic activity. I sense we are very close to a magnetic shift that will begin subtly as erratic fluctuations in the magnetic field strength and position—as the compass needle points. This will be detectable by instruments—probably already is through Defense Department technology. Other indications will be electrical sensations in the lower limbs of the body, erratic animal behavior and lost pets, and increased electronic equipment failures, especially among memory devices. I have seen a vision of what this event will look like. I was looking at the horizon facing magnetic north. The sky became bright and full of color, with rays extending upwards towards the heavens. A large ball of yellow light resembling the sun there appeared and grew in size. At this point in my vision I knew upheavals would begin shortly around the world not just the United States. I then realized this glow had moved westward by some 6-8 degrees. I assume this meant the magnetic pole shift was 6-8 degrees and that the new magnetic north pole was now located where the

compass positions 352-354 are now located...I have previously stated how it will affect electronic devices, aircraft, automobiles, machinery, as well as weather, tectonic stability, and temperature at the poles—a melt-off. I believe we are close to the first of three magnetic pole shifts: time frame '94 -'97.

In his recently released *Future Map of the World*, Scallion states in the text: "New plagues will emerge as the body's electrical system becomes imbalanced by changes in the earth's magnetic field and electromagnetic pollution. When the magnetic field shifts, it will throw off our electromagnetic bodies through the process of induction. The pole shifts will lead to increased tectonic plate movements. As tectonic plates move, they create low frequency infra-sonic waves that can adversely affect the body, making us vulnerable to pronounced mood swings, depression, and something akin to possession."

So, as the electromagnetic frequency of the solar system grows more intense, it will create serious problems for human beings. If they don't vibrate faster, mental and emotional problems will ensue. It will also create havoc among energy-producing machines and appliances that depend on computer chips and electrical power. This is why so many prophets over hundreds of years have predicted that our "artificial light" and "motors" will cease to operate. This is nothing new! Scientists speak of "space weather" and even disturbances known as "sunspots" can create problems on Earth. The last sunspot cycle in 1989 shut down the entire electrical grid in the city of Quebec for twelve hours and cost Hydro-Quebec an estimated ten million dollars. In describing his visions at the Montreal conference, Scallion tells his audience of another vision he had:

Conventional technology is not going to work. We are going to lose our computers and our CD's—all of that material. In the year 2001 they are erased, there is nothing working in the world. There wasn't a single one that I could find working in the year 2001—totally gone. Photography was still there, microfiche was still there, print was still there, but anything magnetic wasn't. And it was because the magnetic field of the earth not only changes position so the compass is pointing in a new direction, but its pulse and frequency has changed so drastically and had a flare-up [Dr. Steinpach's "short circuit"] that was so significant as to render electronic equipment useless. The flip side of it is that consciousness in the year 2001 had this recall of anything that was valid that you needed to know.

More than a decade earlier, Sun Bear wrote:

Also as part of the transformation, we will be learning import-
ant lessons about our over-dependence on technology. As I've said, I don't have anything against the light bulb, but technology has been over-used. When we reach the time technological gadgets no longer work, you may find that you don't need a lot of things that you have now...

As human beings relearn their balance with nature, they will become healthier in body as well as spirit. When people are no longer in stress and out of balance, Spirit will let them live longer...

We are told that after the changes, we'll be learning how to rejuvenate our bodies. This will be easier because we will no longer have people around who are polluting the air, water and earth...

If it is true that electronic equipment will be rendered useless, then this may be God's way of thwarting humanity's capability to do major harm to the earth and to each other—modern weaponry will become ineffective. The spiritual electro-magnetic interference may explain the following passage from the Bible: "If those days had not been cut short [as in short circuit] no one would survive, but for the sake of the elect [God's faithful] those days will be shortened." (Matthew 24:22)

Edgar Cayce would often dream or have visions at the same time he was speaking in a trance. In 1943, when he was given the suggestion to wake, Cayce said "Ugh!" twice, as if viewing something unpleasant. On waking, he said he remembered seeing a whole company of "our boys" wiped out on the African front. Years earlier, in 1934, Cayce was giving a reading for a lady who was suffering from tumors. Upon awakening he told the people present in the room of a vision he had while giving the reading:

Oh, that beautiful music! I was about to have an experience when you woke me up. I heard the most beautiful music. I seemed to get the impression that things are going to happen up in the air that have never been experienced or seen by people before—war, turmoil and strife, Armageddon—wars and rumors of wars; that they will be stopped by the forces in the heavens. [287-16]

To what extent humans will succeed in their attempt to destroy the earth and each other before they are "stopped by the forces in the heavens" is the big question no one can answer. Humanity may find themselves preoccupied with the predicted physical changes taking place on the planet.

Each individual will have to make his or her determination as to whether the predictions herein are plausible. The signs and omens have been elucidated which will lead up to the final prophesied events in the heavens. And, of course, when this happens any doubt will evaporate. But in the meantime, if the precursor signs and omens begin to manifest, at what point along the way does one conclude that the final ones are soon to follow? As individuals carry on the activities of their daily lives, at what point will the urgency of the situation finally strike them?

It is the opinion of the prophets themselves that each person will see things a little differently as he or she is exposed to a variety of situations. The effect on them personally will be the overriding factor. Scallion and Abrahamsen claim the initial response by most will be one of denial. People will choose to rationalize about everything and will attempt to adapt to the changes in order to hopefully become accustomed to them. Most likely this reaction will soon give way to an intuitive uneasiness that will gnaw at them as the changes accelerate. They'll want to take action, but they won't be sure what to do. The natural instinct for survival will be powerful, and advice of every imaginable kind will be rampant. Consequently, people will look more and more to their government and religious leaders for guidance.

The prophets tell us that people will be better prepared to endure the earth changes if they can succeed in raising the vibration of their ethereal body, which in turn will "spiritualize" the physical body including its subconscious or soul-mind. The soul-mind will then become the "guide" as it transmits information from God's Spirit to the conscious mind in order to influence a person's decisions, emotional reactions and behavior. At the same time, the increase in the rate of the person's vibration will positively energize the immune system of the physical body.

Supposedly, during past ages, the separation between the subconscious mind and the conscious mind did not exist. The two minds were able to communicate with each other. Sun Bear claims that before the last pole shift of the earth: "The soft spot we have on top of our heads when we were babies stayed open all during our lifetime. . .through it we were able to receive direct transmissions from the Spirit. Then we got arrogant and *hardheaded* [so] the Creator sealed it over because the human race was not ready to seek the sacred path. . ." Edgar Cayce spoke of the "barrier between the two brains." And in his reading on the Gulf War in 1991, Paul Solomon offered the following explanation about the human condition in past ages and the reason for the prophesied Armageddon:

Man is fascinated by war because he is divided against himself. This race began with a brain that is a single unit. That unit was not for the purpose of creating thought. It was not for the purpose of expanding man's ability to relate to the world around him. It is quite the opposite. The brain is not an instrument to expand man's consciousness into the sensory world around him. It is instead a filter, if you will, a condenser for the purpose of taking the magnitude of what is happening around you and reducing it to a level of tolerance which the physical body can manage.

Thus the brain of man is a reducer, not an expander of consciousness. And as it has become separated upon itself as man confused his rational logic with his intuitive mind and began to argue within himself. . .so did his brain separate one part from the other. It has been his very nature from that day until this, *except* for those who learned to join those hemispheres of the physical brain by creating what you might call "neurons" or passageways of light, of "electricity" of thought, of communication of one side of the brain to the other, and not only integrating one side of the brain with the other, but transcending it with creating a cap, a crown of enlightenment as is symbolized by the crowns, the caps, the skullcaps, the yarmulke, and that worn by Islam as well, of several nations, that symbolize the desire within the heart of man to unify the brain again.

The prophet of the *Grail Message* states:

The instruments within the human body which are at the disposal of the Spirit work like links of a chain. But they all serve in a *forming* capacity *only*, because they cannot do otherwise. Everything transmitted to them they form in accordance with their own special nature. Thus the frontal brain takes up the pictures transmitted to it by the cerebellum and, in accordance with its somewhat coarser nature, first of all compresses them into narrower conceptions of space and time, thereby condensing them and bringing them into the ethereal world of thought-forms, which is of a more tangible substance.

Next the frontal brain forms words and sentences which, through the organs of speech, penetrate as formed sound-waves in the World of Fine Gross Matter, there again producing a new effect brought about by the movement of these waves.

Thus the spoken word is the resultant effect of the pictures transmitted through the frontal brain! The latter can also direct the course of the effect towards the organs of locomotion instead of the organs of speech, whereby words are replaced by writing and action.

This is the normal course of the activity of the human spirit in the World of Gross Matter as willed by the Creator.

It is the *right* way, which would have brought about a healthy subsequent development in Creation, making it utterly impossible for mankind to go astray.

Man, however, voluntarily abandoned the course prescribed for him through the constitution of his body. He stubbornly interfered in the normal working of "the chain" of his instruments by making the intellect his idol. Thus he concentrated his whole energy upon the training of the intellect in an entirely one-sided manner! As a result the frontal brain, having now become the producer, was forced to exert itself out of all proportion to what was required of the other co-operating instruments.

This naturally incurred a heavy penalty! The uniform and harmonious co-operation of all the individual links was upset and hindered, and with it every right development. The excessive strain to which the frontal brain *alone* was subjected for thousands of years forced its development far beyond everything else.

This consequently curtailed the activity of all the neglected parts which, because of their lack of use, were bound to remain weak. Foremost among these is the cerebellum, which is the instrument of the Spirit. Thus it follows that the activity of the human spirit proper was not only severely obstructed, but it is often completely cut off and remains excluded! The possibility of proper intercourse with the frontal brain over the bridge of the small brain is buried, while a direct connection between the human spirit and the frontal brain is utterly impossible owing to the latter's nature. The frontal brain is absolutely dependent on the full activity of the cerebellum, to which it stands *next in succession* according to God's Will, in order properly to fulfill the task assigned to it.

The specific quality of the cerebellum is needed in order to receive the vibrations of the Spirit. It is impossible to bypass it. . .In the one-sided cultivation of the frontal brain lies the hereditary sin of earth-man against his God or, more precisely, against the Divine Laws, which manifest through the right apportionment of the bodily instruments, as in the entire Creation.

The observance of the correct apportionment would have automatically indicated the straight and right road of ascent to the human spirit. As it was, however, man in his ambitious conceit interfered with this machinery of healthy activity, singled out one part and cultivated it specially while disregarding all the others! This was *bound* to bring disproportion and stagnation in its train. If the course of natural events is hampered in such a way disease and failure must ensue, ending finally in wild confusion and collapse.

Through this interference—the unequal cultivation of the two brains—the cerebellum was suppressed through neglect in the course of thousands of years, and thereby the spirit was hampered in its activity. This became the *heredity sin*, because the one-sided over-cultivation of the frontal brain is in the course of time passed on to each child through physical inheritance. Thus from the outset it becomes immensely difficult for the child's spirit to awaken and grow more powerful, because the bridge necessary for this purpose, the cerebellum, is no longer so easy to cross and is even very often completely cut off!

Man has not the faintest idea what irony and strong censure lie in the expressions "large brain" and "small brain" which he created. . .The cerebellum, which is relatively much too small, makes it difficult for the truly serious seekers of today to distinguish between what is genuine intuitive perception within them and what is merely feeling.

In the 1930s, when the field of electromedicine and the use of devices such as electromagnetic bone-fracture stimulators were far in the future, Cayce gave instructions in several readings for the construction of electromagnetic appliances to be used in the healing of certain ailments. The devices suggested by Cayce are still used today by persons interested in alternative therapies. In these readings as in others, Cayce used the terms "electrical" and "electromagnetic" interchangeably. And in explaining the role that electricity played with regard to spiritual matters, he again was far ahead of conventional wisdom and scientific discoveries. Further, when it came to the spiritual part of life, for Cayce the terms "vibration" and "electricity" meant the same thing:

Thus there are the *Vibrations* of the electrical energies of the body, for Life itself is *electrical*. . . [281-27]

Electricity or vibration is that same energy, same power, ye call God. Not that God is an electric light or an electric machine, but that vibration that is creative is of the same energy as life itself. [2828-4]

Know then that the force in nature that is called electrical is that same force as Creative, *or God in action.* [1299-1]

For this is the basis of materiality; for matter is that demonstration of the units of positive and negative energy, when they become spiritual they are *only* positive. [412-9]

As we approach the millennium, the ratio between the positive and negative units of electricity that provide the life force for a person will soon need to change in order to raise his or her vibrations. They will need to "charge" their ethereal bodies with the input of the additional spiritual units that Cayce says are *only* positive. Unfortunately, electromedicine won't be able to help in this case, and neither will a battery charger.

Father Culleton quotes the prophecy of a Church Seeress that is dated in the 1850s. Magdalene Porzat claimed she received messages from the Holy Mother, Mary. Remarkably, she speaks of "spiritual electricity" in the following excerpt:

Listen my children, to what Mary our Mother charges me to announce to you. "Behold the end of time! Behold the end of evil and the beginning of good. What is going to happen is not an ordinary event. It is a grand epoch which is going to commence. It is the third since the Father, who has created us, in order that we may know, love and serve Him. . .

Mary comes from Heaven. She comes accompanied by a legion of angels. *The elect living upon earth should, through spiritual electricity, elevate themselves* in order to go forward. . .

After this, Mary, all powerful, shall change all men into good wheat. . .

It is necessary that God should send His spirit to renew the face of the earth by means of another creation. Behold here the fire from below for burning and changing everything. Behold here, the fire from above. The love of God comes to embrace and transfigure the world. I see the earth rendered level; its valleys are raised; its mountains are lowered; there is nothing more but gentle hills and beautiful vales. Since I am as I am, I see nothing else before us but union and universal fraternity. All men are in reciprocal love. One helps the other. They are all happy.

In the 1980s a nurse and mother of three by the name of Annie Kirkwood began receiving frequent messages from Mary while in prayer and meditation at her home in Texas. She recorded the messages and eventually they were arranged in a broad, systematic order and published in 1991 in *Mary's Message to the World*.

This book contains hundreds of messages of which the following are a few excerpts:

People on planet earth, listen to this message. I, Mary, Mother of Jesus, am alive and concerned for you. My message is to the whole globe and not only to church members. Listen and pay attention to my words sent through this soul [Annie].

Each individual living on earth will have some trials and tribulations to endure, and since these will be worldwide events, I wish to reach as many people as possible. For too long now, my image has hung in churches and homes as one to be worshipped. Only One merits this type of worship—God, our Creator. There is only one place to find Him and that is in your heart and your mind. Make peace with yourself and seek to find God in your heart and mind. Return to the origin of all. Return to your original starting point—God. We all have this in common, that each of us originated in God.

The time is drawing near when you will be shaken and frightened, not because of punishment, but to renew the land and the minds of mankind. The earth will shake and be moved by violent forces which will cause many to lose their physical lives. The process which will cause these earth-changing events has already started. The changes have begun and will continue until completion. The real tragedy during this time would be to lose one's spiritual growth.

The planet earth is being bombarded with forces which will cause it to change its direction in relationship to the universe. As this universe grows and as the galaxies grow, there is a dividing and splitting of galaxies. These changes are universal. Some of these events started millions of years ago. Now, the growth affects your solar system, and the planets will realign to new places and points. During this realignment, the earth will be turned and shaken, and you will have many catastrophic events. . .

My desire is to warn you of the coming trying times. I wish for you to turn to God in your hearts and through your minds, for in this way some of you will survive these catastrophic events by renewing your spiritual values. Only in prayer and meditation will you find solace. Bring all your cares to the altar in your heart. Allow God to heal your hearts, your lives, your spirits, and your loved ones. This healing is your only recourse. Only by prayer and meditation will you be led and guided. . .

Prepare your heart and mind to receive the very Spirit of God. Prepare to judge yourself and make amends for your prejudices, intolerances, fears, envy, animosity and false pride. These are the errors of the flesh. It will be your undoing not to forgive. First, you must forgive yourself. Then forgive all others who have hurt you in the slightest.

Bring peace into your family and your home. Allow this peace to flow out of your home into the world around you. Send thoughts of love to all people on earth. Do not allow countries, religions, or anything to keep you from sending out the Love of God. It is only by love and prayer that you will be safe. . .There will not be a Third World War, for God will not allow you to destroy this beautiful earth with your nuclear arms. You will be too busy sustaining yourselves against the elements to wage war. There will be much destruction of land before the turning of the axis. The forest fires have just begun, the hurricanes have just started, the tornados, the earthquakes, the volcanos and the winds will batter you to such a degree that you will not have the energy or will to wage world war. . .

The coming storms are beginning to be blown across the earth as new vibrations approach earth from the outer corners of the universe. The growth of the universe will be a major cause of the increase in intensity and size of the storms, which will batter your shorelines, your cities, and your plains. In the next few years the intensity of the vibrations of the magnetic field will cause many new and powerful reactions on earth. You have just begun to see the fury of these storms. . .The pressure of the barometric field and magnetic fields will set new records. . .This is not punishment, but the effect of centuries of hatred, anger and fear. The tensions which have invaded man's consciousness will be unleashed on earth. . .

Magnetic fields will play havoc on earth in the last days. Machines will fail and science will not have answers. As the wave of magnetic energy which is traveling in the universe nears earth, some unusual sights will occur in the heavens. There will be lights and sounds picked up from the furthest reaches of the universe. A different energy will enter the atmosphere. This will be one of the causes of the changing weather patterns. . .

In this new energy will be the makings of new stars and a new sun which will enter the immediate solar system. . . Mankind will be glad to have the new era to correct the errors of your civilization's past. Humanity will remember what these errors were. Future generations will learn from your mistakes as a species.

New cells will blossom in the physical body. Humanity will have communication with the spiritual world. New cells will come forth and you will be able to use more of your mind. Mankind will have powers that are not known now. There will be the ability to communicate with all worlds by your mind. Humans will also be able to communicate with the animals in this method. Truly, there will be born a new man and a new species.

Man will enter into a new period of communications with those who live in other parts of the universe. Humanity will put aside its childish fights over land. Man will take pride that as a species and a race he has grown and learned to be united with the universe. This will truly be a glorious way of life.

In future time, man will be as different from the man of today as you are from the cave man. . .I like to think of the coming new era as the "Aftertime," for truly it will be the aftertime when all will live in peace. It is a time for an evolutionary period to come to earth. The coming era in mankind's life is a time of evolution. This will be a period of great growth in the species of man and many species of animals. Some animals that are on earth now will not survive the coming changes. They will go the way of the dinosaur and mammoth. Man will change drastically. He will evolve into a new species.

This evolutionary process will come about because of the need to adjust. The atmosphere will change in components. The solar system will be different. A new sun will be added. This will be a binary solar system [More than two thirds of all stars have stellar companions]. The two suns will activate cells which will draw nourishment from the sun's rays. The need to ingest food will be aided by the nourishment derived from the sunrays.

Man will evolve into a more mental being. He will be able to hear sounds which are not presently heard. He will see through particles of light which are hidden from him now. With his mind, man will hear and speak. He will have better use of his psychic abilities. That which you call intuition will be strongly activated in all mankind. There will be no need for honesty because of the ability to hear mentally. Today man hides his feelings and thoughts. In the Aftertime, man will not be able to hide his feelings or random thoughts. Motives will be known. All dealings will be understood. All thoughts will be heard.

Can you see how wonderful this new way of life will be? Mankind will become peaceful out of necessity. How could you approach another in anger or with malice in your heart? All feelings, all thoughts will be sensed and heard by everyone. People will learn to live in peace. . .

Love will be the answer to all problems, because anger and fear will be seen for what they are. People will speak from the standpoint of love and compassion. Forgiveness will be the accepted mode of conduct. When a person is loving and feels remorse, others will react in love and forgiveness. Like begets like. Love and forgiveness will beget more love and forgiveness. . .

THE SECOND COMING

In the June issue of the *Earth Changes Report*, there is a long article on comets by Janis Hall that includes the following:

> The Florentine painter Giotto di Bondone, having seen Halley's comet in 1301, painted a luminous comet above the baby Jesus in his fresco "The Adoration of the Magi." Perhaps he believed those who claimed that the Star of Bethlehem, which marked the birthplace of Jesus, was actually a comet.

In 1934 Edgar Cayce designated the "Fiery Messenger" as "HIS Star" and he suggests that, for guidance, those persons that seek God and act according to the Will of God will be directed by the spiritual energy of "HIS Star" to "enter into the holy of holies in themselves" through meditation as the Star's energy affects everything on the planet:

> As to the material changes that are to be as an omen, as a sign to those that this is shortly to come to pass—as has been given of old, the sun will be darkened and the earth shall be broken up in divers places—and THEN shall be PROCLAIMED—through the spiritual interception in the hearts and minds and souls of those that have sought His way—that HIS Star has appeared, and will point the way for those that enter into the holy of holies in themselves. For, God the Father, God the Teacher, God the director, in the minds and hearts of men, must ever be IN those that come to know Him as first and foremost in the seeking of those souls; for He is first the GOD to the individual and as He is exemplified, as He is manifested in the

heart AND in the acts of the body, of the individual, He becomes manifested before men. [3976-15]

"He becomes manifested before men"—does this refer to the Second Coming? As the millennium draws near, many people from around the world are expecting a Messiah to appear on the scene. The Buddhists and Hindus are expecting a deity in human form—an Avatar. The Moslems anxiously await the arrival of the Mandhi as prophesied in the Koran.

In Israel, painted signs petition: "WE WANT THE MESSIAH NOW"—and also in Israel, some students of the Jewish religion are convinced that God has recently painted a celestial "sign" in the heavens that means He has responded to their Messiah petition.

In the July, 1994, issue of *The Jerusalem Report* is a long article that speculates about the meaning of a stellar event about to take place far out in space. The comet Shoemaker-Levi, which had disintegrated into twenty-one giant pieces, was about to strike the planet Jupiter in a bombardment-like sequence of collisions. Coincidentally, the first collision took place on July 16th, the eve of the Jewish anniversary of Tisha-Be'av, a day of mourning that marks the destruction of the Jewish Temple by the Romans in 70 CE [Common Era], and the previous destruction of the temple by the Babylonians in 586 BCE [Before Common Era]. According to Jewish tradition, next to Yom Kippur, the anniversary of Tisha-Be'va is considered the most important in the Jewish calendar.

The following excerpts are from the article:

Raphael, Head of Research at Beth Hatefutsoth, Tel Aviv's Diaspora Museum, tracks disaster in Jewish history. He says that forming a connection between Tisha-Be'va and the Shoemaker-Levi comet is logical for those with a bent toward apocalyptic thinking, Jews and non-Jews. "In our day, we are in a period that causes the production of apocalyptic ideas and messianism. We're relatively close to the year 2000 and to the year 6000 in the Jewish calendar. . ."

Some students of Jewish mystical texts have gone so far as to suggest that the coming of this month's comet might also signify the imminent revelation of the messiah—the redeemer said by the Midrash to have been born on Tisha-Be'av.

Christians believe the Messiah has already been here, and is about to make a return visit. But there are differences of opinion among Christian denominations regarding the interpretation of the Second Coming in the New Testament. One of the most interesting of the doctrines has been designated as "The Rapture."

The rationale for the doctrine of the Rapture is based on many Bible passages. In *Apocalypse,* author Grant R. Jeffrey writes: "The Rapture is one of the most important doctrines in the Bible. . .Although this event will remove the living saints to heaven to escape the Antichrist, its primary purpose is to provide all believers, living and departed, with their eternal resurrection bodies. The "translation of the saints" will transform our mortal and corruptible body into a new resurrection body that will be immortal and incorruptible. . ." Most Christians who believe in the Rapture do so based on the statements made by the Apostle Paul in letters he wrote to several of his congregations. In his first letter to the Corinthians (15:49-52), Paul explains:

As we have worn the likeness of the man made of dust, so we shall wear the likeness of the heavenly man. What I mean my brothers, is this: flesh and blood can never possess the kingdom of God, and the perishable cannot possess immortality. Listen! I will unfold a mystery: we shall not all die, but we shall all be changed in a flash, in the twinkling of an eye, at the last trumpet call. For the trumpet will sound, and the dead will rise immortal, and we shall be changed.

In his first letter to the Thessalonians (4:15-17) Paul writes:

For this we tell you as the Lord's word: we who are left alive until the Lord comes shall not forestall those who have died; because at the word of command, at the sound of the archangel's voice and God's trumpet call, the Lord himself will descend from heaven; first the Christian dead will rise, then we who are left alive shall join them, caught up in clouds to meet the Lord in the air.

Writer and lecturer, E.R. Birchmore, is considered a very adept researcher of the Bible and prophecy. The following is his view concerning the doctrine of the Rapture:

According to the prophecies, things are going to get worse before they get better. Does this mean, therefore, that there is no hope, that there is no such thing as free will or spiritual liberation? Not at all. A survey of the dreadful societal judgements recorded in the Bible reveals that in every single case of prophesied catastrophes, a door of liberation is always opened to those who heed the words of prophetic warning. There are many types and historical examples of this. Lot was warned about the coming destruction of Sodom and was allowed to leave the scene because his moral state was different than that of prevailing degeneracy. Noah heeded the prophecies and escaped the Flood. Under the inspired leadership of the prophet Moses, the Hebrews escaped the terrible destruction visited upon the Egyptian and Minoan cultures circa 1500 B.C. Eusebius and Josephus relate that the first-century Christians living in Jerusalem escaped from the city just before the siege and destruction which took place in 70 A.D. and settled in Pella on the northern boundary of Peraea. They obviously paid attention to Jesus' prophecies of the coming destruction and undoubtedly took the appearance of the comet which preceded that awful event as an omen.

The scriptures indicate that the scope and severity of world cataclysms for the endtime have no precedent. The kind of destruction prophesied in Revelation and throughout the prophetic scriptures is global. . .

In Luke 21:36, after describing the cataclysmic events of the endtime, Jesus gives this exhortation: "Watch ye therefore and pray always that ye may be accounted worthy to escape all these things that shall come to pass."

In Revelation 3:10 the faithful are promised deliverance: "I shall keep you from the time of trial which will come upon the whole inhabited world."

The dispensation of people involved in this second exodus is referred to throughout the Bible as those that "escaped" (Isaiah 4:2), "departed" (II Thessalonians 2:3), "taken" (Luke 17:34), "plucked out" (Zechariah 3:2), "delivered" (Ezekial 34:12), exhorted to "come out" (Revelation 18:4), "saved" (Romans 5:9), "caught up" (I Thessalonians 4:16). The last reference is rendered "harpazo" in Greek or "rapere" in Latin and is the word from which our orthodox brethren derive the word "rapture" to describe the event.

The exodus of the elect is also symbolized in the Great Pyramid. . .While reading 19th-century astronomer Piazzi Smyth's book on the Pyramid, I found remarkable corroboration. Writing about the small door 28 feet above the floor of the grand gallery (which *precedes* the time of tribulation depicted in the antechambers of the King's Chamber passage) Smyth wrote: ". . .there is even just before the low passage a *way of escape up aloft* for a few, though not by their own power. This escape is no less than 28 feet above. . .only therefore accessible to something approaching more winged and flying rather than walking beings, leading to a sort of retreat. . .it immediately reminds of what the evangelists in the New Testament promise of the angels being sent to *gather up* the elect *before* the dread period of wars and tribulation on earth begins; and also of those elect thus saved and meeting the Lord in the air and being retained with Him in heaven awhile before His Second Coming to establish His kingdom on earth."

The door opens into a passage leading *above* the "truce in chaos" antechamber, which incidentally has diagonal measurements of 66.6 inches (666) and symbolizes the interim peace and rise of the antichrist. This leads into the "construction chambers" discovered by Howard Vyse. This connects with an utterance from Isaiah: "Come, my people, enter thou into thy *chambers* and shut the *doors* about thee; hide thyself as it were until the indignation be overpast."

This kind of symbolic correspondence is enough to give even the most conceited intellect or skeptic pause.

This prophecy of liberation is also recorded in Gnostic manuscript from Nag Hamadi entitled "The Tripartite Tractate." The text describes a group of people which, ". . .takes its *appointed departure suddenly* and its *complete escape*. . .those who are good whom the Logos brought forth. It has salvation (immediately). . .it will be saved."

Orthodox exegetes who claim that this prophetic doctrine originated with the Plymouth Brethren movement ought to investigate the Nag Hamadi library. They might be surprised to learn that they are off by at least 1,600 years.

In his chapter on the Rapture, Jeffrey presents convincing evidence that covers a broad range of historical data along with other passages in the Bible that support the Rapture doctrine. His conclusions, like Birchmore's, are not difficult to understand. Just before the tribulation, Jesus Christ will return and change the "substance" of the physical bodies of His believers in the "twinkling of an eye" so that their bodies are the same as His "resurrection" body—incorruptible. The bodies of His believers who have died will "rise" and be changed first, followed by the bodies of His believers who are still among the living in the world. Once this is accomplished, the "Translation" of His "saints" takes place. They are "caught up in the clouds to meet the Lord in the air," and without the necessity of a natural death for those of His saints still alive.

Cayce was asked by a member of one of his Bible study groups: "Please explain First Corinthians 15:51. Is the reference here to the body? 'Behold, I show you a mystery. We shall not all sleep, but we shall all be changed.'" He answered:

> Referring to the body; though the individual here speaking (Paul) LOOKED for this to happen in his own day, see? For what is the stumbling block to us today? If we do a good deed we want God to repay tomorrow! So did Paul! Did he not groan continually that the mark, that scar in him, was not removed? Did he not bring those things as said by Peter concerning same? That, "He speaketh many things hard to be understood, that many wrest with to their own destruction." To what did he refer? That their idea (of many who spoke) of time and space was limited; for they had even less conception of same than the weakest among you here! [262-87]

In answering, Cayce does not seem to deny or to support the conclusions of Jeffrey and Birchmore, but simply claims that Paul and many of his followers were incorrect with respect to the "time" of the event.

The meaning of the Second Coming for people who believe in the Rapture is dependent upon the substance of Jesus' body after the resurrection. For these Rapture people, Jesus, in His spiritualized physical body, is presently in Heaven planning His imminent return. However, others who also believe in Jesus Christ have a different interpretation with respect to the substance of Jesus' resurrection body. In his book, *Why We Live After Death*, Dr. Steinpach explains his "ethereal" interpretation:

A positively dramatic account of the existence of such an ethereal body is to be found in the New Testament, according to which after His burial Jesus appeared to Mary Magdalene, and also several times to His disciples. He walked beside them, they spoke with Him, but they did not recognize Him. He entered rooms whose doors were locked—and only when he broke bread with them at the table did they perceive that it was Jesus. This surely testifies quite clearly that He came to them in a different, changed bodily form, in precisely that ethereal body, which they, shaken by the deep experiences of the previous days, were enabled to see at that time. Had it been otherwise, they would surely have recognized Him immediately. But Jesus wished by this not only to tell them that He was risen; He wished to demonstrate to them that life goes on. . .immediately after earthly death."

So many differences of opinion exist with respect to the interpretation of the information in the Bible. At some point we find an individual whose interpretation takes precedence because he has been proven correct by events that have taken place since his death. This is the situation with Edgar Cayce who, although most famous as the "Sleeping Prophet," has also been designated a "Christian Mystic" by numerous scholars of the Bible.

On hundreds of occasions, Cayce was asked questions about the teachings in the Bible. One example of Cayce's perception with respect to the historical information about the early Christian era was first volunteered without his being asked. As he was answering questions about Jesus and His followers, he said that Jesus, Mary, Joseph, John the Baptist, and most other Bible characters with whom Jesus was associated, were "Essenes" who lived in a remote community in the Qumran area of Israel.

The Cayce readings of more than fifty years ago, years before the Dead Sea Scrolls were discovered, claimed that the term Essenes meant "expectancy" among members of the sect. In one reading we find: "Isn't it rather that there were those that ye hear little or nothing of in thy studies—the Essenes—who dedicated their lives, their minds, their bodies to a purpose. . .to them a promise of old. Were there not individuals—men and women— who dedicated their bodies that they might be channels through which such influences, such a body [Jesus] might come?"

The information about this monk-like sect was most likely completely foreign to Cayce. This sect is only briefly mentioned by a few ancient writers such as Pliny, Philo, and Josephus. In his book, *Edgar Cayce's Story of Jesus*, author and researcher Jeffrey Furst states: "Cayce himself had no conscious knowledge of this pre-Christian sect." But today it appears the Dead Sea Scrolls have proven much of the Cayce information correct. The Essenes are credited with writing many Scrolls. They also play a part in the historical exhibits and are considered to be a "third" Jewish sect along with the Pharisees and the Sadducees.

In their thoroughly researched and well-documented book, *The Dead Sea Scrolls Deception*, authors Michael Baigent and Richard Leigh have assembled a great deal of reference material and data about the political and religious controversy surrounding the scrolls. As with most information that deals with translations from historic manuscripts, especially those of a religious nature, there are various explanations and opinions. In their book they quote from the "Biblical Archaeology Review" (B.A.R): "Referring to Jesus' imminent birth, Luke (1:32-35) speaks of a child who will be called 'Son of the Most High' and 'Son of God.' The Qumran fragment from Cave 4 also speaks of the coming of someone who 'by his name shall. . .be hailed [as] the Son of God and they shall call him Son of the Most High.' This, as BAR points out, 'is an extraordinary discovery; the first time that the term 'Son of God' has been found in a Palestinian text outside the Bible."

Baigent and Leigh, in referencing an article from the New York *Times* quote the following: "The origins of some Christian ritual and doctrines can be seen in the documents of an extremist Jewish sect that existed for more than 100 years before the birth of Jesus Christ. This is the interpretation placed on the 'fabulous' collection of Dead Sea Scrolls by one of an international team of seven scholars. . .John Allegro. . .said last night in a broadcast that the historical basis of the Lord's Supper and part at least of the Lord's prayer and the New Testament teaching of Jesus were attributable to the Qumranians." We also find quoted in this book: "If, in any case, we look now at Jesus in the perspective supplied by the scrolls, we can trace a new continuity and, at last, get some sense of the drama that culminated in Christianity. . .The monastery [of the Essenes]. . .is perhaps, more than Bethlehem or Nazarath, the cradle of Christianity."

Cayce was also asked about the "substance" of the resurrected body of Jesus. Did Jesus only appear in His "ethereal" body and was He able to influence only those He chose to "see it?" Was

His pure white, perfect vibration of such a high electrical energy that it was too hot to handle?

On the morning that Christians celebrate as Easter, it is stated in the New Testament that Jesus first appeared to Mary Magdalen, but she did not recognize Him. She even assumes He is the gardener! Next He warns her, "Don't touch me, for I have not yet ascended to the Father. . .but go to my brothers and tell them that I am now ascending to my Father. . ."

In 1935 Cayce was asked: "Why did Jesus say, 'touch me not,' when He first appeared to Mary after the resurrection?" He answered: "For the vibrations to which the glorified body was raised would have been the same as the physical body touching a high power current. Why do you say don't touch the wire? If ye are in accord, or *not* in touch with the earth, it doesn't harm; otherwise, it's too bad!" [262-87].

In 1944, Cayce was asked: "Is the transmutation of human flesh to flesh divine the real mystery of the crucifixion and resurrection? Please explain this mystery." Cayce answered:

Having attained in the physical consciousness the atonement with the Father-Mother-God, the completeness was such that with the disintegration of the body—as indicated in the manner in which the shroud, the robe, the napkin lay [in the tomb], there was then the taking of the body-physical form. This was the manner. It was not transmutation, as of changing from one form to another.

Having as indicated in the manner in which the body- physical entered the upper room with the doors closed (John 20:26), not by being a part of the wood through which the body passed but by forming from the ether waves that were within the room, because of a meeting prepared by faith.

As indicated in the spoken word to Mary in the garden, "touch me not, for I have not yet ascended to my Father." The body (flesh) that formed, that seen by the normal or carnal eye of Mary, was such that it could not be handled until there had been the conscious union with the sources of all power, of all force.

But afterward—when there had been the first, second, third, fourth and even *sixth* meeting—He *then* said: "Put forth thy hand and touch the nail prints in my hands, in my feet. Thrust thy hand into my side and believe." This indicated the transformation.

For as indicated when the soul departs from the body (this is not being spoken of the Christ, you see), it has all of the form of the body from which it passed—yet it is not visible to the carnal [earthly] mind, unless that mind has been, and is, attuned to the infinite. Then it appears in the infinite as that which may be handled, with all the attributes of the physical being; with the appetites, until these have been accorded to a unit of activity with Universal consciousness.

Just as it was with the Christ-body: "Children, have ye anything here to eat?" This indicated to the disciples and the apostles present that this was not transmutation but a regeneration, recreation of the atoms and cells of body that might, through desire, masticate [partake of food] material things—fish and honey in the honeycomb were given. . . [2533-8]

In another reading is the following:

. . .He became the first of those who overcame death in the body [and this] enabled Him to illuminate, to so revivify [impart new life] to that body that He could take it up again, even when those fluids of the body had been drained away by the nail holes in His hands and the spear piercing His side. . . [1152-1]

And Cayce was asked in still another reading:

Question: What changes had to take place in the physical body of Jesus to become a glorified spiritual body?
Answer: The passing of the material life into the spiritual life brought the glorified body; thus enabling the perfect body to be materialized in material life—a glorified body made perfect. [5749-10]

Cayce states it was not until the "sixth meeting" that Jesus consummated the materialization of His crucified body, the "conscious (physical) union with all force," and was able to take food. Thus it may be that Jesus needed some human earth time in order to do this in accordance with the Laws of the material world.

So, Dr. Steinpach's ethereal interpretation may be somewhat correct, but only with respect to the early events of Jesus' resurrection. Therefore the rationale for the doctrine of the Rapture is still open to interpretation. Perhaps the statement by Paul in First

Corinthians in which he says, "Behold, I tell you a mystery. . ." has something to do with the ethereal bodies of the saints being caught up to meet the Lord in the air.

For Cayce, the Spirit of God, or "God's creative force in action" was capable of forming anything in the material world if properly invoked. For Cayce, both the soul of Jesus and the soul of Mary know how to use God's Spirit for creating on the earth plane. They could even create their own material bodies—including the "immaculate conception." One reading on the subject states: ". . .And this is a stumbling stone to many of the wordly-wise" [5749-15]

In another, the question is asked:

Question: Is the teaching of the Roman Catholic Church correct, in that Mary was without original sin from the moment of her conception in the womb of Anne [Mary's mother]?

Answer: It would be correct in any case. Correct more in this. For as from the material teaching of that just referred to, you see, in the beginning, Mary was the twin Soul of the Master in the entrance into the earth.

Question: Then neither Mary nor Jesus had a human father?

Answer: Neither Mary nor Jesus had a human father. . . [5749-8]

The ability of Jesus to form material substance is the basis for the belief in His miraculous conception and resurrection. His ability to heal people, raise the dead, defy gravity by walking on water and ascending to heaven, are also illustrations of Jesus' ability to invoke God's Spirit. Accordingly, the doctrine of the Rapture is based on the assumption that Jesus will invoke God's Spirit on their behalf when He returns to Rapture His saints to heaven. Further, once the Tribulation is over, these very same people will return with Jesus to rule the earth.

If the Rapture theorists are correct, the more we know about Jesus the better prepared we will be when the time comes. For instance, we might be interested in the events that took place leading up to the crucifixion, along with a physical description of Jesus, in order to recognize Him when He returns just as the apostles could after the Resurrection. Few people are aware that there is in existence today, in the Archives of Rome, a description of Jesus. It is included in a report written nearly two thousand years ago, by a Roman, Publius Lentulus, to his Emperor, Tiberias. It reads:

LETTER TO TIBERIAS

There has appeared in Palestine a man who is still living and whose power is extraordinary. He has the title given him of Great Prophet, his disciples call him "Son of God." He raises the dead and heals all sorts of diseases.

He is a tall, well proportioned man, and there is an air of severity in his countenance which at once attracts the love and reverence of those who see him. His hair is the color of new wine from the roots to the ears, and thence to the shoulders it is curled and falls down to the lowest part of them. Upon the forehead it parts in two after the manner of Nazarenes. His forehead is flat and fair, his face without blemish or defect, and adorned with a graceful expression. His nose and mouth are very well proportioned, his beard is thick and the color of his hair. His eyes are grey and extremely lively.

In his reproofs he is terrible, but in his exhortations and instructions, amiable and courteous. There is something wonderfully charming in his face with a mixture of gravity. He is never seen to laugh, but has been observed to weep. He is very straight in stature, his hands large and spreading, his arms are very beautiful.

He talks little, but with great quality, and is the handsomest man in the world.

The description of Jesus in the Cayce readings resembles the one in the letter Publius Lentulus sent to his Emperor:

Question: Please give a physical description of Jesus.
Answer: A picture that might be put on canvas. . .would be entirely different from all those that have depicted the face, the body, the eyes, the cut of the chin, and the lack entirely of the Jewish or Aryan profile. For these were clear, clean, ruddy. Hair almost like of David; a golden brown, yellow red. [5354-1]

The circumstances surrounding another time Cayce described Jesus were unusual because the sleeping Cayce was transported far back into time. Along with a portrait of Jesus, he fills in some of the details leading up to the Crucifixion.

On the morning of June 14, 1932, a 39-year-old lady telephoned Cayce at his home in Virginia Beach from her home in New York City. She had had a sleepless night caused by an eye infection and was in great pain. Her doctor was unable to help, so Cayce gave an "emergency reading" for her. At the end of the reading Cayce was given the usual suggestion to wake up, but he didn't respond. The conductor of the reading tried a second time, and then a third. He still didn't respond. Instead, he began to speak again from his trance state:

The Lord's Supper—here with the Master—see what they had for supper—boiled fish, rice with leeks, wine, and loaf. One of the pitchers in which it was served was broken—the handle was broken, as was the lip of same. The whole robe of the master was not white, but pearl gray—all combined into one—the gift of Nicodemus to the Lord.

The better looking of the twelve, of course, was Judas, while the younger was John—oval face, dark hair, smooth face—only one with the short hair. Peter, the rough and ready—always that of very short beard, rough, and not altogether clean; while Andrew's is just the opposite—very sparse, but inclined to be long more on the side and under the chin—long on the upper lip—his robe always near gray or black, while his clouts or breeches were striped; while those of Philip and Bartholemew were red and brown.

The Master's hair is 'most red, inclined to be curly in portions yet not feminine or weak—*strong*, with heavy piercing eyes that are blue or steel-gray.

His weight would be at least a hundred and seventy pounds. Long tapering fingers, nails well kept. Long nail, though, on the left little finger.

Merry—even in the hour of trial. Joking—even in the moment of betrayal.

The sack is empty. Judas departs.

The last is given of the wine and loaf, with which he gives the emblems that should be so dear to every follower of Him. He lays aside his robe, which is all of one piece —girds the towel about His waist, which is dressed with linen that is blue and white. Rolls back the folds, kneels first before John, James, then Peter—who refuses.

Then the dissertation as to "He that would be the greatest would be servant of all."

The basin is taken as without handle, and is made of wood. The water is from the gherkins, that are in the wide-mouth shibboleths that stand in the house of John's father, Zebedee.

And now comes: "It is finished." They sing the ninety-first Psalm—"He that dwelleth in the secret place of the Most High shall abide under the shadow of the Almighty. I will say of the Lord, He is my refuge and my fortress; my God; in Him I trust."

He is the musician as well, for He uses the harp.

They leave for the garden. [1315-3]

In other readings, Cayce described the events at the garden of Gethsemane, Jesus' trial, and the Crucifixion. However, Cayce never mentioned that a "death warrant" may have been issued.

In the archives of the Cayce foundation there is a copy of an article dated Christmas day, 1924, from the *Lighthouse*, an academic newspaper of a Virginia Beach high school. There are no references concerning the authenticity of the article, but it is included here because it adds another dimension to the story of the crucifixion:

DEATH WARRANT OF JESUS CHRIST

In 1810, some workman while excavating in the ancient city of Amiternum (now Aquila), in the Kingdom of Naple, found an antique marble vase in which lay concealed a copper inscription in the Hebrew tongue. This, when translated, proved to be the death warrant of Jesus Christ. It has been faithfully transcribed and reads as follows:

"In the year seventeen of the Emperor Tiberius Caesar, and the 27th day of March, the city of holy Jerusalem—Annas and Ciaphas being priests, sacrificators of the people of God—Pontius Pilate, Governor of Lower Galilee, sitting in the presidential chair of the pratetory, condemns Jesus of Nazareth to die on the cross between two thieves, the great and notorious evidence of the people saying:

1. Jesus is a seducer.
2. He is seditious.
3. He is the enemy of the law.
4. He calls himself falsely the Son of God.

5. He calls himself falsely the King of Israel.

6. He entered into the temple, followed by a multitude, bearing palm branches in their hands.

"Orders of the first centurion, Tuiluis Cornelius, to lead him to the place of execution, forbids any person whomsoever, either poor or rich, to oppose the death of Jesus Christ. The witnesses who signed the condemnation of Jesus are:

1. Daniel Robani, a Pharisee.

2. Joannus Robani.

3. Raphael Robani.

4. Capet, a citizen.

"Jesus shall go out of the city of Jerusalem by the gate of Struenus."

Most believers in the Second Coming do not expect Jesus to remain in the clouds when He returns to the atmosphere of planet earth. They believe Jesus will continue to descend and actually land on *terra firma* after which He will bring everlasting peace and understanding to the world. The Cayce readings agree:

For He shall come as ye have seen Him go, in the body He occupied in Galilee. The body that He formed, that was crucified on the cross, that appeared to Philip, that appeared to John. . . [5749-4]

Question [in 1933]: Are we entering the period of preparation for His coming?

Answer: Entering the test period, rather. [5749-2]

What Cayce meant by the "test period" suggests that before Jesus returns, humanity will have to be tested in the "school of hard knocks!" But why? There are two schools of thought with respect to the meaning of the Second Coming. One school is convinced that Jesus will return in His physical body and change the world, performing miracles and subduing all evil. The other school believes He will not appear in bodily form, but that the doctrine of the Second Coming properly interpreted simply means a "Christ-consciousness" will infiltrate the consciousness of the human race and change the world. All human beings will eventually learn to love one another as Jesus commanded.

The Cayce readings say that both interpretations are correct to some extent. The sequence of the events needs adjusting and the effect of each Christ-event needs to be understood. For Jesus will return, and the Christ-consciousness *will* bring about a world full of God's Love as professed by the students of the second school of thought. But first, humanity will need experience. As people come to realize that they no longer have control over their lives, most will begin to search for the reason God is disturbing the planet, and why the supernatural events in the heavens are taking place. Many will arrive at the conclusion that humanity has brought the chastisement upon themselves and understand the need for change. Cayce explains:

> For what must be obliterated? Hate, prejudice, selfishness, backbiting, unkindness, anger, passion, and those things of the mire that are created in the activities of man. Then again, He may come in body to claim His own.
> Question: How soon?
> Answer: When those that are His have made the way clear, *passable*, for Him to come. [5749-5]

The Cayce readings on the Second Coming suggest that the purpose of the prophesied millennium events is to create the desire in as many people as possible to "obliterate those things of the mire" and to bring their will in line with God's Will as Jesus Christ did. In a reading on the Book of Revelation, Cayce was asked about the meaning of "the new heaven and the new earth" in the twenty-first chapter:

> When the foundations of the earth are broken up by those disturbances, can the mind of man comprehend no desire to sin. . .Is this not a new heaven and a new earth? For the former things would have passed away. For as the desires, the purposes, the aims are to bring about the whole change, *physically*, so does it create in the experiences of each soul a new vision, a new comprehension. [281-37]

At some point during the "disturbances," when an adequate number of people on the planet are attempting to follow His Way because of an inner longing for the Christ-consciousness on earth, the vibration will be raised enough so that the "way is clear, PASSABLE," and Jesus can return "in body." The number of people that will be adequate to raise the vibration sufficiently, however, is an unknown factor. Cayce said that Jesus was able to form His physical body in the upper room from "the ether waves that were in the room, because of a meeting prepared by faith." However, the ethereal vibration needed for Jesus to materialize at the Second Coming may require the despair and subsequent faith of a much larger number of people. We have seen that Scallion claims it will take "millions."

In 1934, Cayce delivered a talk to his supporters about his personal interpretation and conclusions regarding the Second Coming information in the readings. The following is an excerpt:

I believe that the just people in the world keep it going. The just people are the ones who have been kind to the other fellow. For we may see evidences of the Christ Spirit about us right now, day by day, in kindness, patience, long-suffering, showing brotherly love, preferring our neighbor before ourself. When there are possibly fifty, or a hundred, or a thousand, or a million—then the way may have been prepared for His coming. But all these just men must have *united* in their desire and supplication that the Christ walk again among men.

Ten years later, in, 1943, he was asked while in a trance:

Question: Is there going to be a great spiritual change immediately following this war?
Answer: That depends upon what you—as millions of others, do about it. Do ye choose that such should be? Do ye choose this as the opportunity that people shall be warned that the Day of the Lord is at hand and let every man forsake the old ways and cleave to that which is good? This can only be answered in thyself. [3213-1]

"How soon?" Cayce was asked in a reading:

The time no one knows. Even as He gave, not even the Son Himself, only the Father. Not until His enemies—and the earth—are wholly in subjection to His will, His powers. [5749-2]

The interpretation of this reading is difficult. Cayce may be saying that every human being on earth will become powerless because of the earth changes. In this case, "His will, His powers" may refer to the "Father"—God's will, God's powers. Regardless, the exact timing of Jesus' return is not known. However, other Cayce readings suggest the return of Jesus will occur in the 1998 to 2001 time frame. Once He does return, the next step is said to be "The Last Judgment."

THE LAST JUDGEMENT

In *Spirit Song*, No-Eyes tells Mary Summer Rain:

Summer need see how Great Spirit do stuff. He feel bad too. He give truths to peoples. He give heritage gifts to better see proof of truths. He give peoples free will. He give people long, long rope. He give, and give even more. He give all peoples many chances. . .He give many years' time to peoples. He gonna stop one day. One day He gonna come. He gonna make it stop. He gonna draw final line. He gonna put believers on one side and no believers on other. He gonna let people's vibrations shake and break Earth Mother. Believers be already ready— they be in safe groups. Others be confused—they no ready. They caught full of shame with pants down. They sorry they no listen. He sorry too—but it already too late, time over—it all settled then.

In his well documented book, *The Second Coming*, author Kirk Nelson writes that in one of the Dead Sea Scrolls entitled "The Last Jubilee" there appears a prophecy that predicts "Melechitzedek redivivus" will destroy Satan at the "Final Judgment." It is said in the New Testament Book of Hebrews that Jesus was "a priest for ever after the order of Melechitzedek," who was the Old Testament priest to whom Abraham tithed. Accordingly, the doctrine of the Last Judgment may predate the references to it in the New Testament.

Before the prophecies concerning the doctrine of the Last Judgment are presented, there is another doctrine, much more ancient, that must be considered—the doctrine of "Reincarnation."

Belief in the doctrine of reincarnation is not said to be a prerequisite to being "saved." However, for those who believe in reincarnation and understand the working of its laws, the Last Judgment takes on a much broader and more complete meaning. While reincarnation is usually associated with the Eastern religions, as far back as 1982 a Gallup poll showed that 23 percent of Americans believe in reincarnation.

Reincarnation does not mean that human souls can return to earth and dwell in the body of an animal. This doctrine is known as "Transmigration." Reincarnation simply means that the human soul is granted many opportunities to incarnate in successive bodies on the earth for the purpose of expanding the soul's consciousness so it can make its will one with God's Will.

The historical evidence that reincarnation was an accepted doctrine of Judaism and early Christianity has been extensively documented in hundreds of books including *Dear Amy: Making Sense of the Voyage of the Soul.* In this century reincarnation has so grown in popularity that today numerous leaders, both Christian and Jewish, embrace the doctrine. In addition, thousands of psychiatrists and psychologists now utilize "past-life" regression and therapy in their practices in an attempt to discover if an experience in a specific past life of a person is affecting their present life in some way. The law of physics that states that "for every action there is an equal and opposite reaction" is the physical counterpart of the spiritual law in the doctrine of reincarnation. For members of the Eastern religions this law has been known since ancient times as "karma." Christians point to several passages in the New Testament that they feel supports their belief in the Law of Karma—or "balance" as sometimes referred to.

In Paul's letter to the Galatians he writes: "Make no mistake about this, God is not fooled; a man reaps what he sows." (6:7-9) This admonishment by Paul is similar to the passage in the Old Testament Book of Job (4:8): "This I know, that those who plow mischief and sow trouble reap as they have sown." And there's the quote which warns, "live by the sword, die by the sword"—but not necessarily in the same lifetime. Many point to the passage in Revelation (13:10) as an example of God's perfect justice: "He that leadeth into captivity shall go into captivity; he that killeth with the sword must be killed with the sword. Here is the patience and the faith of the saints." Further, in Matthew, as Jesus is about to be arrested at Gethsemane, He tells one of his defenders who had just cut off the ear of a servant of the high priest, "Put up your sword. All who take the sword die by the sword." (26:52)

According to the doctrine of reincarnation, a person may escape punishment on earth for some misdeed, but "what goes around comes around." In the twelfth chapter of the New Testament Book of Romans, in a letter to newly-converted Christians, Paul tells them: "My dear friends, do not seek revenge, but leave a place for divine retribution; for there is a text [Deuteronomy 32:35] which reads, 'Justice is mine says the Lord, I will repay.'" Many of the prophets quoted in this book accept the doctrine of reincarnation as a fact of life. In *The Revelation of Ramala*, the prophet states:

The concept of reincarnation is recognized all over the World. Many interpretations of its true meaning are to be found but, putting it simply, reincarnation means being born again, living another life again. Many people can accept that their soul, or their spirit, does indeed exist on other levels after the physical act of death takes place, but they find it hard to accept that they have actually lived physical lives before their present incarnation and that they will indeed live again in a physical body at a later stage in the evolution of the earth.

Nothing that I can say will convince any man of the principle of reincarnation who does not within his own consciousness already believe in it, for the belief in reincarnation is a point of consciousness. . .

In your world there often occur acts of great tragedy, as you would describe them. Almost every day you can read in the newspapers of accidents in which people have been killed either in planes or cars, of murders, of tragic deaths and of thousands dying from famine or disease. . .Many people say, "How can God allow such suffering to take place?" and by this they imply that God, or their concept of God, is to blame for the tragedies that take place. If you lived only one life, if you had not lived before and if you were not to live again, then perhaps you might have some justification for thinking that life was cruel, that it was a pointless waste to take a man away in his prime, to remove a mother from her children, to destroy the apparent happiness of life on this earth. But those of you who do believe in reincarnation. . .have recognized that nothing in this world happens by chance and that everything that exists in matter is controlled by forces greater than Man can imagine. . .

If you accept that life on this earth is a school, you must also accept that there have to be term-times and holidays, for when one is young one cannot learn continuously, without a break. Children go to school for a fixed period of time and then have their holidays. That is exactly what happens in life. You go to school on earth for a fixed period of time and then you have a holiday before returning to school again. When you return to school you have within you all the knowledge that you have acquired during your previous times at school. You have within you the experience of all your relationships with your fellow pupils and teachers, the examinations you have taken, the degrees you have obtained, and you will progress onward from that stage. If you have failed some of your examinations, then the opportunity is presented to you to take them again after more schooling. That analogy really is a much simplified description of physical life. . .However, the important factor which has to be considered in all this is that each one of your lives is planned. Not only do you choose the body into which you incarnate, the parents who are to conceive you, the planetary influences under which you are to be born, the country in which you are to live, your way of life and the partner you are to marry, but you also choose the moment of death and the manner in which you are to die.

As I said earlier, this earth is a school, and you learn even when making mistakes. If you face a test and fail, you have to take it again. . .for you cannot progress—and all life is an upward progression, an upward spiral—until you have learned those lessons. . .Therefore, stemming from this fact, it follows from that your behaviour in one life, whether you were a king or a beggar, will greatly affect your next life.

Many of you, I know, are aware of the Law of Karma. Karma has been described as the Law of Cause and Effect. What you do will have an effect. That which you send out will come back to you, if not in this life then in another. If you consider it, this is a very just Law. Everything in the universe, from the stars and the planets above down to nature below, is in balance. Would it not be unjust if Man lived only one life and in that life a person could, for example, murder someone and gain by it. The Law of Creation knows no such thing as imbalance. . .

Let us, for example, suppose that in a fit of anger you have killed someone. Now even if you are truly repentant for what you have done and have learned from that experience, the Law of Karma decrees that you owe that person you killed an equal payment. Now that does not mean that the person you killed has to kill you. That is not payment. It means that because you have killed that person and have perhaps shortened his life, then in another incarnation you would of your own free choice perhaps sacrifice your own physical life to help in that person's development or evolution, either by demonstrating a lesson to him through your own death or else by accepting a physical injury or illness in circumstances which would constitute a test for that person. . .

Be aware that all the incidents in your life have a significance. All those times when you think that fate is just being cruel to you have a meaning. So try to look for it. Think back in your life to what you have done. Examine the incidents that have happened to you. Try to look for the underlying meaning and you will then see and understand the greater purpose of life. There is no such thing as chance. There is no such thing as blind fate. Everything that happens on the surface of this earth happens for a reason. In that you are all born with the divine gift of free choice, as you choose so will you have an effect not only on yourselves but also on those around you. Man has to learn to be responsible not only for himself but for his fellow-men as well. Therefore Karma applies not only to individuals but to towns, to cities, to countries and, of course, to the earth as a whole. . .

I ask you to try to look into life, to see the meaning of the balance in it, to realise that your Creator, Who knows every hair on your head, is aware of everything that is done to you justly or unjustly and is aware of everything you do, justly or unjustly. Realize that as you act so you will cause an effect not only in this life but in your lives to come. You may not harm another brother without that harm coming back to you. If only Man today would be aware of that fact how pleasant life on this earth would be. . .Therefore, please always motivate your actions with the purest and highest spirituality. . .It was William Shakespeare who wrote:

All the world's a stage,
and all the men and women merely players:
they have their exits and their entrances,
and one in his time man plays many parts.

William Shakespeare understood full well that physical life on the earth can be compared to a play, albeit on a slightly larger scale than his little theatrical masterpieces, and that when your eternal spirits incarnate on the physical plane of earth they are simply playing parts, empowering roles in the great drama of life. . .If I release that drama to you, if I tell you what is to happen on the physical plane of life, then where is the point of the drama? You have to experience these events, to handle them and learn from them. You have to invoke your own intuitive energy, to ground and to receive the wisdom of your Creator.

Aron Abrahamsen offered the following information in his newsletter, *The Abrahamsen Report:*

In returning to earth, souls will often decide to seek out the circumstances or conditions they left from their immediate past lives, or perhaps they feel they are ready to deal with a situation left over from a number of lives past. . .many souls choose to work on both. This is done so that they can try to complete the responsibilities and tasks already begun but not finished in a past life.

Upon re-entering earth life everything appears to be new to the conscious mind, but not so to the soul. To the soul the same situation appears as it had before, but now on a different level. Though the culture, language and time frame is different from the previous lifetime, the principles and lessons from the past are the same. Another opportunity has been given to the soul for it to learn and grow. The soul determines/discerns what is best to do regardless of how the conscious mind may oppose it. The Spirit of God instructs the soul concerning the all over picture. Then the soul instructs the conscious mind. This in turn, is to be manifested in the actions of the physical body. This instruction is often relayed to the person in the form of conscience. It can be a long process, depending upon how fast the conscious mind learns and responds to its instruction. In the end though, after perhaps many, many lifetimes there is complete agreement and integration between all aspects and levels of being.

The soul grows one step at a time, a little here, a little there. It can be compared to the painting of a picture. A little at a time the picture is developed and finally it stands there in all its glory and splendor. When this takes place the soul is then ready to take on greater responsibilities so that it can grow further. A challenging facet of the maturing of the soul is that there is always room for improvement.

Edgar Cayce had a long and hard struggle before he finally submitted to the doctrine of reincarnation that had first appeared in a reading without warning. Edgar Cayce's youngest son, Edgar Evans Cayce, a retired engineer living in Virginia Beach has stated: "When Dad awakened from the reading and was told he mentioned a past life of the individual who was asking all of these philosophical questions, he was dumbfounded. He knew as little about reincarnation as he knew about medicine. He was well-versed in Christianity and the Bible, but he had never studied other world religions. Abstract questions of philosophical systems had never concerned him. He was awash in waves of doubt about this new information from his unconscious. He was what today would be called a fundamentalist Christian, attended Church regularly, and was an excellent Sunday school teacher of the Bible."

In a 1937 Cayce reading he lectures: "For to find only that you lived, [another life] died, and were buried under the cherry tree in grandmother's garden does not make thee one whit a better neighbor, citizen, mother, or father. But to know that ye spoke unkindly [in that past life] and suffered for it, and in the present may correct it by being righteous—*that* is worthwhile. What is righteousness? Just being kind, just being noble, just being self-sacrificing, just being willing to be the hands for the blind, the feet for the lame—these are constructive experiences. Ye may gain the knowledge of same [past lives]. For incarnations are a fact. How may ye prove it? In thy daily living" [5753-2].

Fundamental Christian interpretations regarding the Last Judgment are literal in their approach. It could be described as an "either heaven or hell" doctrine. And, if this is true, it seems that, for whatever reason, a large number of people on the planet are not going to be "saved." For those who do believe in reincarnation, the interpretation of the Last Judgment could be described as the "held out" doctrine. Those souls that have decided to act in accordance with God's Will are going to be the only ones allowed to incarnate on the earth during the "thousand years of peace" described in the Bible. From the Book of Revelation, 20:1-6:

Then I saw an angel coming down from heaven with the key of the abyss and a great chain in his hands. He seizes the dragon, that serpent of old, the Devil or Satan, and chained him up for a thousand years; he threw him into the abyss, shutting and sealing it over him, so that he might seduce the nations no more till the thousand years were over. After that he must be loosed for a short while. . .then those who had *not* worshiped the beast. . .came to life again and reigned with Christ for a thousand years, though the rest of the dead did not come to life until the thousand years were over. This is the first resurrection. . .happy indeed. . .is the man who shares in the first resurrection!"

With regard to the above passage, Cayce was asked: " What is the meaning of the thousand years that Satan is bound?"

Answer: Is banished. That. . .in the same manner that the prayer of ten just [persons] should save a city, the deeds, the prayers of the faithful will allow that period when the incarnation of those only that are in the Lord shall rule the earth, and the period is a thousand years.

Thus is Satan bound, thus is Satan banished from the earth. The desire to do evil is only of him. And when there are—as the symbols—those only whose desire and purpose of their heart is to glorify the Father, these will be those periods when this shall come to pass. Be ye *all determined* within thy minds, thy hearts, thy purposes, to be of that number. [281-37]

Edgar Cayce often stated that Jesus Christ belonged to all of humanity, not just the members of the Christian faith. Of course, if we take the doctrine of reincarnation into account, then each soul has incarnated many times over thousands of years as a member of all the religions. So when Cayce says in the above reading that "only those that are in the Lord shall rule the earth," he follows with "whose desire and purpose of their heart is to glorify the Father"—just as Jesus did on the earth. So "in the Lord" applies to any human being who sincerely strives to live in accordance with God's rules which Jesus summed up in the "Golden Rule." In one reading he states: "For the Master, Jesus, even the Christ, is the pattern for every man in the earth, whether he be Gentile, Jew, Parthenian, or Greek. For all have the pattern, whether they call on that name or not. . ." [3528-1].

In April 1944, Edgar Cayce encouraged his followers: "Don't think that there will not be trouble, but those who put their trust wholly in the Lord will not come up missing but will find conditions, circumstances, activities, someway and somehow much to be thankful for" [1467-18].

Gordon-Michael Scallion was told by his source:

After the greater changes occur between 1998-2001, the vibration on the physical earth as well as the inner earth will change. . .only those whose spiritual vibration matches the new earth will find entrance. . .thus the millennium of peace as so prophesied.

In his book, *Why Jesus Taught Reincarnation*, ordained minister, researcher and clinical psychologist, Dr. Herbert Bruce Puryear, explains his interpretation as follows:

During the thousand years of peace, Satan will be bound, that is, no souls who are still rebellious will be permitted to incarnate. . .Those incarnate during the thousand years of peace, under the leadership of the Master, will have prepared a most promising environment into which the others may reenter. . . [the "rest of the dead" Rev. 20:5, now have another opportunity to incarnate]. . .The purpose of the millennium is to establish a planetary classroom of the greatest strength and purity in order to continue the ongoing work of the plan of salvation of *all* of God's children who are entrapped in this system [the "second resurrection"]. . .The reincarnation view makes sense of it all. . ."

This interpretation was offered by the Ramala source in the early 1980s;

Follow that inner light and be true to it. I can reassure you that there is a Plan for this earth, that there is a great Being overseeing that Plan and that no evil thing can touch you if you are but true to yourself. Though many may suffer around you, though many may perish, though there may be droughts and floods, earthquakes and cataclysms, those who are true to that Spirit within will survive, and by survive I do not necessarily mean the survival of the *physical body but the survival of the Spirit* on the higher planes of life. For the Day of Judgement is coming, the time when the wheat must be sorted from the chaff if this planetary system is to move upward on the evolutionary spiral. Now that does not mean that those who are not chosen are faced with extermination. It merely means that they will return to what could be called a *Group Energy* and will allow those who have earned the right to individuality, who have recognized the Divinity of their being, to progress further along their evolutionary paths and so fulfill their potential.

So the "wheat will be separated from the chaff" for a thousand years, after which "the chaff" will be able to incarnate again for another opportunity to transform themselves. In the meantime, the souls that are "held out" will come together in some other dimension—"Group Energy"—for the thousand years. They will be grouped together in some other dimension or special school. The prophet of the *Grail Message*, in his usual harsh manner, explains the thousand years of peace in a slightly different manner:

Man forgot the principal thing! He did not take into account that condition that was also foretold, that *before* the thousand-year Reign of Peace *everything* has to become new in the Judgement. That is the essential foundation for the New Kingdom. It cannot be built up on the existing soil! *Everything* that is old has first to become new.

This does not mean, however, that the old is to be revitalized in its existing form, but the expression "new" implies a change, a transformation of the old!

Now since the human spirits have proved their utter inability to recognize their task in this Creation, since they proved their unwillingness to fulfill it by repudiating and misinterpreting all the warnings given by called ones and prophets, even those of the Son of God Himself, sealing their enmity by the crucifixion, God now *forcibly* intervenes.

Hence the millennium!

Only by *force* can Subsequent [ethereal and material] Creation still be helped, as well as mankind, who have proved that they would never voluntarily be persuaded to take the right path which they must follow in Creation in order to live according to God's Will, and also to work and bring blessing as *the* beings that they really are by virtue of their spiritual nature.

For this reason mankind now, in the Judgement, are being *deprived of their rights*, they are for a time *disinherited* of the right they have possessed up to now, the right that the human will rules over Subsequent Creation, guiding and forming it. Disinherited for a thousand years, so that at last there may be peace, and a striving towards the Light. . .

Disinheriting humanity of all the rights hitherto held in Subsequent Creation therefore makes possible and safeguards the establishment of the long-wished-for Kingdom of Peace. *Thus* does man stand before his God! For *that* must he now render account. That is the meaning of and the necessity for the thousand-year Kingdom of God here on earth. A sad truth, which cannot be more shaming for this mankind! But—it is the only way to help them.

Thus the millennium will become *a school for mankind*, in which they must learn *how* they have to stand in this Subsequent Creation, how to think and act in order to fulfill their appointed task correctly, and thereby to achieve happiness themselves!

To this end the will of mankind as ruler of Subsequent Creation is now suspended for a thousand years, after whatever he has wrongly sown and wrongly guided has been destroyed in the Judgement.

During the thousand years the Will of God alone will reign supreme, to which every human spirit must submit as soon as he has been able to pass through the Judgement.

Such is the millennium and its purpose. In their self-conceit and the delusion of their own importance, mankind have imagined it to be quite different. But they will have to learn and experience it as it actually is!

Therein also lies only a *Grace* of God, to help those who are really of a pure volition!

The prophet in the Ramala teachings claims that at the present time we will need to "transmute" or burn off all karma as a precursor requirement. The following is from *The Vision of Ramala* given in the late 1980s:

Humanity must seek God now. . .must discover within itself and through prayer and meditation develop its divine link with the Source of all Life. Every individual must learn to attune to their own soul wisdom and to act accordingly. I can tell you that the vibratory rate of the earth is being quickened and the transmutation of Karma is being accelerated.

Literally, you will reap in the afternoon what you have sown in the morning, for this the ending of an Age, this is the culminating point of a great learning process. This is humanity's moment of truth, its time of the transformation and transfiguration. The events of the next ten years will challenge the "ungodly" as they have never been challenged before. Those that do not transform will die no matter whether it be through war, natural disaster or disease. Only the pure in heart, those who follow God's Laws, the Natural Order, will survive to see the dawning of the New Age.

Moria Timms writes that Meishu Sama said: "Not only the purification of the human body, but a world-wide purification in every field is impending. This means a general house-cleaning of the whole world and the obliteration of the clouds of negativity accumulated during thousands of years."

The prophets tell us that this is a time when humanity not only must change, but will change. Humanity is about to experience the greatest evolutionary advancement in history. The Ramala prophet suggests that the process has already begun, and counsels:

Those of you who recognize this fact, not knowing when this great moment of transformation will come about but trusting only that it will be a divine act, inspired by Divine will, might ask what is the purpose of your being. As I have said in the past, the analogy of a lifeboat should come to mind. You sail on the great ship of Mother Earth. At present you are sailing in calm waters, for you are living in the rosy days of Western Civilization. . .you have the best of this earth.

See yourselves therefore, as lifeboats of consciousness, as lifeboats designed not for this moment in time but for the storms to come. If I may use an analogy, you are the Noahs of the last great cataclysm. You are receiving your divine inspiration to build your arks, not arks of physical matter but arks of spiritual consciousness—to understand the earth changes that will come, consciousness to understand the death and destruction that must inevitably follow and, above all, consciousness to rebuild human civilization and to ensure its continuing growth in the future.

This Age will see the physical manifestation of the divine principles which you now hold only as ideals, as spiritual concepts in your innermost soul beings. Everything of the highest that you wish was upon earth will be grounded upon her. All things will be possible in the New Age.

The race of humanity that will walk the earth in the Aquarian Age will differ in many respects from today. The human form will be different and will vibrate to a different note. The Angels and the great Masters will actually be present on the earth in physical appearance, and will walk and talk with you. The whole structure of matter, the frequency range in which you live, vibrate and your being will be altered. Therefore only one thing, only one factor, can guarantee your survival, if that indeed is your concern in this natural cycle of change, and that is consciousness, your soul consciousness. For it is your soul that will build the body that you require, that will change the atomic structure of your being and so prepare you for the life of the millennium which is to come—the Golden Age of Aquarius.

Sun Bear tells of a dream he had about the New Age:

After the period of cleansing, we'll be going into the fifth world. The people moving into this world will be from all over the globe, but they will share the same level of consciousness, found in their own individual ways.

I've had dreams in which I'm at a place, and a small group of people comes over a hill. We all embrace and say, "Brother, Sister, you survived." In this world, there aren't any "isms." We don't ask, "Well, what church do you belong to?" or "What this or that you belong to?" None of that matters.

After the cleansing, we will see only people who know how to reach out and learn. We'll see people who are always seeking spiritual knowledge. People will know that their survival came about because they had made a good effort to live in love and harmony.

In the teachings of my people, there are eight degrees of power. The eighth degree is where you are on the same level as the spirits all the time. You talk with them and think with them. During and after the cleansing, many of the great spirit teachers will take human form and walk among us.

In May 1995 Scallion described a vision he had in which he was shown the earth and the human condition after the year 2001:

The other interesting thing I saw was that there were not a lot of people on the planet. It was a significant body, but it wasn't six billion people. What I realized had happened was that the initiation of the planet had also changed which means that in the times that we live in today that virtually anybody can incarnate on this planet. You can be a saint or a sinner and there's a place for you here on the earth. And hopefully us sinners get better and we move up the initiation ladder and move towards a greater light. In the next century, six years from now, I observed that while there are seven rays of souls that have entrance into the earth currently, there are only three in the next 1000 years. And so what happened was that the earth itself had changed its vibration and it meant that in order to incarnate into the earth at this time that you have to have mastered those levels of consciousness. And that's why we have the millennium of peace. It isn't like as if someone is sitting there judging and saying you can come and you can't come, it is a self-judgement system and how you have led your life allows you to enter the world.

Keep the focus on the fact that the world is moving toward a new, bright, spiritual time frame. There has never been a time period on this planet when we have such an opportunity to gain so much so quickly. Because with this rush of this energy that is causing everything to go helter-skelter it is also the same energy that enables us to grow spiritually very quickly. Things that would have taken you ten lifetimes, a hundred lifetimes, you can do in one. So I have reached the point in my life where I see what is happening now as a blessing. And I think if each of us look inward, we will see, and I think we will acknowledge that these things need to happen. What is down the line is so dynamic that everyone would want to come back.

In several of her messages to Annie Kirkwood, Divine Mother Mary said that our solar system would soon have two suns. In July 1976 Aron Abrahamsen told an individual in a reading: ". . .And one will discover by the year 1998 the appearance of a new sun coming into viewpoint of all people on earth. . .not as strong as the present sun, but it will add a great amount of light to the world, indicating that the world is coming into a new consciousness."

In March 1984, *The Economist* reported in an article under the heading "A Companion" the following:

Most stars in the universe are paired. Earth's solitary sun is an anomaly. Or is it? Working independently astronomers at the Lawrence Berkely Laboratory in California and at the University of Southwestern Louisiana now believe that the sun, too, has a companion. Perhaps a tenth of the mass of the sun, the companion star may have an elliptical orbit that brings it relatively close to the sun once every 26M-30M years. Catastrophically close.

In July 1995, Gordon-Michael Scallion reported on an unusual personal experience he felt was very significant for our times as he questioned his "source" about the meaning of the Blue Star:

What I present next is my latest inner-world experience on *The Blue Star*. It is presented in a question and answer format where I am able to ask questions while receiving visions, similar to a lucid dream. This, however, occurs very rarely. If I have had previous visions on a subject and if I am prepared to ask questions, then it happens. As you can imagine, it takes great patience for this phenomenon to occur. In the case of the Blue Star, over thirteen years.

Question: Please explain the following repeating vision I've been seeing since 1979:

In the vision I observed our solar system, that is our sun with all its planets, revolving around another sun—orange in color. As I viewed this movement, a small blue star appeared from behind our sun?

Answer: This is to be. This solar system shall become a binary sun system.

Question: How will this come to be?

Answer: All spheres [planets and stars] have a cycle. For some—like the earth's cycle around the sun—it is relatively short, in this case 365 days. For others the cycle is long, measured in thousands and millions of years. Now, the sun also has a cycle with other spheres. As it moves across the known and unknown heavens, it comes under the influence of other suns, also on their journeys. What you were shown, relative to the blue star, was this star coming into this solar system, making it a binary sun system, for a period of time.

Question: Is its time period related to the previously prophesied "millennium of peace?"

Answer: It is.

Question: Does the blue star remain after this period:

Answer: As part of its cycle it shall disappear behind the sun once more. Though it shall be visible for 1,800 years, in total, and then a new cycle begins.

Question: What will the Blue Star look like during the day and evening?

Answer: During the day it will appear as a silvery light 100 times brighter than any morning star, so as to require a new magnitude scale. (ed. note: in astronomy "magnitude" refers to brightness). During the evening, it will appear as a moon.

Question: Please explain the significance of the part of my vision which showed our solar system revolving around the orange-colored sun?

Answer: Just as the moon is held in orbit by the relationship of the earth and sun to it, your sun is held in orbit by its companion sun.

Question: Is the Blue Star a companion to our sun?

Answer: No, the Blue Star is a companion to Sirius B.

Question: If the companion star is not the Blue Star what is the companion star?

Answer: Arcturus.

Question: And the significance of being shown this companion star?

Answer: These influences shall govern the next root race.

Question: How is this possible? Arcturus is so far away compared to the distance of earth to our sun?

Answer: Distance is only a portion of the dynamics at work here. Alignment between spheres is the greater portion. See it in this way. Your sun governs all in its system including the earth. What occurs with the sun, such as sun spots, magnetic shifts, and its rotation, affects all life, and all spheres in this system. The aurora borealis, or northern lights, is one such visible effect that often disrupts electrical power systems, satellites, as well as animals and humans.

Now these effects occur on the sun which is millions of miles away, yet they affect the earth nonetheless. Just as the earth is affected by this sun, this sun is affected by other suns. At key times, or cycles, the position of the sun, relative to its companion, is affected in varying ways. Its emanations rising and ebbing as a result of inner and outer influences. This in turn causes other spheres, in this system, and others, to adjust accordingly.

Question: This sounds like astrology.

Answer: Astrology is based upon these principles.

Question: How will the Blue Star and Arcturus affect the astrology chart?

Answer: As the Blue Star enters this part of the heavens the charting of same can give added guidance, for this new sun shall have a great effect on the soul.

Remember, astrology only indicates potential patterns, or forces at work. It is the entity [person] alone who determines the outcomes—free will.

Just as the moon governs the emotional body, and the sun governs the personality, the Blue Star shall govern the soul. Do not misunderstand here. It is not that the moon, sun and other planets do not affect the soul currently, they do. But the Blue Star shall affect them differently. The soul learns from its experiences through physical incarnations, as well as non-physical. In the very near future with the addition of another sun in this part of the heavens, a new effect shall be added to the matrix. The vibrations given off by the Blue Star will enable the soul to have an easier time in communication with its host.

Question: Are you saying in the near future people on earth will be able to consciously communicate with their souls?

Answer: They can now. They always have been able to. However most turned away as the human spirit descended deeper into physical matter and the material world held a greater interest than the spiritual world. Shortly, this changes, as the new millennium heralds in a rebirth. God and man shall walk hand-in-hand once again.

Question: Everyone?

Answer: All that are able to return during the New Age.

Question: Some will not be able to return?

Answer: The Blue Star and new vibrations on the earth and sun, shall create a new matrix, or vibration. Where today, for example, all may enter the earth; shortly only those who have developed the necessary spiritual matrix shall find entrance into the earth.

Question: What happens to those who have not developed the necessary vibrations?

Answer: They shall find opportunities for lessons in newly created realms. Should they develop the necessary vibration in those places, then it will be possible for them to enter into the new earth.

Cayce spoke of the star, Arcturus, our sun's "companion," on numerous occasions. He designated it "the beautiful—the wonderful" and said it represented the consciousness or dimension of the universe whereby human souls depart for other evolutionary experiences once they have completed the soul development here.

Scallion's information source states that the Blue Star is the companion of Sirius B. Sirius is the brightest star in the sky. Sirius B is a much smaller star known as a "white dwarf," a star that is in its latter stage of development. Astronomers designate it the companion star of Sirius as it orbits around its mother star. It is extremely dense, said to be a million times denser than water. It is much hotter than other stars, and produces abundant amounts of radiation and extreme ultraviolet wavelengths. If the Blue Star is its companion, then it too may have some of the characteristics of Sirius B. With respect to the star, Sirius, there is an interesting and unusual scenario in *The Wisdom of Ramala*:

. . .I will begin with a story. Whether the story is true or not is for you to decide. You can regard it as a legend, as a myth, if you desire. Hundreds of thousands of years ago there was a planet within a solar system centred on the star which you call Sirius and living on that planet were many races all fulfilling the evolutionary pattern of the God whose spirit was in the star Sirius. Those races lived through many cycles of evolution developing their consciousness and moving upwards on the evolutionary spiral of that solar system. There was, however, one race on that planet which, in spite of the cosmic talents that it had been given, could not and would not use them for the good of the whole. This race of people became more self-centered and used their God-given talents to create power and wealth for themselves. They rarely respected the wishes and the needs of their own race, let alone those of the other races or the planet as a whole.

Because the other beings of that solar system gave freely of love, because they did not oppose the desires of this evolving race, so the evolutionary cycle of the planet became unbalanced and the Lord of that system was faced with the decision of what to do with this race of people. The choice was either to remove it from the planet, to await another cycle, another time, when it could evolve, or else to follow the request of one of the great beings of that race who asked that the race should be given another chance. That being asked that the race should be removed to another solar system where it could evolve and grow more aware of its divinity, where it could more properly use the cosmic talents which it had been given. The Lord Sirius acceded to this request and it was decided to reincarnate this race of people on another planet where the wheat could be sorted from the chaff, where those who did indeed recognize their divine responsibility for right creation, who could live and obey God's Law, who could ground and demonstrate it, would be selected to go forward into the next evolutionary cycle.

So it came to pass that planet in the solar body of Sirius was dissolved and the souls of that race migrated to the solar system in which you now dwell. . .

Scallion is also told that the Blue Star is 100 times brighter than any morning star, and will be visible during daytime. In 2nd Peter, it is stated: "And we have the word of the prophets made more certain, and you will do well to pay attention to it, as a light shining in a dark place, until the day dawns and the morning star rises in your hearts." And John is told in Revelation: "I, Jesus, have sent my angel to gave you this testimony for the churches. I am the Root and the offspring of David, and the bright Morning Star." (22:16)

WHEN THE ANGELS SING

A large, bright comet has entered our solar system. As the astronomers gather their scientific data and their findings are disseminated to the public, there is engaging evidence that this celestial object, Hale-Bopp, has a few characteristics that may qualify it as the prophesied comet/star. Not long after it was discovered, speculation mounted with respect to its size, brightness, and its elliptical course. The January 9, 1996 issue of the tabloid, *The Sun* reported in dramatic style the theories of Johan Oftrbrau, an astronomer from Oslo, Norway. The articles headline read: "Top Astronomer's Grim Warning: COMET HEADS FOR GIANT CRASH WITH EARTH." This article reports the ultimate dooms-day scenario as it describes the vivid and frightening aftermath of the comet's collision with planet earth. The article ends with Oftrabrau's statement: "Of course, I pray my calculations are wrong. . .but I've been a scientist for a long time."

Of course, none of the prophecies concerning the comet allege that it will strike the earth. However, the astronomers have concluded that Hale-Bopp is very large and unusually bright, and this certainty is the first piece of evidence that Hale-Bopp may be the comet/star that the prophets have been expecting.

The second piece of evidence is about "timing" because this particular comet/star is right on schedule as it infiltrates our consciousness and our solar system as the millennium approaches. Of course, there may be others that will also show up. The prophecies speak of "signs" (plural) in the heavens.

Thirdly, and most importantly, the fact that astronomers have determined that it makes a return visit approximately every 3200 to 4200 years completes the prophetic, elliptical cycle. This could place its three previous visits at the time of the Exodus, the time of Noah, and the time of the supposed destruction of Atlantis.

Although it may appear repetitive, a short review is in order with respect to the most significant prophesied characteristic of the comet/star. As we have seen, the Hopi Indians believe their prophesied star named *Kachina* will give off a bluish glow when it makes its appearance in the heavens, and that spirit entities such as angels they designate as "Kachinas" are capable of manifesting on earth in a material form and are the controlling masters of the star.

And again, we find in the *Grail Message* essay "The Great Comet" the assertion:

> Since the event in Bethlehem there has been nothing like it. Like the Star of Bethlehem, the star has also detached itself from the Eternal Realm of Primordial Spirit at such a time as to take effect on this earth exactly when the years of spiritual enlightenment are to come to all mankind.
>
> The star takes its course in a *straight* line from the Eternal Realm of this part of the Universe. Its core is filled with high spiritual power; it envelopes itself in material substance, and will thereby also become visible to men on earth. Unerringly and unswervingly the COMET pursues its course, and will appear on the scene at the right hour, as already ordained thousands of years ago."

Gordon-Michael Scallion wrote in a reading concerning the blue star: "Now, imagine, a star—a blue star, that moves through the heavens at regular cycles, such as a comet, except this celestial object is pure spiritual energy, a star made manifest by spiritual forces—a star composed of light-beings. These angels—souls of the highest level—who by their own spiritual evolution, joined together as a singular Host to serve."

We have also seen that all of the prophecies claim a new, exalted consciousness is going to permeate the human race, and that "angels" will in some way play an important role in bringing about this transformation. As we assemble the pieces of the puzzle it appears that this particular celestial event acts in some manner as the impetus to bring about many material and spiritual changes as we approach the millennium. Accordingly, this period is referred to as Armageddon, the Last Judgment, the Second Coming, and so forth. This may suggest that the prophecies in the Bible about the return of the Son of Man who will be accompanied by His legion of angels may be telling us something that we should seriously consider.

When Jesus was born in Bethlehem, the Bible tells us that two momentous events accompanied His birth: A bright star appeared in the heavens, and a host of angels manifested, ". . .a great company of the heavenly host, singing the praises of God." (Luke 2:13) Edgar Cayce described the scene as follows:

> . . .Then, the herald angels sang. The star appeared that made the wonderment to the shepherds. . .All were in awe as the brightness of His star appeared and shone, as the music of the spheres brought that joyful choir, "Peace on earth! Good will to men of good faith."
>
> All felt the vibrations and saw a great light—not only the shepherds above that stable but those in the Inn as well. [5749-15]

If Jesus is about to return, it is not unreasonable that the event will once again be announced by a bright star and that He will be accompanied by a host of angels. However, the Bible passages referring to this event suggest that the angels will be singing hymns that vibrate in a discriminating or selective manner. The passages in the Book of Matthew support many of the prophecies already presented:

> Jesus told them another parable: "The kingdom of heaven is like a man who sowed good seed in his field.
>
> "But while everyone was sleeping, his enemy came and sowed weeds among the wheat, and went away.
>
> "When the wheat sprouted and formed heads, then the weeds also appeared.
>
> "The owner's servants came to him and said, 'Sir, didn't you sow good seed in your field? Where then did the weeds come from?'
>
> " 'An enemy did this,' he replied. The servants asked him, 'Do you want us to go and pull them up?'
>
> " 'No,' he answered, 'because while you are pulling the weeds, you may root up the wheat with them.
>
> " 'Let both grow together until the harvest. At that time I will tell the harvesters: First collect the weeds and tie them in

bundles to be burned; then gather the wheat and bring it into my barn.'" (13:24-30)

Jesus spoke all these things to the crowd in parables; He did not say anything to them without using a parable.

So was fulfilled what was spoken through the prophet (Psalm 78:2): "I will open my mouth in parables, I will utter things hidden since the creation of the world."

Then He left the crowd and went into the house. His disciples came to Him and said, "Explain to us the parable of the weeds in the field."

He answered, "The one who sowed the good seed is the Son of Man."

The field is the world, and the good seed stands for the sons of the kingdom. The weeds are the sons of the evil one, and the enemy who sows them is the devil. The harvest is the end of the age, and the harvesters are angels.

As the weeds are pulled up and burned in the fire, so will it be at the end of the age.

The Son of Man will send out His angels, and they will weed out of His kingdom everything that causes sin and all who do evil. (13:34-41)

This is how it will be at the end of the age. The angels will come and separate the wicked from the righteous. (13:49)

For the Son of Man is going to come in His Father's glory with His angels, and then He will reward each person according to what he has done. (16:27)

At that time the sign of the Son of Man will appear in the sky, and all the nations of the earth will mourn. They will see the Son of Man coming on the clouds of the sky, with power and great glory. And He will send His angels with a loud trumpet call, and they will gather His elect from the four winds, from one end of the heavens to the other. (24:30-31)

Shortly before his death, Edgar Cayce told a lady who was a writer and had come to him for advice:

What is needed most in the earth today? That the sons of men be warned that the day of the Lord is near at hand, and that those who have been and are unfaithful must meet themselves in those things which come to pass in their experience. [5148-2]

On another occasion, Cayce was giving a reading when he told a young lady: "*It is never too late to mend thy ways.* For life is eternal and ye are today what ye are because of what ye have been. For ye are the co-creator with thy Maker, that ye may one day be present with all those who love His coming. For He forgiveth those who trespass against Him. It is the nature as manifested in His Love for His fellow man" [5284-1].

Finally, in another reading Cayce said:

Then, as that coming into the world in the Second Coming—He will come again and receive His own, who have prepared themselves through that belief in Him and acting in that manner; for the Spirit is abroad, and the time draws near, and there will be the reckoning. . .He that hath ears to hear, let him hear that music of the coming of the Lord in this vineyard, and art thou ready to give account of what thou hast done with thine opportunity in the earth. . .Then make thine paths straight, for there must come an answering. [364-7]

In 1940, as World War II was breaking on the horizon, a group of Edgar Cayce's followers had gathered at Cayce's home in Virginia Beach. At this occasion, Thomas Sugrue, the author of Edgar Cayce's biography *There is a River*, inspired the group as he read a poem that imparted his views and expectations for the Golden New Age:

THE NEW TOMORROW

And in that time, so the prophets have written; when the Twentieth Century shall have passed away, *and the sign of the God-man is in the sky* [His Star]; peace shall reign upon the earth and no man shall hate his brother.

Neither shall there be war, nor pestilence, nor poverty, nor any other of the shameful things which man has done unto himself since first he knew shame.

And a great land shall have risen out of the ocean of the Atlantic, and many islands also, to care for those who were forced from their homes in the land that destroyed itself, that was called Europe.

Nations that are great shall have perished, and all men seeking to be brothers shall have put their hands to a common pledge, and raised up a single force to rule them: the force of wisdom.

Then wisdom shall sit in the palaces of cities, and on the mountain tops, and breathe in the hearts of men.

Wise men shall sit in judgement, and order the ways of their brethren, and listen for the voice of God.

For wisdom is the knowledge of God, and of His whereabouts, and of His laws and His mercy, and the beauty of His creations.

So wisdom brings peace, and teaches love, and sets the face of man toward his spirit.

And in that time these things shall be, and the earth and the sky and the sea shall open to man their secrets.

Atoms shall put their shoulders to the wheels of commerce, so that the trees may grow unharried, and rest in their graves of coal and oil without hindrance.

Sound from heaven shall bend itself to the ears of man, that he may hear the music of the spheres, and understand the rhythms of his soul.

Colors and perfumes shall rise up from the sea to fashion beautiful images, and nourish the dreams of the young.

And through all the land, love, like a famished child, shall sit down to a feast, and rise up filled with joy.

No soldiers shall march; no guns shall sound; no bitterness or lies shall do disservice to the lips of anyone.

No debts shall be made; yet all promises shall be fulfilled. Death shall come to meet no man; all men shall go to meet death.

In the spring forget-me-nots shall blanket the fields, and the hearts of maidens shall turn to the hearts of men, and the sun shall follow its course in the heavens.

And God shall be pleased a little, looking at man, and tint the roses with a deeper red, and raise the skylark in the sky.

In the 1940s Edgar Cayce had an inspirational experience while he was taking a walk in the night air. In a letter to a friend he wrote the following:

> The changes are at hand in the earth I am sure—have you noticed the evening sky—there are so many of the major planets visible at one time, and the sight is really awe-inspiring. Believe it is said this hasn't happened as now since the year 1—so guess there is being enacted something that will in a few years bring a new message to this old world. All are so prone to think of just a few days making such changes, but the preparation takes time—and we are usually forewarned by the nature of things, but realize it after it has passed.

If the prophecies are correct that this is a "Star" that embodies enormous spiritual or electromagnetic energy and is capable of doubling the earth's frequency to "over 15 cycles per second" as Scallion claims, then the size may not be of any great consequence and its color and brightness may manifest in unexpected ways. Regardless, from this point forward, there may be abundant and diverse follow-up information given by astronomers, religious leaders, government officials, students and researchers of the millennium prophecies and, of course, by a slew of latter-day prophets. Maybe Edgar Cayce was right: by 1998 we will all begin to fully understand.

It is said no important future event occurs without humanity first being told the signs and omens. When prophecies from many persons, from different countries, times and cultures, are comparable, it is unlikely the prophets have been reading each other's mail. Prophecy is unselfishly offered for our awareness and contemplation. If Edgar Cayce was right, then the time is drawing near when we may want to consider the matter seriously.

BIBLIOGRAPHY

Abd-Ru-Shin, *In the Light of Truth: The Grail Message*. Stuttgart, Germany: Stiftung Gralsbotschaft Publishing Co., Grail Foundation Press, Gambier, OH, 1971.

Abrahamsen, Aron. *The Abrahamsen Report*. St. Augustine Beach, FL.

The American Heritage Dictionary. New York: American Heritage Publishing Co., and Houghton Mifflin Co., 1992.

Ausubel, Kenny. *Seeds of Change*. New York: Harper & Row Publishers, San Francisco, 1994.

Baigent, Michael and Richard Leigh. *The Dead Sea Scrolls Deception*. New York: Summit Books, 1991.

Berlitz, Charles. *Doomsday, 1991 A.D.* New York: Doubleday and Co., 1981.

Brinkley, Dannion and Paul Perry. *Saved By the Light*. New York: Random House, 1994.

Cayce, Hugh Lynn. *Earth Changes Update*. Virginia Beach, VA: A.R.E. Press, 1980.

Carter, Mary Ellen. *Edgar Cayce on Prophecy*. New York: Warner Books, 1968.

Cheetham, Erika. *The Man Who Saw Tomorrow*. New York: Berkley Books, 1981.

Culleton, Rev. R. Gerald. *The Prophets and Our Times*. Rockford, Illinois: Tan Books and Publishers, 1941.

Dupont, Yves. *Catholic Prophecy, The Coming Chastisement*. Rockford, IL: Tan Books and Publishers, 1970.

Encyclopedia of Witches and Witchcraft. New York: Facts on File, 1990.

Farr, Sidney. *What Tom Sawyer Learned From Dying*. Charlottesville, VA: Hampton Roads Publishing Co., 1993.

Fowler, Cary and Pat Mooney. *Shattering*. Arizona: University of Arizona Press, 1990.

Funk and Wagnall's New Encyclopedia. New York.

Furst, Jeffrey. *Edgar Cayce's Story of Jesus*. New York: Berkley Publishing Group, 1987.

Hall, Manley P. *The Secret Destiny of America*. New York: Philosophical Library, 1944.

Hieronimus, Robert. Ph.D. *America's Secret Destiny*. Rochester, NY: Destiny Books, 1989.

The Holy Bible: King James Version. London: Oxford University Press.

The Holy Bible: New International Version. International Bible Society, 1984.

James, D. Clayton. *The Years of MacArthur*. vol. 3, 1941-1945. Boston: Houghton Mifflin Co., 1975.

Jeffrey, Grant R. *Apocalypse*. New York: Bantam Books, 1992.

Jochmans, J.R. *Rolling Thunder: The Coming Earth Chages*. Albuquerque, NM: Sun Publishing Co., 1980.

Kay, Tom. *Dear Amy: Making Sense of the Voyage of the Soul*. Charlottesville, VA: Hampton Roads Publishing Co., 1994.

Kirkwood, Annie. *Mary's Message to the World*. New York: Putnam Berkley Group, 1991.

Layton, Rear Admiral Edwin T., S.S.N (Ret.). *And I Was There*. New York: William Morrow & Co., 1985.

LogosNews. Oak Harbor, WA: Logos Research Systems.

Metaphysical Bible Dictionary. Unity Village, MO: Unity School of Christianity.

Montgomery, Ruth. *A Gift of Prophecy*. New York: William Morrow & Co., 1965.

Mother Shipton's Prophecy Book. North Yorkshire, England: Mother Shipton's Cave, Ltd.

Nelson, Kirk. *The Second Coming*. Virginia Beach, VA: Wright Publishing Co., 1986.

Nexus. Mapelton, Australia and Kempton, IL.

The New English Bible. England: Oxford Univeristy Press, Cambrige Univeristy Press, 1970.

Penick, James L. *The New Madrid Earthquakes*. Columbia, MO: Univeristy of Missouri Press, 1981.

The Prophesie of Mother Shipton: In the Raigne of King Henry the Eighth. 1641.

Puryear, Herbert Bruce, Ph.D. *Why Jesus Taught Reincarnation*. Scottsdale, Arizona: New Paradigm Press, 1992.

The Revelation of Ramala. Suffolk, England: Neville Spearman, 1978.

Ritchie, Dr. George G., Jr.. *My Life After Dying*. Charlottesville, VA: Hampton Roads Publishing Co., 1991.

Scallion, Gordon-Michael. *Earth Changes Report*. Chesterfield, NH: Matrix Institute.

Sitchin, Zecharia. *The 12th Planet*. New York: Stein and Day, 1976.

———. *Genesis Revisted*. New York: Avon Books, 1990.

Stearn, Jess. *The Door to the Future*.

———. *The Sleeping Prophet*. New York: Bantam Books, 1968.

Solomon, Paul. *The Meta-Human*. Charlottesville, VA: Hampton Roads Publishing Co., 1990.

Steinbach, Dr. Richard. *Why We Live After Death*. Stugart, Germany: Stiftung Gralsbotschaft Publishing Co., Grail Foundation Press, Gambier, OH, 1980.

Storl, Dr. Wolf D. *Culture and Horticulture*. Kimberton, Pennsylvania: Dynamic Farming and Gardening Association, 1979.

Sugrue, Thomas. *There Is a River*. Virginia Beach, VA: A.R.E. Press, 1942.

Summer Rain, Mary. *Phoenix Rising*. Charlottesville, VA: Hampton Roads Publishing Co., 1987.

———. *Spirit Song*. Charlottesville, VA: Hampton Roads Publishing Co., 1985.

Sun Bear with Wabun Wind. *Black Dawn/Bright Day*. New York: Simon & Schuster, 1990.

Timms, Moria. *Beyond Prophecies and Predictions*. New York: Ballentine Books, 1994.

The Vision of Ramala. Essex, England: C.W. Daniel Co., 1991.

Wheeler, W. Alexander, Ph.D. *The Prophectic Revelations of Paul Solomon*. York Beach, ME: Samuel Weiser, 1994.

The Wisdom of Ramala. Essex, England: C.W. Daniel Co., 1986.

INDEX

Hampton Roads Publishing Company
publishes books on a variety of subjects,
including metaphysics, health, integrative medicine,
visionary fiction, and other related topics.
For a copy of our latest catalog, call toll-free,
(800) 766-8009, or send your name and address to:

Hampton Roads Publishing Company, Inc.
134 Burgess Lane
Charlottesville, VA 22902